C+Suite Leadership
For Christ

C+SUITE

LEADERSHIP

FOR CHRIST

ERIN O. PATTON

XULON PRESS

Xulon Press
2301 Lucien Way #415
Maitland, FL 32751
407.339.4217
www.xulonpress.com

Paperback ISBN-13: 978-1-6628-4421-8
Ebook ISBN-13: 978-1-6628-4422-5

Thank You... Holy Spirit

TABLE OF CONTENTS

INTRODUCTION

The dispensational course of mankind has been time stamped by periods of rebellion, confusion, uncertainty and chaotic voids. Its weighted impacts on our public and private affairs adequately measured by the correlating depths of instability. Tethered, more so when calamity abounds and skewed even further with volatility in no short supply.

Invariably, though, opportunity conspires its way through the fell clutch of circumstance. Inevitably, yielding to a much higher demand curve toward change.

Change itself, now an outlier from the status quo. Searching for a better fit, a better place. Reaching an entirely new dimension. Settling on a new brand of leadership.

More compassionate, more caring. LEADERSHIP.
More thoughtful, more considerate. LEADERSHIP.
More collaborative, more collective. LEADERSHIP.
More or less, loving and selfless. LEADERSHIP.

In the C+Suite, the writing on the wall clearly spells change. All signs of the times are pointing to the need for a transformative power operating outside of and bigger than ourselves. Group think is seeking an infinite wisdom far greater than our finite knowledge.

Regardless of the external or internal forces at play, be it natural calamity, global pandemic or darker forces operating behind spiritual powers and principalities, business as usual will no longer suffice. Getting "back to normal" is far off in the distance and starts to ring hollow along empty office corridors.

Makes no difference how the car got in the ditch. Be it the blind leading the blind, or what profits a man, woman, company, board, or organization to gain the world. And lose its heart. And soul. And good people. No matter how you cut it, slice it, downsize or try to hide it, accruing the wages of sin and incurring the inflated costs of greed, abuse of power and one too many ego trips, impacts the bottom line.

When facing such macro neglect and marginal deficits of leadership, the best available option to course correct and cross the gulf is mainly achieved by seeking heavenly assistance. And with that, hatching a new game plan. With a new playbook for the C+Suite. Out with the old, in with the "new man" in Christ.

It is our public contention and private witness that leaders have been born, and future leaders made, for a time such as this. It is our deepest, vastly held belief that Almighty God has pre-destined and called forward such a generation of leaders down from eternity into time before the foundations of the world.

Appointed by God's sovereign, unilateral authority and divine providence, these elected leaders are on a divine assignment to fulfill prophecy and change history. They, we, are uniquely purposed, poised and chosen to usher in a new business model for leadership in the Messianic Age and Millennium. Modeled after kingdom principles, this Faith-centric model of transcendent leadership walks after the spirit, and refuses to be ruled by the carnal desires and instincts which dominate the day.

This model doesn't leave Christ on the outside, looking inside the ivory tower. Nor does it leave the keys to the kingdom in the car, left unattended. On the contrary, this blueprint for leadership is designed to make Christ the very cornerstone of the C+Suite. With this transformative style of leadership, people's lives, careers and fortunes are changed forevermore. From the inside out. This type of leadership is not confined to a religion, but conforming to a way of life and cultural norms based upon the character, conviction and inarguable attributes of "Christlikeness."

LEADERSHIP that follows the full proof pattern laid out for us in scripture, with accountability found from the boardroom and the conference room to the break room and the mailroom. Righteous presence is felt. On-site or offsite. Core values and vision are clear top to bottom.

DISCIPLESHIP that succeeds as the standard for succession planning and advancement. This new leadership dimension and business model prioritizes and places value and emphasis on human capital as its primary growth strategy.

FELLOWSHIP that can go livestream and grow organically, non-denominationally, by the water cooler or in the parking lot. The good news spread virtually by Zooming in, or Zooming out.

ENTREPRENEURSHIP and the start-up success path begins and ends with a "WE." Founders view God as their silent partner and lead, seed investor. Thereby, thinking / planning / acting on a generational basis, not making plans based on individual exits.

PARTNERSHIP alignment centered around an ethical, spiritual framework. Human Resources recruitment becomes Faith-driven. Retention becomes Faith-centric. Spawning a Kingdom mentality that permeates throughout, self-actualizing into a shared, aspirational collective state above individual title, office or rank. This culture emphasizes giving, over taking. Praying, and receiving in the spirit. Sewing and reaping. Resource allocation and revenue generation are rooted in principles of seed time and harvest time.

Just as Emotional Intelligence fundamentally shifted the narrative and thinking surrounding the Organizational Behavior discipline and in much the same fashion that Meyers-Briggs set new precedent, normalizing personality frameworks around leadership, we offer our proprietary Christ Quotient (CQ) and Christ Type personality profile as the Millennium standard.

We are living in an age and society where protecting and harboring feelings is exalted above and beyond proclaiming the truth.

Indeed, along the path to modernism, countless Christians somehow were convinced in order to follow Christ, one must become sheepish, quiet and withdrawn. In the process, confusing the Lamb's meekness as the Lion's weakness. Instead, we know God's strength is perfected in us (2 Corinthians 12:9).

With this, our brokenness becomes transmitted into boldness in our leadership and influence. Beyond totem pole leadership, and tossing the weight of titles and authority around, our commitment to Christ Type leadership naturally admonishes us to his brand of servant leadership. His example teaching us how *not* to misappropriate our gifts and influence.

In this regard, we approach this subject humbly, knowing and believing God to be no respecter of persons. As believers, we inherit the faith to share it but not own it. Together, we assume this mantle of leadership so that Christ may be fully exalted corporately. While we write from a Christian perspective, this transformation of leadership can be recognized and experienced by anyone, regardless of your faith and religion, and even if you practice no religion at all.

BOOK 1

LEADERSHIP

Chapter 1:
The Transformative Power of God

"I form the light and create darkness, I bring prosperity and create disaster; I, the Lord, do all these things."

Isaiah 45:7 (NIV)

God does his best work in the dark. One might further testify, when it comes to Leadership, the greatest leaders aren't born. They are made, quiet as kept, in the dark. Like Moses, often hidden from view. In plain sight.

In other words, great Leadership may appear suddenly but doesn't happen overnight. The full picture of Leadership develops, transforms (and transfigures) over time.

"So God created man in His own image, in the image and likeness of God He created him; male and female He created them."

Genesis 1:27 (AMP)

From the very beginning, God was quite deliberate and clear about what the image of leadership looks like. He, literally, prescribes its core essence and aspirational value in his own terms. Beyond physical appearance, though, this authoritative expression of leadership resembles God's moral likeness. HIS character.

You are undoubtedly familiar with the saying, "leaders don't create more followers, they produce more leaders." Essentially, what we're suggesting here is the creator of the universe was divinely inspired as being the first to subscribe to this philosophy, existentially.

As such, God's self-fulfilling prophecy and desire for men and women in Leadership is to transform their finite attributes into the infinite expression and fullness of his image. Ultimately, conforming to His style, and personifying His type of a leadership.

> *"In all things shewing thyself a pattern of good works: in doctrine shewing uncorruptness, gravity, sincerity,"*

> *Titus 2:7 (KJV)*

From this perspective, we begin to transpose Leadership in light of God's intentional process, not Man's isolated happenstance. We start to perceive that ALL of our business affairs, decisions, works and activities are a fine pattern woven together into the fabric of a much broader tapestry. ALL matters are guided by God's sovereign hand. ALL things are timed, purposed, arranged and orchestrated by *His* divine providence.

Spotlight On ♥ Divine Providence

Divine Providence is God's sovereign authority of governance and strategic planning mechanism through which His boundless wisdom, love, and counsel cares for and directs all things in the universe. As CEO of the cosmos, the doctrine of divine providence soundly asserts that God is in complete command and control of all things. And all time.

On the summary of roles, responsibilities and qualifications for His position, Divine Providence sits atop the list. Which, incidentally, makes us under-qualified for the role. He is sovereign over the universe as a whole (Psalm 103:19), the physical world (Matthew 5:45), the affairs of nations (Psalm 66:7), human destiny (Galatians 1:15), human successes and failures (Luke 1:52), and the protection of His people (Psalm 4:8). This doctrine soundly stands polar opposite to the idea that the universe is evolved and governed by chance or fate.

What does this have to do with you, your business or organization? Everything. From the Presidential chamber to the C+Suite and the board room, to the task force committee and assembly hall, it is through divine providence that God raises up and divinely appoints leaders, anointed for particular tasks at specific times, to accomplish His will.

And so it is.

To ensure that His divine plan, purpose and prophecy are fulfilled, God governs our macro affairs and operationalizes our micro works with the day-to-day, natural order of things. As much as Man fancies himself to be supreme, co-opting God's laws of nature such as "survival of the fittest" and falsely categorizing them as tenets of leadership fit, we are left to reasonably conclude this is nothing more than God's work at play in the universe.

Quite literally, when the dust settles, we find the laws of nature have no inherent power, or ruling authority themselves. Rather, they are the principles God has set in place to govern how things normally work. They are only "laws" because God decreed them.

Hence, they are only leaders because God declared them. As such, there is no leadership role or power structure of major or minor significance that God has not authorized, permitted, discontinued or abruptly brought to cease and desist altogether.

> *"The Lord said to Samuel, "How long will you grieve for Saul, when I have rejected him as king over Israel? Fill your horn with oil and go; I will send you to Jesse the Bethlehemite, for I have chosen a king for Myself among his sons."*

> *1 Samuel 16:1 (AMP)*

When God told Samuel he had rejected Saul and his reign was over, it was over. It didn't matter how much the Prophet wanted Saul to reign on, as return on the sweat equity he invested in anointing Israel's inaugural kingship. It didn't matter how much Israel rejected Theocracy and desired their own succession of kings from among the people. God was pre-determined to bring all of those things into proper alignment for his purpose.

For this purpose, he told Samuel to fill his horn with oil and go to the little town of Bethlehem. Along the same time continuum that Ruth, Naomi and Boaz were headed there. These separate, but (literally) related confluence of events, were essential to God's strategic plan to turn the Leadership Key of David. From the Root of Jesse.

Two branches, representing the Levitical priesthood and royal tribe of Judah, from which the King of Kings and Lord of Lords would come. Christ, in the Greek translation, meaning "Christos: The Anointed One."

It bears witnessing here that "the anointing" is God's great equalizer which pre-determines the organizational flow chart for divine providence. The chosen vessel is but the means of transport. In a real sense, Samuel was carrying David's anointing. And David's anointing was rightfully in Samuel. Anointed as he himself *was*, Samuel was still in mourning, rightfully attached to anointing the wrong man in Saul.

Obedience is pre-requisite for divine providence. Samuel's acquiescing to Saul's failed brand of leadership despite God's explicit instructions, would have meant no David. Lest divine providence, Samuel refusing to anoint David would have been a deterrent to God's divine plan further down the seed line to anoint Christ as the Messiah.

This seemingly small caveat on the "flow of anointing" speaks volumes beyond the pulpit for entrepreneurship, generational wealth, family businesses and succession planning. Henceforth, making overall informed and transformative leadership decisions with ramifications that are bigger than one's self. In a nutshell, can God trust you with another man's anointing?

> *"And if ye have not been faithful in that which is another man's, who shall give you that which is your own?"*

> *Luke 16:12 (KJV)*

Measuring The Christ Quotient (CQ)

⚜ C+Humility
"Acts of Divine Providence"
Peter & Cornelius

> *"For through him we both have access to the Father by one Spirit."*

> *Ephesians 2:18 (NIV)*

Humility is the access code for the gatekeeper to enter through doors of expansion. In fact, it is pre-requisite for accessing the next dimension. Christ, Himself, taking up residence at the door. Let's examine this core attribute of CQ at work in the life and times of Peter and Cornelius. The Great Book of Acts represents a manifold paradigm shift beginning to operate in the hearts, minds and spirit of the new covenant church. Here, we find Peter and Cornelius in the midst of all three.

The foundational aspect of the book of Acts documents the history of the early church. It's emphasis being on the fulfillment of the Great Commission, as the apostles are now serving as the ascended Christ's witnesses in Jerusalem, Judea and Samaria. We find them spreading the power of the gospel (and encountering opposition) to transform lives throughout the world. Moreover, the book of Acts sheds light on the powerful gift of the Holy Spirit which comforts, guides, empowers, teaches, and serves as our Counselor - covering the transitional time between the ascension of Christ and the completion of the New Testament canon. In turn, the apostolic miracles were God's means of authenticating His message through the men who penned the Bible.

The book of Acts also serves as a transition from the Old Covenant to the New. This transition is highlighted in several key episodes. First, there was a change in the administration of the Holy Spirit, whose primary function in the Old Testament was the external "anointing" of God's people, among them Moses (Numbers 11:17), Gideon (Judges 6:34), and Saul (1 Samuel 10:6–10). After the ascension of Jesus, the Spirit came to dwell in the very hearts of believers (Romans 8:9–11; 1 Corinthians 3:16). In essence, the indwelling and abiding presence of the Holy Spirit is the gift of the true and living God to those who come to Him in faith.

The power and the paradigm then shifted from Immanuel (Christ), "God *with us*," to (Holy Spirit) "God *within us*." All of us. Jews, Greeks and Gentiles alike. All of which was somewhat problematic for His most faithful servants who were unable to wrap their ego, minds (and inflated sense of entitlement) around it.

Although many faithful servants were used to preach and teach the gospel of Jesus Christ, the Apostle Paul was the most influential in spreading the good news. Before he was converted, though, he over-zealously disdained and persecuted Christians. His dramatic conversion, being struck down (and struck blind) on the road to Damascus, is a highlight of the book of Acts. Paul's conversion in Acts 9 is a dramatic example of the power of God unto salvation (see Romans 1:16) and the opening of spiritually blinded eyes.

"Meanwhile, Saul was still breathing out murderous threats against the Lord's disciples. He went to the high priest and asked him for letters to the synagogues in Damascus, so that if he found any there who belonged to the Way, whether men or women, he might take them as prisoners to Jerusalem. As he neared Damascus on his journey, suddenly a light from heaven flashed around him. He fell to the ground and heard

a voice say to him, "Saul, Saul, why do you persecute me?" "Who are you, Lord?" Saul asked. "I am Jesus, whom you are persecuting," he replied. "Now get up and go into the city, and you will be told what you must do."

The men traveling with Saul stood there speechless; they heard the sound but did not see anyone. Saul got up from the ground, but when he opened his eyes he could see nothing. So they led him by the hand into Damascus. For three days he was blind, and did not eat or drink anything."

Acts 9:1-9 (NIV)

Paul had been blinded by a pharisaical misinterpretation of the law and his own self-righteousness. After he met Christ, the "scales fell from Saul's eyes"(Acts 9:18) and his boasting of his own goodness was replaced by his glorying in the cross of Jesus Christ (Romans 3:27; Galatians 6:14). Many other "eye opening" miracles were performed during this transformative time to signify God's new message for his chosen leadership. Thus, bringing us to Peter, Cornelius and their obedient acts of humility in alignment with God's divine providence.

"Now at Caesarea [Maritima] there was a man named Cornelius, a centurion of what was known as the Italian Regiment, a devout man and one who, along with all his household, feared God. He made many charitable donations to the Jewish people, and prayed to God always. About the ninth hour (3:00 p.m.) of the day he clearly saw in a vision an angel of God who had come to him and said, "Cornelius!" Cornelius was frightened and stared intently at him and said, "What is it, Lord (sir)?" And the angel said to him, "Your prayers and gifts of charity have ascended as a memorial offering before God [an offering made in remembrance of His past blessings]."

Acts 10:1-4 (AMP)

Meanwhile, down by the sea, we discover God was also stirring things up in the life of Peter.

> *"The next day, as they were on their way and were approaching the city, Peter went up on the roof of the house about the sixth hour (noon) to pray, but he became hungry and wanted something to eat. While the meal was being prepared he fell into a trance; and he saw the sky opened up, and an object like a great sheet descending, lowered by its four corners to the earth, and it contained all kinds of four-footed animals and crawling creatures of the earth and birds of the air. A voice came to him, "Get up, Peter, kill and eat!" But Peter said, "Not at all, Lord, for I have never eaten anything that is common (unholy) and [ceremonially] unclean." And the voice came to him a second time, "What God has cleansed and pronounced clean, no longer consider common (unholy)."*

> *Acts 10:9-15 (AMP)*

Peter's vision in a dream of the unclean animals in Acts 10:9–15 was a sign of God transitioning from the exclusivity of Old Covenant to the New Covenant's unity of Jew and Gentile into one body, and one universal Church. The Old Covenant law had served its purpose (Galatians 3:23-29) so now both Jews and Gentiles were united in the New Covenant of grace through their faith in the death and resurrection of Christ. The "unclean" animals in Peter's vision symbolized the Gentiles, once referred to as "dogs" even by Christ, who were now deemed "cleansed" by God through the sacrificial Lamb of God. They were saved by His grace through their Faith, as evidenced by God and witnessed for us in the life of Cornelius.

As we go deeper, we can fully appreciate the finer details of God's microscopic divine providence at work.

While Peter is having juxtaposing visions and conversations with God that were reshaping and perplexing his biased views, an Angel of The Lord is instructing Cornelius to send his servants down to

Joppa and invite Simon (Peter) to his house for dinner. Such an association was not only rare but quite unheard of, and unnatural for a zealot like Peter.

Peter is in the midst of downloading the New Covenant update that would increase his CQ through obedience and yielding in humility to the Holy Spirit. Simultaneously, we find humility and the early fruits of the indwelling Holy Spirit being cultivated just the same within Cornelius. Our text carries us esoterically into the very domicile of divine providence. Right up to the front doorway of the home of Cornelius. This man of great wealth and stature (rightfully considered a door of access himself), laying prostrate on the floor out of respect for Peter in the presence of a house full of unsuspecting guests. What an enormous act of humility! In an instant, Cornelius recognized the significance of casting ego aside in this divinely appointed moment and yielding to the newly chris-tened operation of the Holy Spirit.

In real-time. Just as the not so ordinary, yet self-described ordinary man was coming into alignment. In this moment, through a quintessential act of humility and divine providence, the disciple upon whom Christ said He would build His church was now officially leading the new church in prayer and sharing the message of salvation (Acts 2:42).

> *"Opening his mouth, Peter said: "Most certainly I understand now that God is not one to show partiality [to people as though Gentiles were excluded from God's blessing], but in every nation the person who fears God and does what is right [by seeking Him] is acceptable and welcomed by Him.*
>
> *You know the message which He sent to the sons of Israel, announcing the good news of peace through Jesus Christ, who is Lord of all— you know the things that have taken place throughout Judea, starting in Galilee after the baptism preached by John— how God anointed Jesus of Nazareth with the Holy Spirit and with great power; and He went around doing good and healing all who were oppressed by*

the devil, because God was with Him. We are [personally] eyewitnesses of everything that He did both in the land of the Jews and in Jerusalem [in particular].

They also put Him to death by hanging Him on a cross; God raised Him [to life] on the third day and caused Him to be plainly seen, not to all the people, but to witnesses who were chosen and designated beforehand by God, that is, to us who ate and drank together with Him after He rose from the dead. He commanded us to preach to the people [both Jew and Gentile], and to solemnly testify that He is the One who has been appointed and ordained by God as Judge of the living and the dead.

All the prophets testify about Him, that through His name everyone who believes in Him [whoever trusts in and relies on Him, accepting Him as Savior and Messiah] receives forgiveness of sins." While Peter was still speaking these words, the Holy Spirit fell on all those who were listening to the message [confirming God's acceptance of Gentiles]."

Acts 10:34-44 (AMP)

As humility gets displayed as a dominant personality trait and characteristic in measuring Christ Quotient (CQ), we discover God can do amazing things through ordinary people when empowered through the Holy Spirit. The book of Acts reveals how God took a band of fisherman and used a group of "uncommon commoners" to turn the world upside down (Acts 17:6). Only God can take a Christian-persecuting murderer and transform his leadership and influence into the most prolific Christian evangelist through time, authoring close to half the books of the New Testament.

Only God's divine providence can explain how the persecution endured by Christians would stimulate and ignite the hearts and minds of the leadership fueling the rapid growth of the early church. Only God could, literally, use the door of a charitable Gentile (like Cornelius) to open the eyes and views of His most ardent followers (like Peter) to see beyond their cultural and dogmatic bias into a new dimension, new covenant, new dispensation of grace and new administration of the Holy Spirit. With humility, God is able to perform exponential miracles and go "exceedingly, abundantly above all that we ask or think, according to the power that works in us" (Ephesians 3:20-21).

In brass tacks, this means changing the hearts and minds of our C+Suite in order to change our corporate culture into one that is more inclusive and tolerant of differences. It means empowering our leaders with the Holy Spirit to power our people. And, it means stoking passion to spread the good news of salvation through Christ that is available for everyone.

If we try to accomplish God's work in the world in our own power, surely we will fall short of the intended mark and desired outcome for the "new church." Like the disciples in the book of Acts, we must faithfully proclaim the gospel, humbling ourselves by trusting God for the results and by devoting ourselves to the adherence, teaching and fellowship of the apostles, "even to the breaking of bread and to prayer together as one body" (Acts 2:42).

Can God trust you with other people's anointing? When it's not your time, but theirs. Even when it feels out of season and your blessing becomes their promotion. Even when your appointment takes you inside to break bread in someone else's house you have nothing in common with. Can God trust you to carry a message to someone, even when it disagrees with your stance, or position? Even when it's intended for someone who looks the same but thinks differently than you. Even when it's not who you expected, or what you expected, when you show up. Even if it doesn't turn out the way you thought it would.

Truth be told, God searches the heart, not the outer appearance. So what exactly does that look like in a leader? It looks like David.

Christ ↑ Type

David

Though he was a gifted Psalmist and Writer, David's most significant qualifications and credentials for leadership aren't found in black and white. Nor, put down on paper. He didn't look the part. He wasn't tall, dark and handsome like Saul. He was a bit undersized so he didn't come flexing with military might as advertised, like His brother Eliab. David was a good chaser, though. And he was a man after God's own heart.

He penned intimate prose to Him. Glorified Him. Pursued Him. Singing romantic songs of praise and worship from the mountaintops while tending to sheep. It was in this very context, he defined and forever etched The Lord in our minds as The Good Shepherd.

> *"The LORD is my shepherd; I shall not want. He maketh me to lie down in green pastures: He leadeth me beside the still waters. He restoreth my soul: He leadeth me in the paths of righteousness for his name's sake. Yea, though I walk through the valley of the shadow of death, I will fear no evil: for thou art with me; Thy rod and thy staff they comfort me."*

> *Psalm 23:1-4 (KJV)*

God made David king not because he grew up in, or knew his way around the palace. Not because of his experience with protocols as a ruling authority. Not based on how studied and versed he was on military matters of warfare. David's leadership qualities and credentials were more intangible. Far less tangible.

Like Christ, David's sole purpose was to carry out God's will. In fact, they both delighted at the thought of being in God's will at all times. Leaders of the David Christ Type are not traditionally groomed for their role or position. They are called into leadership, a most unlikely choice, seemingly coming out of nowhere. Most likely, they have not "been prepared" but "come prepared" for the challenge.

In fact, they innately perceive challenges to be masked as opportunities. Like David, rising to the occasion and defeating Goliath. They take one for the team. They make the moment; they don't miss the moment. This mantra defines their core leadership characteristic.

The key leadership trait for this Christ Type is the sincere, active pursuit of their relationship with God above all other affairs. This exudes from within their nature, permeates the organization or culture around them and frames their decision making process. In seasons of prosperity or seasons of pain. They remain the same.

Steadfast.

Even while he was suffering in the throes of self-inflicted defeat, resulting from the treacherous actions surrounding his entanglement with Bathsheba, David subjected himself to God's will throughout. This is particularly telling in light of David accepting Nathan's prophesy that his child with Bathsheba would die at the hand of God for his sinful transgression, stooping so low to have her husband Uriah killed in battle.

> *"But when David saw that his servants whispered, David perceived that the child was dead: therefore David said unto his servants, Is the child dead? And they said, He is dead. Then David arose from the earth, and washed, and anointed himself, and changed his apparel, and came into the house of the LORD, and worshipped: then he came to his own house; and when he required, they set bread before him, and he did eat."*
>
> *2 Samuel 12:19-20 (KJV)*

It is also here, perhaps, we find nothing more telling regarding God's divine providence and flow of anointing. Nothing quite so indicative of the fact that God truly does search the heart. Nothing as comforting and reassuring than discovering our Heavenly Father's true love story for His children never ends.

And it always begins with what happens next.

In David's case, we all know what happens next. David may have lost one son due to his foolish indiscretion. But God counted David's faithfulness as righteousness. Giving him (and Bathsheba) Solomon next in return. Who was Solomon? The only of David's sons to also be anointed King of Israel. He was only the wisest man who ever lived.

"And God gave Solomon wisdom and understanding exceeding much, and largeness of heart, even as the sand that is on the sea shore. And Solomon's wisdom excelled the wisdom of all the children of the east country, and all the wisdom of Egypt. For he was wiser than all men; than Ethan the Ezrahite, and Heman, and Chalcol, and Darda, the sons of Mahol: and his fame was in all nations round about. And he spake three thousand Proverbs: and his songs were a thousand and five. And he spake of trees, from the cedar tree that is in Lebanon even unto the hyssop that springeth out of the wall: he spake also of beasts, and of fowl, and of creeping things, and of fishes. And there came of all people to hear the wisdom of Solomon, from all Kings of the earth, which had heard of his wisdom."

1 Kings 4:29-34 (KJV)

Like his father, Solomon was a king after God's own heart. He was less motivated by the trappings of power than catching hold of God's will. For this reason, Solomon was a divinely anointed and appointed leader.

"In Gibeon the LORD appeared to Solomon in a dream by night: and God said, Ask what I shall give thee. And Solomon said, Thou hast shewed unto thy servant David my father great mercy, according as he walked before thee

in truth, and in righteousness, and in uprightness of heart with thee; and thou hast kept for him this great kindness, that thou hast given him a son to sit on his throne, as it is this day. And now, O LORD my God, thou hast made thy servant king instead of David my father: and I am but a little child: I know not how to go out or come in.

And thy servant is in the midst of thy people which thou hast chosen, a great people, that cannot be numbered nor counted for multitude. Give therefore thy servant an understanding heart to judge thy people, that I may discern between good and bad: for who is able to judge this thy so great a people? And the speech pleased the Lord, that Solomon had asked this thing.

1 Kings 3:5-10 (KJV)

Are you a leader that actively pursues God in your daily operation? Do you seek 360 Godly counsel for His will before making decisions? Are you a God chaser, and willing to shout about it? Are you the one that everybody counted out, except God who counted you in? Have you been underestimated and under-qualified most of your life? Do you love God with all your heart? Like David.

Spotlight On 💡 Divine Alignment

If anointing is the predetermined equalizer in matters of leadership for God's divine providence flowing in a supernatural direction from heaven to the earthen vessel that carries it, then it naturally follows that divine alignment be prerequisite.

For man, timing is everything. For God, purpose is the only thing. As the clock with no hands, our Creator doesn't rely on time, only purpose.

Seeing as though God's ways and thoughts are above ours, it also stands to reason that our thought process around timing serves as a natural impediment to God's supernatural flow. Hence, under-mining our ability to line up against the infinite wisdom of His divine providence in any given leadership situation. Given our finite knowledge and carnal visibility.

Given that our human resources functions and executive search firms are largely searching for talent, not hearts. Given candidate pools espousing their outer talent, not inner works. Given our pre-disposition toward "influencers" and "disruptive" leaders moving people with their voice, or call-to-action, but seldom from their hearts. Given our natural tendency (in the flesh) to operate out of divine alignment (in the spirit).

Sounds like utopian jazz until you actualize this natural fact in supernatural, rhythmic terms. God simply won't use the flow of his anointing on a heart that's tuned – or turned – in the wrong direction. Like Saul. Once God's chosen one to lead the nation of Israel who, up until then, was a collection of scattered tribes without centralized leadership. As a vital function for living in turbulent times, leaders would arise but the Israelites had never officially consolidated themselves and power as one unified nation.

Because of the constant threat of war with the Philistines and a desire to be like the surrounding nations, the people pressed Samuel to appoint a king to rule over them (1 Samuel 8:5). The people had rejected God as king, having even forsaken Him to serve other gods (1 Samuel 8:6–8). God told Samuel to anoint a king as the people had asked, but also to *"warn them and show them the ways of the king who shall reign over them"* (1 Samuel 8:9). Thus, it became Samuel's task to anoint a king from among the people and Saul became the first king over the tribes of Israel (1 Samuel 10:1).

Let the magnitude of that opportunity sink in for a moment.

Talk about being in the right place at the right time. Talk about being the man. Next to the man. Talk about no pressure. We've all been there. How many times were you in a similar position to be the first, or find yourself on the receiving end of a once in a lifetime opportunity? How did you handle it? If you could do it over again, what would you do different? Was God navigating, or did you simply bring him along for the ride, if at all? Or, somewhere in between?

In either event, through the life of Saul, we are afforded a glimpse of the essential truths divine alignment places upon leadership continuity and sustainability. First and foremost, our odds for success increase exponentially when we obey the Lord and seek to do His will. From the outset, Saul was perfectly positioned to be the benchmark by which future kings of Israel would all be measured. For his part, all Saul had to do was align his will (and heart) with God and his rule would undoubtedly have been honorable and pleasing to God.

Instead, he disobeyed. And disregarded direct orders from God. What's worse, he tried to cover up his transgression by lying to Samuel and, in essence, directly to God (1 Samuel 15). This act of disobedience was the last straw, leading God to withdraw His Spirit from Saul (1 Samuel 16:14). This break between God and Saul is arguably one of the saddest occurrences in scripture.

The second lesson, which cannot be overstated, is not to misappropriate our influence and abuse the power given to us or the people God is entrusting to us. Without question, King Saul abused the power and position God had bestowed upon him. Pride can creep into the most well-intended hearts and minds of leaders when people begin serving, honoring and even idol worshiping them.

If we are not careful, becoming the beneficiary of such "star treatment" can take us out of alignment and have us make believing we are rather unique and truly something special. When this occurs, we forget that God is the one who is really in control and that He alone rules over all. We lose sight of the fact that He put us in the position. Indeed, God chose Saul because he was humble. Over time, though, that humility was usurped by a self-serving and self-destructive pride that would ultimately go before the fall of his rule.

"It is repulsive [to God and man] for Kings to behave wickedly, For a throne is established on righteousness (right standing with God). Righteous lips are the delight of kings, And he who speaks right is loved. The wrath of a king is like a messenger of death, But a wise man will appease it. In the light of the king's face is life, And his favor is like a cloud bringing the spring rain. How much better it is to get wisdom than gold! And to get understanding is to be chosen above silver. The highway of the upright turns away and departs from evil; He who guards his way protects his life (soul). Pride goes before destruction, And a haughty spirit before a fall."

Proverbs 16:12-18 (AMP)

Perhaps, the most universal key learning for us to glean from Saul is to always error on the side of leading the way God wants us to lead. 1 Peter 5:2–10 is the ultimate guide for shepherding the people God has placed under our charge and entrusted to our care. *"Be shepherds of God's flock that is under your care, serving as overseers—not because you must, but because you are willing, as God wants you to be; not greedy for money, but eager to serve; not lording it over those entrusted to you, but being examples to the flock."*

While Saul would be allowed to serve out the remainder of his life as king, he was plagued by an evil spirit that tormented him (1 Samuel 16:14–23). His final years were also profoundly tragic as he battled manic depression. And here's the shout. There was a young man brought into the king's court named David who became the soothing musical influence on the troubled king.

Saul would embrace David as one of his own, but this changed as David became a fine military leader in his own right. In fact, a popular song of the day was *"Saul has slain his thousands, and David his tens of thousands"* (1 Samuel 18:7).

When Saul realized that God was with David, he sought to kill David. To no avail. It's here we fully comprehend the manner in which God's divine providence springs forth forth from his unconditional, sovereign will. For which, he neither consults or requires cooperation from man.

Rather than swing the royal pendulum back and forth between the wishes of the people and misaligned leaders like Saul (which he forewarned them against), God chose to make a king out of a shepherd boy instead.

✎ *Leadership Key of David*

"Anointment Comes Before Appointment"

While the proverbial being in the "right place, at the right time" is of vital concern in matters of divine alignment and divine providence, we also yield to one subtle, yet profound caveat to this timeless euphemism. Which is to say, "right place, right time" *correlates to* but doesn't necessarily *correspond with* "right now." In other words, being in the right place at the right time is a self-fulfilling prophecy that is constantly occurring along the eternal continuum of time. Measured by incremental moments of now. And then.

Even if we are oblivious to the moment. And most certainly when we are blind to the broader ramifications playing out further down the line.

It bears repeating. God is magnificently big on vision but painstakingly short on details. He will show you the big picture, to make sure you see it and believe it. Well before it shows up, and actually exists. God will give you the individual pieces before solving the whole puzzle while reverse engineering your process orientation. He will reveal His hidden hand, while keeping the other one (just) out of plain sight. The anointing itself, being part of God's ever unfolding mystery, kept unto Himself.

Yes, God will start the future flow of anointing and make a royal appointment in the midst of your present, peasant circumstances. He will make presidential moves, before taking the pauper out of you. You can be cursed now. And show up blessed then. You can be in the midst of a bad day, bad decision, bad quarter, bad season or bad administration and trust that He is busy working all things together for your greater good.

In the meantime, and in between time. Until the appointed time. In fact, if there were a mantra, positioning statement or condition as it were to describe God's call to leadership, it would boldly declare and decree *"Anointment Comes Before Appointment."*

David was anointed by Samuel at the tender age of 15, but sized up to walk in palatial shoes he would ultimately not fill until much later. This reality of doing leadership business and advancement God's way can be both stifling and abhorrently confusing. Especially, considering generational shifts occurring around emerging leaders and choices of an entitlement generation.

Whereas, there once was tremendous merit to be found in striving for upward mobility from the mail room to the board room, such true process integration and ascending vertically into an organization today has all but gone. Going well beyond passé. Such depths of patience and humility have grown way past impractical. In the current paradigm, horizontal movement is perceived as stifling to career growth and leadership potential.

Once tried and true methods of leadership "modeling" have become virtually non-existent. Buried beneath layers of instant gratification, privilege and patience.

Whatever happened to the notion of being a forerunner? David was a forerunner. Anointed, and appointed (horizontally), three times. From Prophet, to Priest to King. The Key to David's Leadership Key is the complete foreshadowing of the horizontal administration and vertical integration of Jesus Christ into the Kingdom.

We must also subject ourselves to the harsher realities of divine alignment, divine providence and their correlating effects upon transformative leadership. Which is to say, distinguishing between what God sanctions and determining what He allows. Such discussion invariably involves going to the depths of revealing God's aforementioned hidden hand and the invisible operations of the spiritual realm. Including what role evil powers, principalities, dark forces and wickedness from high places plays in all of this.

> *"Let every person be subject to the governing authorities. For there is no authority except from God [granted by His permission and sanction], and those which exist have been put in place by God."*

> *Romans 13:1 (AMP)*

Be that as it may, we begin with the premise that a man or woman meritoriously ascends to a leadership position of founder, chief executive or administrator, president, corporate officer, pastor, king, queen, dictator, or manager. But only with God's approval. And according to His higher purposes. Operationalized through the process of divine alignment. Bound by (and within) the supernatural framework and methodology of His unilateral divine providence.

All of the above, exceeding our finite ability to reason or reconcile beyond a certain point.

> *"For My thoughts are not your thoughts, Nor are your ways My ways," declares the Lord. "For as the heavens are higher than the earth, So are My ways higher than your ways And My thoughts higher than your thoughts."*

> *Isaiah 55:8-9 (AMP)*

Nevertheless, we often perceive the Holy Scriptures to somehow be fictitiously divorced from present day realities born of a true and living God. As if, God retired from office. As if, He hasn't foretold us all things. As if, He's not the same today, yesterday and tomorrow. As if, we forgot God's propensity to raise up a leader to serve as a catalytic destroyer of another nation only to destroy that leader and his nation once they pass the unrepentance point of no return.

> *"Therefore thus says the Lord of hosts, 'Because you have not obeyed My words, behold (hear this), I will send for all the families of the north,' says the Lord, 'and I will send for Nebuchadnezzar king of Babylon, My servant [to enact My plan], and I will bring them against this land and against its inhabitants and against all these surrounding nations; and I will utterly destroy them and make them a horror and a hissing [that is, an object of warning and ridicule] and an everlasting desolation."*

> *Jeremiah 25:8-9 (AMP)*

In this, the cyclical nature of divine providence, we refer to the great book of the Prophet Jeremiah regarding Judah and Babylon. In one fell swoop, we witness God exacting judgment and prophecy upon both. Going beyond our purview to see the end from the beginning. In His infinite, all knowing wisdom as it is written.

> *"This whole land will be a waste and a horror, and these nations will serve the king of Babylon seventy years. 'Then when seventy years are completed, I will punish the king of Babylon and that nation, the land of the Chaldeans (Babylonia),' says the Lord, 'for their wickedness, and will make the land [of the Chaldeans] a perpetual waste. I will bring on that land all My words which I have pronounced against it, all that is written in this book which Jeremiah has prophesied against all the nations. (For many nations and great Kings will make slaves of them, even the Chaldeans [who enslaved other nations]; and I will repay [all of] them according to their deeds and according to the work of their [own] hands.)"*

> *Jeremiah 25:11-14 (AMP)*

God is serious about his Kingdom business. Because we cannot reasonably know or even possibly fathom God's higher purposes until He reveals them, we have to trust Him. We must accept the fact that He is carefully curating and thoughtfully managing the various processes at the same time. Multi-tasking for the sake of the world. On both a macro and micro level. As Daniel told king Nebuchadnezzar of Babylon, *"He [the Most High God] changes times and seasons; He sets up kings and deposes them…"*

When Mao Zedong implemented "The Great Leap Forward" program in 1958, he did not anticipate his vision and the totalitarian actions of the China Communist Party (CCP) would transform China from an agricultural-based economy into a communist society. His success metrics never factored in mass starvation within five years. His decisions resulted in the deaths of millions of people. God allowed Mao to rule in dictatorship over China for decades even though God foreknew the horrific outcome. This is because Mao's choices fit within God's prophetic plans for the future of China and the world.

Such dichotomy is difficult to grasp and accept conceptually because we are unable to see the end from the beginning as God does. In fact, the end of the book reveals the time coming when God allows the devil himself to rule over the whole world (Revelation 13:11-18).

From this perspective, we are able to draw some distinctions along the fault line of demarcation between what man does and God allows. Indeed, history reveals to us that perpetual prosperity is not the inalienable right for any leader or nation operating recklessly, without fear of rebuttal. Any nation, corporation, pastoral leadership team, military regime, executive administration or board of directors is subject to flourishing or disappearing depending on the behavior and wisdom of its appointed leaders.

With few permissible exceptions for causality as indicated above, God enables the most enterprising leaders to prosper for as long as their governance is honorable and reflective of making wise choices.

Studies have shown that even the most introverted leadership types will influence on average 10,000 people in their lifetime. One need not be a mathematician to calculate the aggregate, weighted impact rendered on any organization through the intentional decision making process. Good, bad and indifferent. Imagine the net present value of shifting the deliberate mindset and thought leadership of your organization toward an abiding Faith-centric, Christ-consciousness. God's universal law of "cause and effect" and principles of seed time and harvest time cannot be broken. They shall forever remain.

> *"While the earth remains, Seedtime and harvest, Cold and heat, Winter and summer, And day and night Shall not cease."*

> *Genesis 8:22 (AMP)*

Whatever we sow, we reap (Galatians 6:7-8). This principle holds true for individuals and organizations. Which leaves us to ponder the who, what, when and why God allows.

And for just how long?

When a leadership structure willfully advocates and exalts evil works and deeds, a patient God signals His disapproval by removing His blessings (or hand) from them before rendering judgment. God truly desires for His leaders to be successful. Thus, He gives ample warnings to encourage repentance, correction and cooperation which is a function of His conditional will. If there is no change in behavior, God's unconditional will then operates with full autonomy. His fair and righteous judgment, with recompense follows. Sometimes fast, sometimes slow.

Always, when we least expect it. Therein, lies the snub.

Because God's sovereign operation proceeds after the counsel of His own will, we are now left stymied. Our leaders find themselves unprepared and otherwise somewhere in the midst of taking, lying, hiding or stealing another inch. Trying to cheat God out of another mile.

Until we receive the breaking news.

> *"You have abandoned (rejected) Me," says the Lord. "You keep going backward. Therefore I shall stretch out My hand against you and destroy you; I am tired of delaying [your punishment]!"*

> *Jeremiah 15:6 (AMP)*

Though largely ignored by failed leadership, God sends catastrophic signals before disaster strikes. Problems stemming from disobedience and lack of self-control spring forth in due season like dandelions, forcing management to hunker down to reap what has been sown by its corrupted leadership. Killing precious time in the weeds responding to rumors and mitigating legal exposure instead of cultivating growth.

Specifically, sexual misconduct starts at the top and runs rampant throughout the organization. Unfortunately, the buck doesn't stop there. The up-spike in the "Me Too" movement down-spiraling careers, ruining stakeholder relationships, destroying marriages and wreaking havoc on innocent families in its path.

One of the tell-tale signs of a nation, organization or culture's imminent plunder is the onset of idolatry – the most lethal form of leadership. When the people we place in positions of power become immoral, with blatant disregard for God's divine presence or providence, you can bet the Southfork Ranch the end is near as God removes himself (and his face).

> *"And in that day I will become angry with them and forsake them; I will hide my face from them, and they will be destroyed. Many disasters and calamities will come on them, and in that day they will ask, 'Have not these disasters come on us because our God is not with us?' And*

> *I will certainly hide my face in that day because of all their wickedness in turning to other gods."*
>
> *Deuteronomy 31:17-18 (NIV)*

The Bible offers many cautionary tales for leadership. First and foremost, God will use anyone and is "no respecter of persons." Everything belongs to Him. The Lord created man, the Earth and all things consisting of, for His good purpose and good pleasure (Philippians 2:13). He will allow for the demolition of dynasties and self-destruction of porously infected strains of self-indulgent leadership when it becomes woefully clear they are reprobate, unfit and no longer serve a purpose. The most transformative leaders are raised up, to come and go.

Management teams and regimes rise and fall over time. Because our Father loves all of His children, He blesses each leadership structure with a span of time to prosper and do well. This surety, or grace period expires when the leadership authority becomes reprobate, degenerate, rebellious and unfit for self-rule. When God determines the extended mercy for that structure's rule or operation as a continuing concern has no redeeming value toward His divine providence (having fallen out of divine alignment), He marginalizes them or destroys it.

Our fundamental Sunday School understanding of the great flood of Noah's day presents us only part of the picture. God was angry, and rightfully so, as *"every inclination of the thoughts of the human heart was only evil all the time."* God also preserved Noah's family because they were pure, and had not defiled or corrupted themselves.

Thus, ensuring the continuity of our His divine plan for the ages, preserving the seed line through which Christ would come and sustaining ongoing Kingdom operations. God operates in the inter-generational good faith of future generations as much as He does in the present generation. When it becomes evident to Him that the promise of future generations and corresponding leadership

administration will be compromised by the behaviors, disobedience and carnal instincts being passed down, He resets the current
condition.

When any governing authority violates God's laws and leaders willfully become dishonest, cruel, lewd, or act oppressively to maintain
or abuse their power, they hasten God's judgment.

God warns all government rulers and those in positions of authority
that they will ultimately have to give an account for their actions.
(Psalm 2:10-12).

One need only to look at the throngs of leaders across the landscape whose lives, families, careers, businesses, ministries, political aspirations, reputations and very freedom have been destroyed
under judgment for sexual harassment, sexual sin and perversion.
Surely, these individuals were given ample warning and opportunity to repent before consciously or subconsciously rejecting (and
grieving) the Holy Spirit.

Throughout scripture, we find many cases where God himself
hardened the hearts of leaders or gave them over to "reprobate
minds" and going after the desires of the flesh. Part of seeing the
end from the beginning is also recognizing that all souls belong to
the Father. Ultimately, we take comfort in knowing these matters
have been placed in the trustworthy, unfailing care of God's divine
providence. Guided by His sovereign hand firmly on the Potter's
Wheel. Molded through an unusual set of pre-destined and pre-
ordained circumstances.

Before the foundations of the world.

Transformative Leadership is truly one of God's most precious
treasures revealed. We bear witness to discovering God truly does
his best leadership work in dark places. It's an inside job. Far
removed from the assembly. Outside the corridors of the C+Suite.
His best plans laid well in advance of the appointed time for the
preset lights to come on. Long before press releases get crafted and

both cameras and eyes start to roll. The stage has already been set. Sound the horn. The high call has gone out. How will you respond? As we shall explore next, the call to leadership is rarely timely, and not always pretty, even when nurtured and transformed through the most ideal set of circumstances.

Transformative Power of God

Leadership Summary

• **God's desire is to transform finite attributes of leadership into the infinite expression and fullness of his image**. This, in accordance with and being conformed to His example and type of Leadership. This theocratic expression of leadership resembles God's moral likeness and character. This process of self-fulfillment invariably produces more leaders, not followers.

• **Divine Alignment is the calling card for God's divine providence.** From this perspective, we transpose matters of leadership in light of God's intentional process, not isolated consequences. We recognize ALL of our business affairs constitute a fine pattern. We perceive our marketplace activities to be guided by God's hand and woven together into the public and private fabric, revealing his much broader tapestry. ALL managed and orchestrated by His divine providence.

• **God doesn't rely upon time, only purpose.** This affirms the saying, "God may not be there when *you* want but He's *always* on time." The clock with no hands is set to His standard time. Transformative leaders operate with such discernment and divine purpose as their guideline.

• **God is in command and control of ALL things.** Undoubtedly, considering the aforementioned human propensity to get in our own way, much less His, God reveals Himself through divine providence to be more chess master, less checkerboard king. In effect, commanding the board while playing to His strengths as both.

• **With one slight of hand, He silently makes careful, calculated moves**. God's leadership moves are plotted in advance with such precision as to render the opposition defenseless. Their best counter moves playing directly into His hands. Choreographed in a way that confounds our enemies. Synchronized in such a way as to dictate each and every piece on the chess board to the point of maximum utilization. That's called leadership checkmate.

• **With the other slight of hand, He boldly reconciles everything back to himself.** Everything, including what was taken. God also moves swiftly, in sovereign checkerboard fashion. Sequencing His moves all the way downstream with complete authority when the time of appointment gets near. "King ME, He says!" And repeats it. Over and over. Again.

• **King David is the perfect illustration of both God's divine providence and divine alignment in play.** His royal sequence best characterized as a not so friendly game of *"chess AND checkers."* Call it Kingdom (Re)Building 101. No mistakes allowed. Be that as it may, though, God still operates within the framework of man's free will. As such, the key players must exercise their own free will in order to play their leadership position. In other words, David had to come *to* Bethlehem in order to get in position for the flow. It didn't come to him. Samuel said he wouldn't rest until David came into alignment. The oil of anointing was to flow in that sequence from David to Jesus.

• **The Leadership Key of David is in his modeling what was to come and foreshadowing the Messiah – the real King**. David was the forerunner. Mary's water broke in Bethlehem, and the wax first melted over David in Bethlehem. David stood where Jesus was to be born. Joseph got tired in Bethlehem for a reason. Through a series of God-ordained events thousands of years apart, we find it necessary for them both to be in the right place at the right time. We find the full pattern of the administration of Christ, stitched and woven through this course of events that would change the entire fabric of history.

• **When it is your time, it is your time (as the Holy Spirit is your witness).** David was a Christ type of leader who instinctively knew that being in the right place, at the right time, was to be in God's will. He understood that having the right attitude was as critical as being in right alignment. The oil of the Holy Spirit didn't flow over Eliab or any of David's other seven brothers whom, on the surface, it appeared to be better served. Instead, Samuel waited and his horn held the oil until the wax melted over David.

• **The anointing comes before the appointing.** David's anointing by Samuel was years before he was appointed. Saul died, David became king. Transformation doesn't happen overnight. Leaders of David's type have to grow into it. They are groomed by a Jonathan. And prepared to shift into it. Even while seemingly stuck in a neutral position. All the while, going with the flow.

• **Leadership isn't always how it looks to you**. God chooses His leaders based on different standards than the C+Suite is accustomed to. God identifies candidates using a much different set of leadership criteria, attributes and credentials. God searches for willing hearts, then activates talent. Far too often, we search for talent but fail miserably to locate the hearts and minds within leaders who think on greater things. What do your leadership ranks reflect? Have you been working on talent improvement exclusively, or working toward improving the leadership hearts and minds for your team, organization or enterprise?

• **Transformative leaders know to get low because its "bigger than you."** Christ type leaders like David know how to think big and play small. They know how to come in high, but get down low. Conversely, the smallest leaders have the greatest demands and place them upon their people. Christ got low because He already knew He was big enough. He didn't need anyone to validate His stead. For transformation to permeate your organization, culture or enterprise, you need leaders who think bigger than their title, rank or promotion. You need leaders who believe it's about prophecy and legacy. Leaders that know it's about what's going to come *through you, not from you.* Especially, when carrying someone else's anointing.

• **Leadership transformation happens at the door of expansion.** The hallmark of a transformative leader is not in their "know how" to confidently access and open doors, but in their recognition of humbling themselves when they approach elevated doors of expansion. They know how to recognize the one who stands at the door, and realize the dimension it leads to is palatially bigger than the door itself.

• **The enemy hates alignment.** As a transformative leader, you are not being attacked *because of you* but because of what's going to *come through you* once you fall into alignment. For this reason, the enemy hates alignment. It's about the territory. The House of Saul grew weaker and weaker (in the flesh) while David grew stronger and stronger (in the spirit). No doubt, as leaders get up under the anointing, the house and territory gets stronger and vice versa.

• **Destiny is waiting on your next move.** Given our natural inclination to ego trip over ourselves, God is big on vision but short on details. He told Samuel, *"fill your horn and go."* The Bible also says *"the steps of a good man are ordered by the Lord, and he delighteth in his way."* Leaders of the David Christ Type model for us that God's word indeed *"is a lamp unto my feet."* Even as we press toward the mark of the high calling and hasten our pace to see down the road to our expected end, God brings us along step by step.

• **Divine Providence requires higher levels of discernment to distinguish God sanctions and what He allows.** As the saying goes, the "higher the level, the higher the devils." And, subsequently, "to whom much is given, much is expected." While evil may appear to run rampant, and haphazard, God allows for this in the course of redemption, fulfillment of prophecy or final judgment. Leaders, institutions, authorities and organizations who ignore this indisputable fact do so at their own peril.

• **Submission and humility are essential for transformative leaders to cooperate with God's conditional will.** In order for God's divine providence to come to pass, Samuel had to come out of his own will as a man after Saul's heart, and submit to coming into alignment with God's will and purpose to anoint David (a man after God's heart) as king. The act of submission – coming under God's mission - should be the cornerstone of humility and obedience upon which every leader suitable for the task, job or assignment is built upon.

Chapter 2:
The Call To Leadership

"And we know that in all things God works for the good of those who love him, who have been called according to his purpose. For those God foreknew he also predestined to be conformed to the image of his Son, that he might be the firstborn among many brothers and sisters. And those he predestined, he also called; those he called, he also justified; those he justified, he also glorified."

Romans 8:28-30 (NIV)

Because God holds Leadership in such high regard, He places His personal imprint upon our leadership abilities. In fact, God democratizes leadership such that He calls upon every believer to participate in the process by leading others – even as we follow Him.

By doing so, He elected to create human beings with the free will capacity to choose and follow Him, each answering the call to leadership, without Him forcing us to do so. Fundamentally, God designed the Art of Leadership with everyone in mind, not as an exclusive club with membership reserved for a few. On a more cooperative level, the access point for leadership and influence is broadened for each and every person who accepts Him.

"You are the salt of the earth. But if the salt loses its saltiness, how can it be made salty again? It is no longer good for anything, except to be thrown out and trampled underfoot. "You are the light of the world. A town built on a hill cannot be hidden. Neither do people light a lamp and put it under

a bowl. Instead they put it on its stand, and it gives light to everyone in the house. In the same way, let your light shine before others, that they may see your good deeds and glorify your Father in heaven."

Matthew 5:13-16 (NIV)

Just as *"many are called but few are chosen,"* everyone in your organization is not properly equipped, suited or qualified (yet) to lead others. Naturally, there are innate qualities and unique skill sets that transfer quite seamlessly into positions of growth and confer leadership. However, this does not mean other individuals lack the potential or substance to be *made* and formed into effective leaders or wield positive influence, in pivotal or seasonal times of transition either.

That being said, it does mean there is a definite *"it"* factor involved in the anointing and high call. Through close examination of the scriptures, we observe a set of clear attributes and intangible characteristics that God's called leaders have in common.

4 C's of the High Calling:

1.) Charisma - those anointed by God to lead have a way of lighting up a room, warming up a crowd and displaying a unique set of natural gifts. Chief among their gifts is a certain magnetism and exceedingly abundant gift of being a people person, not a people pleaser.

2.) Character - the anointed leader is the one who does the right thing when nobody else is looking because they know God is *always* watching. The closer the leader gets to the anointing, the more they assume the Godly character, falling into pattern like Christ. The nature and character of the Most High shone His glory on the face of Moses. You can, especially, sense God's presence once the leader is called into their assignment.

3.) Conviction - God is not a passive-aggressive type of leader. Neither are his anointed ones. They always stand for something, and rarely fall for anything. Most of all, they stand for what is right. And know how to repent when they're wrong.

4.) Competence - we serve a God of supreme intelligence and high excellence. Those leaders pursuing the high call do so in learning mode, with a results-orientation and "failure is not an option" mentality.

Upon closer examination, the call to leadership also reveals a consistent, tangible pattern moving and operating throughout biblical times. As we will explore in much further detail in the chapter on Discipleship, God's raising up of one, followed by an immediate and deliberate process of preparing another, is the masterful art and science of succession planning in the Kingdom.

Whenever God prepares to call a leader, there are two components. There is both an inward component and outward component of the calling. God's hand, or grip, upon the leader is the *"justification"* part that Paul refers to in Romans 8:30. Through it, the individual recognizes that he or she is destined for the appointment and occupying the position of leadership. Without possessing, or necessarily requiring, all of the details.

The outward component is where God *"glorifies"* those he's called by *raising them up* to heavenly dignity in the sight of men. And very presence of their enemies. In the process, all parties involved are brought under submission to the undeniable fact that God's hand is resting upon the individual. And the individual is firmly in God's grip.

This makes hell very nervous, as it should.

Only our Heavenly Father can anoint or appoint an individual to lead and transform nations, large corporations and small organizations, in times of transition. It is of particular importance for spirit-informed leaders to demonstrate through faithful action to those they serve, support and lead that their authority comes from above. Thereby, placing no one else below.

Only after an individual demonstrates such an elevated form of self-awareness, refining their influence into Christ-like character, are they ready to be fully exalted. This is purely determined by God. Your highest level of education completed, or number of degrees hanging from the wall won't determine it. Your list of certifications won't change it. Six Sigma statistics won't predict it. We have a strong tendency to place our faith in mechanics, methods and techniques for process improvement.

We are creatures of habitually initiating processes of hiring flawed people to improve upon flawed processes of identifying flawed people for positions of leadership. Our process improvement is inevitably impaired, as our natural selection is determined by default popularity contests. Style points over character substance.

Truthfully, we cannot (and should not) separate our manner of lifestyle from our matters of leadership. Fortunately, God uses slightly different metrics to ensure His leadership success outcomes. Thankfully, God measures an individual's willingness to *sacrifice himself* for others. God makes it plain that leaders must give up certain things, and think less of themselves, in order to gain more of Him.

In order to do so,
the called leader must be willing to pursue *moral purity.*
the called leader must be presenting themselves a *"living sacrifice,"* as their reasonable service.
the called leader must be *"quick to listen, slow to speak and slow to become angry"* (James 1:19).
the called leader must be committed to acting *relationally,* compromising *self-motives.*
the called leader must be *in the world* but not *of the world.*
the called leader must be a believer that knows *"He that is in me is, indeed, greater than he that is in the world"* (1 John 4:4).
Only after being enabled and powered by the in-dwelling of the Holy Spirit, is that individual ready to be fully ordained, respected and backed by peers. The word *"ordain"* comes from the Latin word to *"set in order, to arrange, appoint or regulate."* True

ordination does not precede ministry, or functional leadership, it follows it. God does the calling, justifying and glorifying but the people, nation or organization confirm the call through the process of ordination.

Which, we suggest, is anything but ordinary.

When God decided to raise up the nation of Israel, He called upon one man. Abraham. When it was time to deliver His people out of Egypt, He didn't call for a straw poll as part of the process. God called out "Moses, Moses."

Like most, Moses made a variety of excuses to avoid answering the call.

> *"Therefore, come now, and I will send you to Pharaoh, and then bring My people, the children of Israel, out of Egypt." But Moses said to God, "Who am I, that I should go to Pharaoh, and that I should bring the children of Israel out of Egypt?" And God said, "Certainly I will be with you, and this shall be the sign to you that it is I who have sent you: when you have brought the people out of Egypt, you shall serve and worship God at this mountain."*
>
> *Exodus 3:10-12 (AMP)*

Moses' Life Mission and His Five Big Excuses

(Exodus 3:11-4:14)
Source: Maxwell Leadership Bible

When pressed, most of us can conjure up a litany of reasons why we aren't prepared or unable to lead effectively. Just as Moses did. When God called him, he instantly thought of five reasons why he couldn't lead.

Excuse One: Who Am I? (3:11). Moses struggled with his identity. He just didn't feel qualified; he thought God had picked the wrong leader. God's response: It doesn't matter who you are. I am with you (3:12).

Excuse Two: Who Are You? (3:13). Moses felt a lack of intimacy. He didn't know God well enough to describe Him to the people and lacked convictions concerning his relationship with God. God's response: I AM WHO I AM. I AM ever present. I AM everything you need (3:14).

Excuse Three: What if they don't listen? (4:1). Moses felt intimidated. He worried about the people's reaction to him. God's response: When I'm finished, they'll listen (4:2-9).

Excuse Four: I've never been a good speaker (4:10). Moses fretted about his inadequacies. Who would listen to him if he couldn't even speak well? God's response: Guess who made your mouth? (4:11, 12).

Excuse Five: I know you can find someone else (4:13). Moses felt inferior. He compared himself to others - even his brother - and decided that he came up short. God's response: OK, I will let Aaron go with you...but I'm still calling you to go (4:14).

When Moses went up to the mountain, never to return, the wilderness operation didn't stall. God didn't enlist a search committee to exhaust a long, arduous process. When it was time to cross into the promised land, the children of Israel followed Joshua - the one who was following in the biggest shoes of all to fill.

"No one will be able to stand against you all the days of your life. As I was with Moses, so I will be with you; I will never leave you nor forsake you. Be strong and courageous, because you will lead these people to inherit the land I swore to their ancestors to give them."

Joshua 1:5-6 (NIV)

As we shall delve deeper into later during our discussion on succession planning, whenever God is preparing a generational paradigm shift, He calls forth a leader down from eternity into time to step up, step in and step out on faith. The grandest requirement for the job is to be of good courage, and great patience. In cases such as this, the call always comes before the crowd gathers. In fact, God plucks one from among the crowd who also stands apart from the crowd.

Because called leaders are pre-destined through time for turbulent times of transition, merger or acquisition, they are not supposed to fit in. They are called to break the mold. Typically, they are being asked to lead a group, management team or band of employees into the unexpected. Usually, they are being forced to build bridges to somewhere they haven't quite been themselves.

Inevitably, they are expected to merge cultures, customs, and processes. Along the way, minor points can lead to major frustration. These leaders must be able to lead past confusion and through resistance. They must be nimble enough to navigate their way past diverse backgrounds, a multitude of opinions, varying degrees of organizational tension and constant internal mumblings. All while staring down the face of external opposition.

Fortunately, this is not breaking news to God. Realizing the complexities born around leadership in times of transition, God raises up a multi-faceted leader through an equally convoluted set of experiences that uniquely poise and enable them to get the job done. Knowing the nature of the internal and external resistance to confront His chosen leadership given the task ahead, He sequences their success path, failures (and shortcomings) accordingly. He fortifies them with the adequate measure of grace, matching the key ingredients of talent, before serving them up.

Before they ever take control, God assumes command of their lives. Once called, God never sets a leader up to fail. Man may fail himself through the faculty of his own devices, but it won't be because God didn't equip and empower him with the proper tools to be successful. Most certainly, as the Bible more aptly puts it,

He *"pre-qualifies and pre-ordains"* the called. Those He foreknew. Which is to say, those He loved and chose before the foundations of the world. Those leaders He predestined to be conformed to the image of His Son. And those He predestined, He also called. And those He called, He also justified. And those He justified, He also glorified (Romans 8:30).

Notice in the above verse, God's foreknowing comes before the predestination AND calling of the leader. Hmmm. Is it possible God made that executive decision long before you chose your Chief Executive? We submit that it is not only very possible, but quite likely, your next Chief Administrative Officer is coming under the administration of the Holy Spirit. Your Co-Founder is making their way through the early stage of predestination to kick start your start-up.

The turn-around specialist you've been waiting for is taking another sanctification turn or two before being ready for you. Which is to say, having already fully apprised Himself of the chosen time of predestination to call the leader forth, God carefully orchestrates and arranges the order of things in their background and journey equal to the task of transformation. He bobs and weaves them through their variety of roles and multi-national exposure.

He pre-calculates their interpersonal, cross-cultural and cross-functional lifetime experiences in such a way that the sum of their interactions ends up being much bigger than where they came from. Adding up to be enough to address core constituents and key stakeholders, while resonating with the masses. Having been matured and quickened with a wide enough range of associations to render an inter-generational, multiplier effect.

Like Moses.

Possessing the uncanny, beautiful blend of being born Hebrew, but raised in Pharaoh's palace so he was taught how to walk (and talk) like an Egyptian. Moses was too Egyptian, and too close to the boss, to be readily accepted by his own kind.

At the end of the day, though, there was enough Hebrew in Moses for him to be around Pharaoh and still be uncomfortable in his own skin. Never quite fitting in with either group. Somehow, able to be taken in and blend right on in, between both. That was Moses.

> *"When the child grew older, she took him to Pharaoh's daughter and he became her son. She named him Moses, saying, "I drew him out of the water."*

> *Exodus 2:10 (NIV)*

When God calls the predestined leader forth, He *is drawing them out* as much as calling them out. What comes *out* of them is the uniqueness in style, personality, influence, character, background, perspective and upbringing that God placed *in* them for a time such as theirs. In times of transition, this process can initially feel as foreign and frightening to the leader as it can be for those he or she has been called to lead. As it would be with Moses.

Spotlight On 💡 Predestination

> *"Now a man of the tribe of Levi married a Levite woman, and she became pregnant and gave birth to a son. When she saw that he was a fine child, she hid him for three months. But when she could hide him no longer, she got a papyrus basket for him and coated it with tar and pitch. Then she placed the child in it and put it among the reeds along the bank of the Nile. His sister stood at a distance to see what would happen to him."*

> *Exodus 2:1-4 (NIV)*

In retrospect, it is absolutely amazing to see how a small papyrus basket floating on the banks of the Nile River could play such an extraordinarily large role downstream in the lives of the ordinary men and women that would fulfill prophecy and chart a new course for history. This finely anointed child, wrapped inside, having been called down from eternity through time. God's pre-ordained, pre-destined deliverer of Israel from the wicked hand of Pharaoh.

The very seed line of Abraham, through which the Messiah would come. Moses, himself, born into life-threatening conditions. For a time of persecution such as this. As the saying goes, "the watched pot never boils." Suffice it to say, when it comes to His called upon chosen few, God masterfully prepares His predestined leaders in the crock pot of divine providence. Setting both the time and temperature to reach a precise moment. The savory seasonings of leadership influence, charisma, humility and patience marinating and simmering in the process.

Heat and pressure, both equally distributed throughout. When it's ready, the aroma calls you. What was drawn out, now draws you. As the aforementioned scripture in the Book of Matthew makes clear, flavor and taste is of prime importance to God in matters of leadership. Therefore, what goes into the process is necessary to the outcome. No matter how long the wait. No matter how starved we may be for leadership. Or, how hungry we may be for our seat at the table.

It is what God does in us while we wait to be served up that readies the course. The perfect patience God worked in Moses enabled him to lead his own stiff-necked people through a wilderness of frustration. What happens to us and around us while we wait is vital to the outcome. In the end, our waiting deepens our relationship with God and matures our perspective on leadership – through *His* lens. It also enhances our understanding of seasons and ability to withstand the heat brought about during times of transition.

By standing the test of time, our preparedness becomes the best indication of our readiness. Our having been made to endure also validating us to seize the opportunities and challenges from others who have gone before us, bound for the same pre-destination. In this regard, we are also reminded of others before Moses who waited years for God to "complete" their predestined leadership process in pure Biblical terms:

- Noah waited some 120 years before the predicted rains and flood came.

- For Job, it took 60-70 years of what undoubtedly felt like a lifetime to receive justice.

- Abraham, whose faith was counted unto righteousness and would ultimately gain him entrance into the Faith Hall of Fame, entered in covenant with God to become the father of many nations at the ripe old age of 99.

- Joseph had teenage dreams of ruling over his family but would first be sold into slavery and spend another 14 years in prison for a crime he didn't commit before rising to the rank of second in command to the king of Egypt.

In each of the above cases, both the chosen leader and the appointed time were carefully calibrated to coincide with a precisely calculated moment of destiny. This is not fate. This is not chance. This is not the luck of the draw. This is fact, not fiction. Effectually, it has been written.

> *"In Him also we have received an inheritance [a destiny—we were claimed by God as His own], having been predestined (chosen, appointed beforehand) according to the purpose of Him who works everything in agreement with the counsel and design of His will, so that we who were the first to hope in Christ [who first put our confidence in Him as our Lord and Savior] would exist to the praise of His glory."*

> *Ephesians 1:11-12 (AMP)*

This profound illustration of predestined leadership in times of transition not only applies to the early patriarchs and God's Elect. It applies now, more than ever, to those early adopters predestined and purposed to answer the call to usher in a new, incorruptible brand of leadership and be birthed amongst His first fruits *corporately.*

We could not present a thoughtfully crafted position on predestination without making mention of the critical importance of the role of the midwife in the process. Thereby, providing protection, nurturing, birthing and guardianship of predestination.

In much the same regard as we saw Samuel carrying the horn filled with the oil of anointing for David in the last chapter, God entrusts, anoints and predestines midwives to be in the right place, at the right time to deliver upon His promise. Like Moses.

> *"When she opened it, she saw the child, and behold, the baby was crying. And she took pity on him and said, "This is one of the Hebrews' children." Then his sister said to Pharaoh's daughter, "Shall I go and call a wet-nurse from the Hebrew women to nurse the child for you?" And Pharaoh's daughter said to her, "Go ahead." So the girl went and called the child's mother. Then Pharaoh's daughter said to her, "Take this child away and nurse him for me, and I will give you your wages." So the woman took the child and nursed him."*

> *Exodus 2:6-9 (AMP)*

What would have happened to Moses if not for the obedience of the God-fearing women who refused to obey Pharaoh's wicked command to murder all Hebrew male newborns to counteract the growing number of Hebrew slaves? Despite their fears, and the king's threats, brave Hebrew midwives like Shiphrah and Puah continued to risk their own lives to deliver the male Hebrew children. Indeed, their submission to the will of God spared the life of Moses, who was hand-picked and predestined by Almighty God to deliver the children of Israel into the Promised Land.

What would have happened to God's promise to nurture the seed line and protect the blood line of Abraham through which Messiah would come had it not been for the quick wit of Moses' sister Miriam to convince Pharaoh's daughter to allow her to fetch his (Moses) mother to nurse him all the way into the palace?

Who is it that changes the course of history and determines generational outcomes in times of transition? We can now bear witness to this predestined, preordained juncture and highly strategic inflection point in God's divine plan for the ages. These pre-sorted women from different cultures, separate identities and opposite social strata ALL coming together accordingly to answer the call.

Clearly chosen. Choosing to place themselves in position to play an instrumental role in the fulfillment of Messianic prophecy that is still shaping our world as we know it today. The need for this type of sacrificial leadership in this last hour is great. Their uncompromising actions to do the right thing and follow the LORD's commands above everything else paving the way for the Christ type of leader who would do just that.

Who was Moses that God predestined him to lead the Hebrews out of Egypt? Of His faithful predecessors, how did Moses become the only one God would speak to face to face? Boasting no claim or unique insight into God's rationale, we do present the clear supposition that it was no crowning event. Instead, it was a gut-wrenching and soul-searching process. From Day 1.

> *"Therefore, come now, and I will send you to Pharaoh, and then bring My people, the children of Israel, out of Egypt."*
> *But Moses said to God, "Who am I, that I should go to Pharaoh, and that I should bring the children of Israel out of Egypt?"*

> *Exodus 3:10-11 (AMP)*

One can only extrapolate how such a conversation might go over in today's Ivory Tower...

"Moses, welcome to the team! Glad you decided to accept the offer. I made you an offer you couldn't refuse, for a reason. I brought you in to be *my* turn-around specialist. Reporting directly to me. Now, as you can see, things are in a bit of a transition. We're changing the culture around here and taking the family business back private after falling into the wrong ownership hands. In order to do so, we're also relocating all of our personnel to new territory.

That's why you're here. No need to sit down. As Board Chair, you have my full support and clear marching orders. No ad-libbing, though. Stick to the script. By the way, those ratchet jaws murmuring in the lobby? Those are *your* people. As much as they complain, they seem to like working here. Good luck with that. Now, hurry, go gather your team. We have a big meeting coming up. By the way, if anyone asks, tell'em I sent you!"

Clearly, if ever there were a definitive calling card for the Christ type of leader, it would be just that. "I Am That I Am" sent them.

> *"Then Moses said to God, "Behold, when I come to the Israelites and say to them, 'The God of your fathers (ancestors) has sent me to you,' and they say to me, 'What is His name?' What shall I say to them?" God said to Moses, "I AM WHO I AM"; and He said, "You shall say this to the Israelites, 'I AM has sent me to you.'"*

> *Exodus 3:13-14 (AMP)*

Christ ↑ Type

Moses

Moses is one of the most prominent figures in the Old Testament. While Abraham is called the "Father of the Faithful" and the recipient of God's unconditional covenant of grace to His people, Moses was the man chosen to bring redemption to His people. God specifically chose Moses to lead the Israelites from captivity in Egypt to salvation in the Promised Land.

Moses is also recognized as the mediator of the Old Covenant and is commonly referred to as the giver of the Law. Finally, Moses is the principal author of the Pentateuch, the foundational books of the entire Bible. Moses' role in the Old Testament is that of a Christ type foreshadowing the role Jesus plays in the New Testament. As such, his life is definitely worth examining.

Moses' life was typological of the life of Christ. Like Christ, Moses was the mediator of a covenant. Again, the author of Hebrews goes to great lengths to demonstrate this point (Hebrews 3:8-10).

The Apostle Paul also makes the same points in 2 Corinthians 3. The main difference is that the covenant Moses mediated was temporal and conditional, whereas the covenant that Christ mediates is eternal and unconditional. Like Christ, Moses provided redemption for his people.

Moses delivered the people of Israel out of slavery and bondage in Egypt and brought them to the Promised Land of Canaan. Christ delivers His people out of bondage and slavery to sin and condemnation. He brings them to the Promised Land of eternal life on a renewed earth when Christ returns to consummate the kingdom He inaugurated at His first coming. Like Christ, Moses was a prophet to his people. Moses spoke the very words of God to the Israelites just as Christ did (John 17:8).

Lastly, Moses predicted that the Lord would raise up another prophet like him from among the people (Deuteronomy 18:15). The early church taught and believed that Moses was speaking of Jesus when he wrote those words (John 5:46, Acts 3:22, 7:37).

In so many ways, Moses' life is a precursor to the life of Christ. As such, we can catch a glimpse of how God was working His plan of redemption in the lives of faithful people throughout human history. This gives us hope that, just as God saved His people and gave them rest through the actions of Moses, so too will God save us and give us an eternal Sabbath rest in Christ, both now and in the life to come.

As Moses grew into adulthood, he began to empathize with the plight of his people. Upon witnessing an Egyptian beating a

Hebrew slave, Moses intervened and killed the Egyptian. Later, Moses attempted to intervene in a separate dispute between two Hebrews. One of the Hebrews rebuked Moses for the prior incident with the Egyptian. Realizing that his criminal act was made known, Moses fled to the land of Midian.

The next major incident in Moses' life was his encounter with God at the burning bush (Exodus 3—4), where God called Moses to be the savior of His people. Despite his initial excuses and out-right request that God send someone else, Moses agreed to obey God. God promised to send Aaron, Moses' brother, along with him. Moses and Aaron went to Pharaoh in God's name and demanded that he let the people go to worship their God.

After the final plagues came upon Egypt with Pharaoh's stubborn refusal to let them go, Moses led the Hebrew people in Exodus to the edge of the Red Sea where God provided another saving miracle by parting the waters and allowing the Hebrews to pass to the other side while drowning the Egyptian army (Exodus 14). Moses brought the people to the foot of Mount Sinai where the Law was given and the Old Covenant established between God and the newly formed nation of Israel (Exodus 19—24).

When God finally did call him into service, Moses was resistant. Moses, now 80 years old, became overly timid. When called to speak for God, Moses said he was "slow of speech and tongue" (Exodus 4:10). Some commentators believe that Moses may have had a speech impediment. Perhaps, but then it would be odd for Stephen to say Moses was "mighty in words and deeds" (Acts 7:22). Perhaps Moses just didn't want to go back into Egypt and fail again.

This isn't an uncommon feeling.

How many of us have tried to do something (whether or not it was for God) and failed, and then been hesitant to try again? There are two things Moses seemed to have overlooked. One was the obvious change that had occurred in his own life in the intervening 40 years.

The other, more important change, was that God would be with him. Moses failed at first not so much because he acted impulsively, but because he acted without God. Therefore, the lesson to be learned here is that when you discern a clear call from God, step forward in faith, knowing that God goes with you! Do not be timid, but be strong in the Lord and in the power of his might (Ephesians 6:10).

If you are a Moses Christ type of leader, your success path and journey is marked by leading high-profile organizations, ministries, cross-functional teams, global business units and multi-national corporations through high-stakes transition. When it comes to mergers & acquisitions, you are the most likely candidate to succeed.

In fact, you have come to know, trust and believe that you have been chosen and predestined to be in the right place at the right time. Although you have been called to a seemingly insurmountable task, your initial resistance eventually gives way to your personal "burning bush moment" and call to leadership of a special group of people that comes out of it. Your passion runs hot, and your frustration level equally high.

Ultimately, your success comes from your ability to build consensus across multiple constituent and stakeholder groups. Your fortified nature engenders the full support of your management team, directors, advisory board and internal champions. Your formidable strength perseveres in the midst of adverse conditions, despite the constant threat from competition and other external forces beyond your control.

Like Moses, you overcome your flaws and deficiencies by the supreme confidence that comes from your faithful assurance in who has called you out and sent you. By name. Like Christ, your commitment to the covenant made between you and your God keeps you going. Not because of what's happening now, but because of what comes next.

Without a doubt, Moses provides the most astute student of leadership with a definitive case study on heeding the call to leadership. More so, it is instructive to the process surrounding it. As we established from the outset, God does His best work in the dark. His greatest treasures of leadership are hidden and kept out of sight, and the limelight, before He exposes them.

The ability to turn this into that, happens in the dark. God does a little "something something" with a lot of darkness. If He can draw Moses out over the cloak of darkness, He can draw the VP out of your shady past. If God can change Jacob's name to Israel after boxing with Him and wrestling with an Angel through the night over His calling, He can change the title on your business card overnight.

> *"Then He said, "Let Me go, for day is breaking." But Jacob said, "I will not let You go unless You declare a blessing on me." So He asked him, "What is your name?" And he said, "Jacob." And He said, "Your name shall no longer be Jacob, but Israel; for you have struggled with God and with men and have prevailed."*

> *Genesis 32:26-28 (AMP)*

Point being, God knows you're going to wrestle with Him when He calls, so He quietly takes you to a private place and starts to work on you. God knows what you are going into is going to change what comes out of you, and how folks look at you, so He hides you from the public. The resurrected Christ came over the course of three nights, just as Jonah was three nights in the belly of the big fish. Are you three days away from resurrecting your career?

There's something about getting us alone, and working in the dark, that appeals to God. In order to draw out of us what He's placed in us, He needs our full, undivided attention. Our contention here, is that the call to leadership involves three, distinct phases:

1.) **God incubates you** during the initial phase, or incubation period. God will hide the called leader to begin to hatch his purpose behind your calling. In order to do so, God begins to *purge* the leader of counter-productive qualities, habits, tendencies, associations and limited thinking that no longer serves the individual or broader mission. As with a boot camp or accelerator program for the entrepreneur, the goal of the incubator phase is market readiness. And not a minute too soon.

2.) **God inoculates you** from external threats, internal attacks as well as the enemies and dark forces from high places whose mission is to stop yours. Once called, God also *protects* His leaders by preventing harmful, outside distractions from reaching them that compromise the inner work being performed during the incubation period. It's important to point out that, during this phase, largely preventative measures of divine providence are being taken by God behind the scenes, unbeknownst even to the leader.

3.) **God isolates you** to set you apart, before elevating His called leaders. As previously stated, according to God's Word, those He called, he also justified." God isolates His leaders to justify them. This phase often includes a wilderness experience, or probation period. Such justification can be found in Jacob's wrestling with and Moses' resisting of God's call. Both revealing the tussle and struggle that occurs behind the scenes before the curtain raises on the covenant.

Bear in mind, all of the phases above are occurring *before* the promise turns into promotion. Without fail, because He predestined the call, God makes a point to bring the leader to and through periods of frustration that must be endured during each phase. This is prerequisite to the actual predestination in order to "set them apart" and ensure they never really fit in.

Further, given the transitional magnitude and high stakes nature behind the call, God tempers isolation in each phase before fully embellishing upon it in the final phase. Throughout, God admonishes and prunes the leader on the winepress. Thereby, crushingly rein-forcing the painful point that the predestined leader simply can't run with the herd or get away with the same things as everyone else. Particularly, as the time of promotion nears. Whereas, some lack of conformity to God's molding may be tolerated in the incu-bation and inoculation phase, the isolation phase is defined by less variance and degrees of freedom in matters of discipline, integrity and obedience.

Undoubtedly, the leaders that God calls to usher us in and through times of transition are held to a much higher standard. With higher levels of scrutiny. And, with that, higher stress levels. Bringing increased levels of accountability. Spawning higher levels of attack. Fiery trials will consume more and more of the leader's unwanted properties - building our heat resistance and refining our leader-ship qualities in the process. In essence, "to whom much is given, much is expected." It follows as no mystery, then, why so many are called but even fewer are chosen.

Like Moses.

✎ *Leadership Key of Moses*

"Heeding The Call"

As every called leader like Moses throughout both the scriptures and modern age can attest, "hiding" from the call, "hearing" the call and "heeding" the call are distinctly different phases. For the most part, we find ourselves vacillating somewhere in between.

Then, suddenly it happens. In an instantaneous moment, you walk right into it. Bam. And bump into your calling. Whereas, before you weren't exactly sure. This time He's clearly calling YOU out. By name. Opportunity knocking, at the most inopportune time. Right, smack dab in the middle of the mess. He calls upon you to dust off your own linen and be the clean-up man.

He's planted you there, Esther, in a dry season such as this so you can hold court with the king and become queen of the land (Esther 4:14). In the process, rescuing your people from a sure fate of destruction and despair. Having been groomed, strengthened and prepared to use your newfound power and influence to intercede on their behalf. Hiding selfish motives, and displaying honor. Showing obedience and demonstrating faithfulness to the call.

Like Moses.

Perhaps, initially, while on wilderness probation. Running from your past. Stumbling into a generational opportunity. Right when you're just getting comfortable in your own skin. But still quite comfortable, demonstrating your strong preference for blending in. Could very well be that He is calling you right on His time, but it comes at a time you are least expecting. Or, when you're not quite living right. So, a piece of you hopes it's wrong. Not because you don't believe that it's your calling. It's just not a good time. For you. But there is no way around it. God's divine time waits for no man.

And it's not that you don't believe that it's Him calling because you are Holy Spirit quickened to believe in Him now more than ever. He is revealing Himself to you in real time, and ways you can't accurately explain, nor legitimately deny. What's more, you have the unbelievable privilege of experiencing Him even greater now. While believing in yourself a little less.

Like Moses.

And you find yourself in a real Catch 22 because you don't believe you can level up to such a high calling. But He does. So you can't possibly ignore it. This is where things get real. And we learn what it really means to keep it real. And fear God. For real. This is where we gain some increased knowledge, deeper understanding and pro-verbial wisdom from it.

"The fear of the LORD is the beginning of wisdom, And the knowledge of the Holy One is understanding."

- Proverbs 9:10 (KJV)

Like Moses.

If you remain still, the Holy Spirit makes the announcement quite clear. For whom the bell tolls, though, we may still find ourselves in a relative state of confusion. Candidly speaking, when the high call comes, we can't understand why He's called us. To underscore the premise above, God is quite deliberate, mysteriously careful and boldly intentional in revealing Himself and message to the receiver in ways only he or she will understand.

Clearly, God does this to shred any doubt that it is Him calling on the other end. Still, we practice avoidance routinely. We invent new and improved ways to preoccupy ourselves from listening. Yet the Holy Spirit keeps calling. Quietly guiding us away from the external noise, distractions and destruction going on around us – so that we may go within. This is the quiet place we find ourselves in where His still, small voice blows gentle like the wind.

"and after the earthquake a fire; but the LORD was not in the fire: and after the fire a still small voice. And it was so, when Elijah heard it, that he wrapped his face in his mantle, and went out, and stood in the entering in of the cave. And, behold, there came a voice unto him, and said, What doest thou here, Elijah?"

1 Kings 19:12-13 (KJV)

Before Elijah answers, we pause here to interject a word of wisdom. You might call it "Heeding The Call 101." Like a good Father, when God asks his children a question, you can bet your old life that He already knows the answer. God is testing you. More specifically, He's not just curious to know if you heard him. Rather, He is keen on knowing that you're an active listener based on your response. This point can't be understated.

In order to heed the call to leadership, particularly in times of transition, it is absolutely critical that God trust in the obedience of your ear. Transformative leaders are active listeners. Not only are they sensitive to the needs expressed by their colleagues, constituents or congregation, they are actively engaged in the process of hearing what God is saying to them about the people they are leading that He has entrusted to their care.

Like Moses, we find Elijah in this passage of scripture in 1 Kings facing a conundrum with the children of Israel as confusion abounds and disobedience and murmurings increase. Both signals, and leadership, are getting crossed. In situations like this, the called leader must demonstrate the ability to tune out these distortions to static and tune into God's frequency. By having ears to hear, we respond by seeking God's direction for our dilemma.

> *"And he said, I have been very jealous for the LORD God of hosts: because the children of Israel have forsaken thy covenant, thrown down thine altars, and slain thy prophets with the sword; and I, even I only, am left; and they seek my life, to take it away."*
>
> *1 Kings 19:14 (KJV)*

As Elijah finds out in the continuing verses (1 Kings 19:15-18), just as the Lord knows the answer before He asks the question, He has the "Dear Abby" for our dilemma and saline for our solution. He sends the reinforcement we need to replenish the call by backfilling our deficiencies. He raises and calls Elisha up to be a prophet for Elijah. He prepares Aaron to be a spokesperson for his younger brother. So, why is it that we still keep searching for excuses? Why are we always trying to find an easier, softer way to avoid Him?

Like Moses, we find Hagar on the run. Lord knows we like to hide in the wilderness. Promising God that we will take the call but just need to get back to Him. As soon as possible. Eventually. Maybe. However, we only end up running headstrong and head first into another question from Him, with a foregone conclusion. We can't keep running away.

> *"But the Angel of the Lord found her by a spring of water in the wilderness, on the road to [Egypt by way of] Shur And He said, "Hagar, Sarai's maid, where did you come from and where are you going?" And she said, "I am running away from my mistress Sarai."*

> *Genesis 16:7-8 (AMP)*

The point we are illustrating here with these Biblical character references and witnesses is that we serve a God of impossible. And He is just that. Impossible to ignore. If He knows where to hide me. Surely, He knows where to find me. We serve El-Roi. The God who always sees Me.

> *"Then she called the name of the Lord who spoke to her, "You are God Who Sees"; for she said, "Have I not even here [in the wilderness] remained alive after seeing Him [who sees me with understanding and compassion]?"*

> *Genesis 16:13 (AMP)*

Our calling is found in the back and forth of going from belief to disbelief. Our thoughts and vision get established between what our eyes can, and choose not to see. Betwixt flashes of His brilliance and glimpses of His glory. Our Faith gets put to the ultimate test through fiery tests, trials and tribulations. With a burning bush. When God calls us out twice. In a single word, it's scary. It's exciting. It's frightening. It's enlightening. It's devastating. It's captivating. It's illuminating. All at once.

Like it was, for Moses.

> *"Now Moses was tending the flock of Jethro his father-in-law, the priest of Midian and he led the flock to the far side of the wilderness and came to Horeb, the mountain of God.*

There the angel of the Lord appeared to him in flames of
fire from within a bush. Moses saw that though the bush
was on fire it did not burn up. So Moses thought, "I will
go over and see this strange sight—why the bush does not
burn up." When the Lord saw that he had gone over to look,
God called to him from within the bush, "Moses! Moses!"
And Moses said, "Here I am."

Exodus 3:1-4 (NIV)

Here I Am.

These three, simple words spoken by a complex man drawn off of simplicity.

Here I am...But I'm still on the run.
Here I am...But I'm not quite ready.
Here I am...But they're not quite ready for me.
Here I am...But I don't like the position I'm in.
Here I am...But me and the position are in over my head.
Here I am...But I'm not sure who I am.
Here I am...But I'm coming anyway.

Here I Am.

These three, simple words chronicling a pivotal, mountaintop moment for generations (and the Messiah) to come. Whenever God calls his leader out by name, twice, it is a sign of covenant between God and the leader. When God calls leadership forward, he does so from the Heavenly, unleashing his power down from eternity into time.

> *"God has spoken once; Twice I have heard this: That power*
> *belongs to God."*

Psalms 62:11 (AMP)

It is "thy will being done." Spoken and bound on Earth. Echoing from Heaven. *"Abraham, Abraham." "Joshua, Joshua." "Adam, Adam." "Moses, Moses."* It is God's calling *to* the coming and our subsequent coming *to* the calling that establishes the covenant. Even if it means us coming to our calling confused, conflicted and all.

Either way, God knows it will take some time for us to finally arrive.

Here I Am.

These three, simple words unlocking for us the leadership key and affirming the high call upon the life of Moses. The man who would heed the call, eventually scribe The Ten Commandments and pen the first five books of the Bible. The one who would become a forerunner for Christ. The obedient servant that would lead the disobedient children of Israel through the wilderness up to, but not into, the Promised Land.

In an ironic twist of fate, and process of self-discovery, Moses would also find himself on the other side looking in. As we will bear witness to shortly, he was unable to enter and possess the land because of his own disobedience to heeding God's command. First, though, we rewind to the third chapter of the Book of Exodus. Here, we find Moses "auditioning" to answer the high call. Literally. Rehearsing to play the Good Shepherd's role, for which his current circumstances tending to the flock of his father-in-law Jethro bear no special resemblance.

So it seems.

Upon first glance, Moses is going through the motions - albeit next in line to run the family business. Executing another routine task in the day to day, mundane life of a shepherd. Having married Zipporah, the Midianite, his life was comfortable but not necessarily brimming with infinite possibilities. From the outside looking in, Moses does not appear to be burning at all with passion, or consumed by desire at the ripe old age of 80.

So it seems.

Until this burning bush appears. The Bible says Moses thought it strange that the bush was on fire but did not burn up. So he turned around to see why the bush had not become consumed. So Moses is staring intently at the bush. And the bush is staring back at him.

No doubt, perplexed, Moses must have been thinking, *"what in God's name is going on **inside** this burning bush?"* And, likewise, the angel of the Lord inside the bush is thinking, *"what on Earth is going on **inside** this man on fire?"*

These two bush men now having something serendipitously in common. Both of them are on fire. But neither one of them appears to be totally consumed.

So it seems.

Which begs the parallel question: How many leaders in pivotal times of change and transition aren't positioned correctly for the pivot? Not so much physically, but mentally. Mainly because they perceive themselves to be stuck in a neutral position or status quo. Having blown it, missed it, failed or flopped at it. On the wrong side of their own history, and back side of opportunity.

Not dying on the mountain - but scaling it sideways. With slow, to no upward mobility. And negative thoughts and circumstances from the past playing catch up to each other. Leaving little room for advancement.

So it seems.

However, upon further reflection, we catch an awe-inspiring glimpse of the foreshadowing of the high call of God. We bear further witness to the ironic move of God's divine providence orchestrating the life of Moses through a mirror image of events and responsibilities taking him from shepherding sheep to the unenviable task of leading God's little flock out of Egypt.

Let's go deeper...

Moses is shepherding his father-in-law Jethro's flock in the wilderness for 40 years, which is also characterized throughout scripture as the time period of probation. Moses would later lead and shepherd the children of Israel through that same wilderness for, *you guessed it*, 40 years! That being their probationary period coming out of Egypt. This exact, same wilderness where they wandered, murmured, complained and contemplated returning to Pharaoh's house.

> *"Then all the congregation of the children of Israel moved on from the Wilderness of Sin by stages, according to the commandment of the Lord, and camped at Rephidim, but there was no water for the people to drink. Therefore, the people quarreled with Moses and said, "Give us water so we may [have something to] drink."*
>
> *And Moses said to them, "Why do you quarrel with me? Why do you tempt the Lord and try His patience?" But the people were thirsty for water; and the people murmured against Moses and said, "Why did you bring us up from Egypt to kill us and our children and our livestock with thirst?" So Moses cried out to the Lord for help, saying, "What shall I do with this people? They are almost ready to stone me."*
>
> *Exodus 17:1-4 (AMP)*

This same wilderness of sin, where they would backslide back and forth between following Moses into new covenant with God and going back to their old, idol worshipping ways. This same wilderness that would breed frenetic fights with frustration and devout bouts with doubt. Foreign territory for all involved, without a doubt.

So it seems.

Upon deeper introspection, the most biblically sound and astute will recognize another striking parallel in this correlation of the call of Moses. In Exodus 3:1, we find that Moses leading Jethro's flock to the "far side" of the wilderness until he came to *Horeb*, the mountain of God.

This being the same mountain, in the same wilderness, where God would stand before Moses and issue the command for him to strike the rock and nourish the thirsty flock of Israelites. That moment of truth taking the temperature and full measure of Moses, the patriarch.

Measuring The Christ Quotient (CQ)

♛ C+Self-Awareness
"The Case for an Exodus: Leading Through Frustration"
Moses & Aaron

> *"Behold, I will stand before you there on the rock at Horeb; there you shall strike the rock, and water will come out of it, so that the people may [have something to] drink." And Moses did so in the sight of the elders of Israel."*

> *Exodus 17:6 (AMP)*

This mile marker in the wilderness of Moses' growing frustration would foreshadow the pivotal moment that would cost the promised leader the Promised Land. This public display of harkening to God's voice in a show of obedience eventually giving way to anger and causing God's foot soldier to break rank, file and Messianic order.

Moses is encountering a most common leadership dilemma in the most unusual place. He is trying to lead his people out of physical bondage, but they remain bound by mental enslavement.

Any leader worth their salt will tell you that there is nothing more disconcerting or debilitating in times of transition than moving an organization, culture and process two hard fought steps forward, just to have the people take two steps back.

Nothing hinders progress in the C+Suite more than the constant tug of war involved in shifting mentalities between where leadership is trying to go and the staff's inability to grasp it. Having become set in their ways of working, even when it's clearly working against them, the rank and file demonstrate an unwillingness to let go of what they once knew. In fact, it's the only thing they know. And the only way they know how to do it.

When in doubt, they revert backward. Shackling themselves back to the status quo. In the process, often turning their backs or deaf ears toward their leadership. Their stubborn nature causing the leaders to fight through and work through a stubborn stalemate of frustration. Still, leaders in times of transition must lead in diplomatic fashion, as failure is not an option.

In the case of Moses, the people are frustrated with him and he is frustrated with the people. The Israelites are frustrated because Moses has led them out of Egypt into the wilderness. They were hungry for Manna, and thirsty for water. Not only were they murmuring and complaining, the Hebrews were even plotting to kill Moses.

Imagine that.

The same wilderness Moses sought refuge as a fugitive for murdering an Egyptian man threatening the life of one of his fellow Hebrew brothers, now has his life being threatened by his Hebrew brethren for leading them away from Egypt and the genocidal grip of Pharaoh.

In the same environment Moses spent years searching for Himself, he discovers a keen insight into leadership in times of transition. People, teams, boards, directors, staffs, partners, employees, and even families can play follow the leader - until they've been led into trouble. Led into uncertainty. Running into job insecurity. Bumping into leaner, tighten the belt buckle sort of times. In the midst of hiring freeze, furlough and probationary times such as these.

As we alluded to previously, the called leader responds to the high call because of the emotional investment. Often, because of the opportunity to do something as a labor of love, out of love for the people. They become invested in their mutual success. And good fortune. As a result, these leaders take things very personal, which breeds frustration.

It's one thing to be angry, disappointed or frustrated with people you don't know. It's another thing looking past internal dynamics you don't love. However, when you've been with the company long enough to remember the kids of your colleagues from the time they were knee high to a grasshopper to them now sending them off to college, it becomes highly personal.

It becomes a family affair.

Such was the dilemma for Moses.

Fast forward, and the people are thirsty in the wilderness and requesting water again. *I don't know about you Moses, but sounds like a set-up to me.* Faithfully, Moses did his usual best by first seeking Godly counsel. This time, however, God provides Moses with a distinctly different set of instructions – yielding a decidedly different outcome.

> *"Take the rod; and you and your brother Aaron assemble the congregation and speak to the rock in front of them, so that it will pour out its water. In this way you shall bring water for them out of the rock and let the congregation and their livestock drink [fresh water]."*
>
> *Numbers 20:8 (AMP)*

Moses now finds himself on the same rock of Horeb, on the far side of the wilderness, where he led Jethro's flock. Facing ongoing opposition and mounting fury with his own people. The disobedient children of Israel are escaping Pharaoh's wrath but running head-strong into Moses.' The insidious nature and hallmark of leading through frustration is the inevitability of frustration finding a way to express itself. With less than a moment's notice. Exacerbated, when there are unresolved *internal* issues.

> *"So Moses took the rod from before the Lord, just as He had commanded him; and Moses and Aaron gathered the assembly before the rock. Moses said to them, "Listen now, you rebels; must we bring you water out of this rock?" Then Moses raised his hand [in anger] and with his rod he struck the rock twice [instead of speaking to the rock as the Lord had commanded]. And the water poured out abundantly, and the congregation and their livestock drank [fresh water]."*

> *Numbers 20:9-11 (AMP)*

Instead of holding his peace, Moses let the rebels have it. Out of patience. Out of character. Out of order. Moses was supposed to "speak to the rock" but struck it instead. Twice. Instead of speaking to the rock and feeding the people, he spoke to the people out of frustration. Instead of taking it to God, he took his frustration and inner-conflict out on them.

This lack of water, manifesting itself into a perceived lack of trust in the leadership. And Faith starvation by the leaders. This show of non-belief, in the sight of the sons of Israel, establishing God's rationale why Moses and Aaron would not lead the Israelites into the promised land.

> *"But the Lord said to Moses and Aaron, "Because you have not believed (trusted) Me, to treat Me as holy in the sight of the sons of Israel, you therefore shall not bring this assembly into the land which I have given them."*

> *Numbers 20:12 (AMP)*

For Moses, this bittersweet ending after sojourning through the wilderness of transition, falling the longest yard short of the land flowing with milk and honey. For Moses, this bittersweet taste left in the mouth of the man with unbridled passions and ears to hear, yet unable to tame his own tongue. When all was said and done, the end result of speaking to one too many untamed ears.

> *"I am the Lord your God, Who brought you up from the land of Egypt. Open your mouth wide and I will fill it. "But My people would not listen to My voice, And Israel did not [consent to] obey Me."*

> *Psalms 81:10-11 (AMP)*

Moses was not alone. His brother Aaron also proving the high calling comes with a high cost. Almighty God called Aaron and his sons to serve as the first order of Israel's high priests, the highest of all honors. Thus, giving them all access to the very presence of God in the Holy of Holies. Such a calling requires a certain level and maintenance of holy attainment. Their conduct was to be above reproach. Scripture makes God's expectations for the position quite clear.

The Lord set Aaron apart for his Holy work.

However, Aaron ultimately chose to live and lead otherwise. Like so many of us, despite the high calling, Aaron struggled to reconcile his position of higher authority with the need for validation and acceptance of others. Instead of elevating them to a higher standard, he would eventually succumb to the lowly, depraved wishes of the people.

As a result, he failed at the most critical juncture by leading the rebellious Israelites into a pagan worship service, which was an abomination in the eyes in the sight of the Lord. Moreover, it costs thousands of lives of many Israelites.

The failure of a leader battling frustration or the flesh, usually results in consequences and repercussions far greater than the misgivings of a non-transformative figure. When leaders fall from grace, their followers pay the price. Like it or not. Love them or leave them. Their teams are left to pick up the pieces. The organization is forced to pick up the legal tab.

Has God made it clear to you that he expects more from you than others around you? If so, chances are you are being called to an even higher level of leadership than you may have initially expected or anticipated. This can feel intimidating but is to be expected.

God's high calling is well-orchestrated, strategically timed and divinely aligned in such a way that reconciles past, present and future events. His will gets accomplished through major miracles or seemingly minor occurrences. All designed to initiate the uninitiated and conform the non-conforming to His well-defined pattern.

In retrospect, we can look back and see the pattern. In the case of Moses, so much can be said about this sequence of events which took place in the Wilderness of Sin, in stages. So much was definitively done on this mountain of God known as the rock of Horeb where Moses both auditioned for, then played the part of the good shepherd. Answering the call. And failing miserably by ignoring it.

Still, heeding the call through it all.

Tirelessly fighting the good fight. Atop this very mountain, holding his arms up high but falling down in fatigue. Aaron and Hur helping raise them back up just as Moses was raising Joshua up to experience the thrill of his victory while agonizing on the inside over his own defeat.

"So Moses said to Joshua, "Choose men for us and go out, fight against Amalek [and his people]. Tomorrow I will stand on the top of the hill with the staff of God in my hand." So Joshua did as Moses said, and fought with Amalek; and Moses, Aaron, and Hur went up to the hilltop. Now when Moses held up his hand, Israel

prevailed, and when he lowered his hand [due to fatigue], Amalek prevailed. But Moses' hands were heavy and he grew tired. So they took a stone and put it under him, and he sat on it. Then Aaron and Hur held up his hands, one on one side and one on the other side; so it was that his hands were steady until the sun set. So Joshua overwhelmed and defeated Amalek and his people with the edge of the sword."

Exodus 17:8-13 (AMP)

This precious stone on the hilltop of Horeb symbolizing Christ, our rock. The water that flowed from it, coming from the one and only thirst quencher. When God instructed Moses to "speak to the rock," instead of the people, He was telling him to speak to Christ so that the living water would flow from Him and the Israelites would never thirst again

"Jesus answered, "Everyone who drinks this water will be thirsty again, but whoever drinks the water I give them will never thirst. Indeed, the water I give them will become in them a spring of water welling up to eternal life."

John 4:13-14 (NIV)

By quenching his own thirst of disbelief, Moses would not only break rank with the Father, he broke the flow of the Messianic pattern. By speaking to the people out of sheer frustration. By stooping to their unbelief. By believing he had to prove himself. By doing so, he effectively struck the rock. In other words, Moses went low, when he should have gone high. Instead of patterning himself on God's coat tails, he succumbed to the depths of his own insecurities that were crystallizing as doubts around his effectiveness as a leader.

Moses had every right to be frustrated. Any leader that invests so much personal "faith capital" into the enterprising effort of turning things around has a right to digress themselves. Any leader with enough self-awareness to divest themselves from their own selfish needs to ensure success outcomes for the greater good has a right to feel some type of way when the feeling isn't mutual.

Any leader able to keep his cool in the heat of battle is within his or her right to lose it every now and then. Any leader with the presence of mind to make sure cooler heads prevail in the boardroom by interceding on behalf of the people and talking the Chairman off the fence with a sharp axe to grind, is within his own right to legitimate beef.

> *"The Lord said to Moses, "How long will these people treat me disrespectfully and reject Me? And how long will they not believe in Me, despite all the [miraculous] signs which I have performed among them? I will strike them with the pestilence (plague) and dispossess them, and will make you into a nation greater and mightier than they." But Moses said to the Lord, "Then the Egyptians will hear of it, for by Your strength You brought up these people from among them, and they will tell it to the inhabitants of this land. They have heard that You, Lord, are among these people [of Israel], that You, Lord, are seen face to face, while Your cloud stands over them; and that You go before them in a pillar of cloud by day and in a pillar of fire by night. Now if You kill these people as one man, then the nations (Gentiles) that have heard of Your fame will say, 'Because the Lord was not able to bring these people into the land which He promised to give them, therefore He slaughtered them in the wilderness.' But now, please, let the power of the Lord be great, just as You have declared, saying, 'The Lord is slow to anger, and abundant in lovingkindness, forgiving wickedness and transgression; but He will by no means clear the guilty, visiting (avenging) the wickedness and guilt of the fathers on the children, to the third and fourth generations [that is, calling the children to account for the sins of their fathers].' Please pardon the wickedness and guilt of these people according to the greatness of Your lovingkindness, just as You have forgiven these people, from*

Egypt even until now." So the Lord said, "I have pardoned them according to your word;"

Any leader who is wise enough and humble enough to check their ego at the door to follow the advice of his father-in-law to help him delegate his way through it, has a right to be the only one our Heavenly Father addressed face-to-face.

That would be Moses.

"Moses' father-in-law said to him, "The thing that you are doing is not good. You will certainly wear out both yourself and these people who are with you, because the task is too heavy for you [to bear]; you cannot do it alone. Now listen to me; I will advise you, and may God be with you [to confirm my advice]. You shall represent the people before God. You shall bring their disputes and causes to Him. You shall teach them the decrees and laws. You shall show them the way they are to live and the work they are to do. Furthermore, you shall select from all the people competent men who [reverently] fear God, men of truth, those who hate dishonest gain; you shall place these over the people as leaders of thousands, of hundreds, of fifties and of tens. They shall judge the people at all times; have them bring every major dispute to you, but let them judge every minor dispute themselves. So it will be easier for you, and they will bear the burden with you. If you will do this thing and God so commands you, then you will be able to endure [the responsibility], and all these people will also go [back] to their tents in peace." So Moses listened to his father-in-law and did everything that he had said."

Exodus 18:17-24 (AMP)

Any leader that knows their performance is ultimately being judged by Almighty God and answers to the great I Am deserves to take their righteous place, flaws and all, in the hallowed "Hall of Faith." The face of a great leader forever etched in our minds by the image of this one, humble man. More humble than all men who were on the face of the earth (Numbers 12:3). Living testament to the fact that great leaders are *born AND made.*

That would be Moses.

> *"By faith Moses, after his birth, was hidden for three months by his parents, because they saw he was a beautiful and divinely favored child; and they were not afraid of the king's (Pharaoh's) decree. By faith Moses, when he had grown up, refused to be called the son of Pharaoh's daughter, because he preferred to endure the hardship of the people of God rather than to enjoy the passing pleasures of sin. He considered the reproach of the Christ [that is, the rebuke he would suffer for his faithful obedience to God] to be greater wealth than all the treasures of Egypt; for he looked ahead to the reward [promised by God].*
>
> *Hebrews 11:23-26 (AMP)*

What does the Leadership Key for Moses mean for unlocking the full potential for you, and your leadership who have been called forward to lead your organization through these perilous times of transition and most certain uncertainty?

It means that in a world of social media sensations, digitally searching for followers, you can find God's chosen leaders are still in analog mode. Manually searching for themselves. And it is only upon searching for themselves, they begin seeking God. And find out their assignment.

It means that, quiet as is kept, if you are close enough to be in the presence or midst of paradigm shifting leadership greatness, you will testify to the fact that great men and women don't seek to lead, they are called to it. And hesitate, before they respond to it. What moves them is the idea behind the movement, not the leading of it.

It means that, in fact, because they are so self aware, actively looking to lead a multitude to or through any level of uncertainty or conflict is usually the least foremost thing on their mind. He was conflicted himself. Moses' own people knew he was a Prince before he saw himself as one.

Raised to walk and talk like an Egyptian, but his blood ran hot with his Hebrew heritage. The conflict he saw outside on the street between the Egyptian and his Hebrew brother was a reflection of the identity conflict raging on his inside.

It means the ones you are most connected to may be those you have never bonded with or identified with. So they look at you and your leadership as being suspect.

To keep it real, right or wrong, they view you as being less than authentic. Less qualified to lead them because you can't relate to their everyday struggle. To keep it 100, they can't relate to the one going on inside you either.

It means, like David, Moses was anointed before he ever knew he was appointed. Moses had no more desire to lead the Children of Israel into the promised land than Rev. Dr. Martin Luther King's desire to long suffer for the same. In Dr. King's case, facing persecution and imminent threats upon his life, also coming to grips with the fact that he "wouldn't get there" with them.

Still, neither could resist God's gravitational pull. Neither would be able to deny God's surety or inherent promise of freedom for the multitudes of ALL of His people that was inherent in the outcome and waiting on the other side.

> *"The Lord is not slack concerning his promise, as some men count slackness; but is longsuffering to us-ward, not willing that any should perish, but that all should come to repentance."*

> *2 Peter 3:9 (KJV)*

It means the task, team or business you are managing today is the practice run for the times of transition, shift and assignment ahead. It means you can never be over-qualified for God's calling and assignment. It means the leader that still has a burning desire has yet to be consumed.

It means the most capable leader knows where his or her capabilities come from. It means not only recognizing that as a function of possessing a high self-awareness quotient like Moses, but also being quick to admit our shortcomings like the Apostle Paul. God's strength is *being* made perfect through our weakness and imperfections.

> *"On behalf of such a man [and his experiences] I will boast; but in my own behalf I will not boast, except in regard to my weaknesses. If I wish to boast, I will not be foolish, because I will be speaking the truth. But I abstain [from it], so that no one will credit me with more than [is justified by what] he sees in me or hears from me."*
>
> *2 Corinthians 12:5-6 (AMP)*

It means called leaders must be able to tune into God and tune out the noise, naysayers and constant chatter surrounding them (and within) to be rock solid in this hour. It means the success path through times of transition is never a straight line. It's crooked. And controversial. It's a SWOT analysis marked by constant, external threats. And tainted by internal weaknesses. Disguised as opportunities. Hidden from plain sight. It means that the leadership life is a lot like a delivery room. God is constantly drawing *out* of us, the things we never knew were *in* us. It only took a moment to pull the baby Moses out of the water but it took 40 years of him being on the run as an outlaw, hiding from the long arm of justice and reach of Pharoah's judgment, to get the man child out of him.

The man with no rule over the power of his spirit, seeking an escape from the powerful man he once thought himself to be heir apparent to. Indeed, it took an epic fight with frustration over decades of pushing and pulling the leader Moses out of the baby. It took what it took because it takes what it takes. It takes pain for God to push you and birth something new out of you when you're still in labor.

It takes time for God to raise you up, then pull you out. It takes courage to go back to where you were running from, and tell your Pharaoh, or whatever is holding them back, to let your people go.

And, by doing so, serving notice on your past to do the same.

Like Moses.

We can all draw strength from that.

10 Commandments For The C-Suite

I. Believe upon The Lord, Your God. And keep Him first in all of your business affairs and business practices so that you may prosper righteously.

II. Thou shalt not worship your internal leaders or make idols of your external clients, partners, directors and investors.

III. Don't take your success in vain. In all things, acknowledge the source behind your administration of talents, your abundant giver of gifts and chief allocator of resources.

IV. Thou shalt take time, make time and allow time for the Holy Spirit to manifest itself, permeate your culture and be expressed from within your management team. Remember to keep time off from work and mental health days sacred.

V. Show honor to your executive leadership, subordinates and fellow administrative co-laborers just the same. Respect the shared interests of ALL stakeholders.

VI. Thou shalt not kill the environment, destroy or disrupt the prized vestiges of community or compromise the safety of your neighbors for the sake of profits. Thy shall feed thy flock and give back to those in need.

VII. You shall not commit adultery or engage in sexual perversion, harassment or otherwise inappropriate personal and intimate affairs.

VIII. Thou shalt not steal intellectual property, engage in corporate espionage or the pre-emptive or pre-meditated divulging of trade secrets with others outside your organization.

IX. Thou shalt not bear false witness against, or slander the reputation of anyone inside or outside of the C-Suite, boardroom and broader assembly.

X. Thou shalt not covet thy customer, thy competitor, or their goods and services, but adhere to the foundational economic principles of healthy competition and fairness.

The Call To Leadership

Leadership Summary

• **Moses serves as the pre-eminent case study on predestination.** God first predestines and calls a *leader out* to perform a specific assignment only that leader is uniquely qualified to perform based on diversity of background, exposure and experiences.

• **Like a crock pot, the chosen leader is called to the appointed time.** His or Her leadership calling is carefully calibrated with the right amount of pressure, temperament and temperature to reach crescendo at a precise moment in time.

• **Whenever God calls a leader out for a specific assignment to lead a flock, He gives them an emotional investment in the work.** Moses "bought into" the idea of freeing the Hebrews from bondage even before God called him to the task.

• **God affirms the leader through others, sends help and raises up successors.** When Moses told Jethro about his encounter at the burning bush, his father-in-law affirmed him and helped him "manage up and down" (Exodus 18:1-12). Moses also asked for and received help from his brother Aaron as spokesperson, Hur in the heat of the battle and Joshua as his successor.

• **God foreshadows the monumental task a leader shall perform through the mundane**. What appeared to be a routine responsibility of shepherding his father-in-law Jethro's flock on the mountain of Horeb turned out to be a foreshadowing, and turning into a generational pivot that would change everything, as Moses would lead the little flock of Hebrews out of bondage.

• **Nothing the predestined leader has encountered will be wasted.** God used everything in Moses' background to help him fulfill his calling. From the formal education he received in Egypt and knowledge of what made Pharaoh tick, to his time on the run in the wilderness.

• **Leaders that are set apart, must stand apart.** Sounds fairly elementary, but the lesson remains largely unlearned. Given the high stakes and high visibility associated with the task and position, chosen leaders simply can't do whatever everyone else does. When leaders fall from grace, their followers pay the price and their organization is left to pick up the pieces.

• **God hides his hidden treasures and refines the leader's character in obscurity**. God *incubates*, *inoculates* and *isolates* leaders in well-crafted stages before promoting them. Moses received 40 years of seminary education in the desert. God's greatest treasures of leadership are kept hidden, out of sight and the limelight, before being exposed.

• **As the call upon Moses' life can attest, "hiding" from the call, "hearing" the call and "heeding" the call are distinctly different phases.** For the most part, we find ourselves vacillating somewhere in between. Somewhere, caught up in between not being able to ignore it and not answering. It may not appear to be the best timing for us but it is absolutely the right time in God's eyes.

• **We serve a God of impossible and He is just that.** God is impossible to ignore. He is firm and resolute when calling leaders out by name, in covenant, twice. It also bears repeating that He is just as resolute in encouraging them that He shall neither leave them, nor forsake them.

• **God instills in the leader the value of hard work and vision.** Moses may not have worked much in the Egyptian palace, but he learned its worth in the desert! Moses also called the vision of the promised land long before the Hebrew slaves did.

• **God will give his leader a burning bush moment to stoke their fire and passion.** Moses was staring at the bush. But the bush was staring back at Moses. God extracts the finer properties of leadership and burning desire out of the called leader, while consuming that which is not useful.

• **God's high calling is well-orchestrated, strategically timed and aligned.** God's divine providence operates in such an incomprehensible way that reconciles past, present and future events - in the sight of witnesses. This is accomplished through major miracles or seemingly minor occurrences.

• **Knowing how to delegate, when to delegate and with whom to share the load lifts the spirit of heaviness from the leadership.** Moses set his own ego aside to follow his father-in-law Jethro's advice to share his leadership role and divvy up his responsibilities with others. He then gave them the authority to do the work. For example, delegating the task for Joshua and Caleb to be one of the twelve spies not only made inheriting the Promised Land a team effort but would prove to be an essential decision in God's succession plan.

• **The role of the midwife is critical in the process of predestination and birthing the call to leadership.** From Moses' sister to Pharaoh's daughter and the faithful obedience of the Hebrew midwives, these courageous women's protection, nurturing and guardianship ensured the Messianic prophecy and bloodline was delivered from umbilical cord to umbilical cord.

• **The fight with frustration is the biggest foe for leadership in transition.** Moses not only fought against the rebellious nature and mindless chatter and complaining of the Israelites, but also battled his own insecurities and anger management. While this would cost him dearly, his faithful service, reverence and honoring God would reward him greatly in the end. This, evidenced and witnessed for us by the *Song of Moses,* first captured in the Book of Deuteronomy, and later in the Book of Revelation, as the song that the Saints will be singing and rejoicing in, as they go marching in.

Song of Moses

"Listen, O heavens, and I will speak; And let the earth hear the words of my mouth. Let my teaching drop as the rain, My speech distill as the dew, As the light rain upon the tender grass, And as the spring showers upon the herb. For I proclaim the name [and presence] of the Lord; Ascribe greatness and honor to our God! The Rock! His work is perfect, For all His ways are just; (A God of faithfulness without iniquity injustice), Just and upright is He."

Deuteronomy 32:1-4 (AMP)

BOOK 2

DISCIPLESHIP

Chapter 3:
Succession Planning

"So Moses went and spoke these words to all Israel. And he said to them, "I am a hundred and twenty years old today; I am no longer able to come in and go out [as your spiritual and military leader], and the Lord has said to me, 'You shall not cross this Jordan.' It is the Lord your God who will cross ahead of you; He will destroy these nations before you, and you shall dispossess them. Joshua is the one who will go across before you [to lead you], just as the Lord has said."

Deuteronomy 31:1-3 (AMP)

We now turn our attention to discipleship, the next dimension of leadership. First, though, we offer a word of cautious optimism. No doubt, thought leadership and perspective abounds around this core tenet of Christianity. Discipleship is symbolically emblematic of the fundamental life, time and teachings of Jesus Christ.

"Therefore go and make disciples of all nations, baptizing them in the name of the Father and of the Son and of the Holy Spirit, and teaching them to obey everything I have commanded you. And surely I am with you always, to the very end of the age."

Matthew 28:19-20 (NIV)

Our contention is to approach discipleship *in theory* as a necessary byproduct and inherent function of *systemic* succession planning.

Our intention is to triangulate discipleship with mentorship while demonstrating the application of both for the C+Suite as well as their broader ramifications for the marketplace and as an enterprise solution.

In this process of discovery, we hope to arrive at the conclusion that leadership and discipleship are not fit, nor intended to be mutually exclusive. Where leadership is art, discipleship is exact science. Mentorship is the natural blend, or occurrence, of both.

While there is no shortage of subject matter experts, conferences, coaches, consultants, theories, principles, models and studies from which to consider the vast leadership vacuum that is the 21st Century, they all fall woefully short of connecting the dots to the main source. Truth be told, the best resource for leadership training, development, mentorship and succession planning today remains unchanged from thousands upon thousands of years ago. Its wisdom and mastery preserved, in tact, through the ages and dispensations of time.

For the earnest student of leadership, there is no greater text on succession planning than the greatest book on leadership fit to print – the Bible. There is no better teacher than the master Himself. Anything else, will eventually become less than civilized. Christ left His indelible mark of leadership and discipleship on the church to impact the Kingdom while doing the work of eternity. What we've largely failed to do, is expand the definition of the church body beyond the church building itself.

As mentioned in our introduction, God is calling for a Christ type of leadership that goes beyond the pulpit into office buildings, lofts, virtual work spaces and HQ places. This is not a new call to action reprising old, self-righteous religious labels and traditions of men. Nor, is it equidistant to the false Christianity movement. Rather, it is a natural call to leadership that God has placed within each of us and extracts through the most unnatural, undesirable set of circumstances.

As we just discovered in the life and leadership of Moses, God will draw the leader out of you. Over time. Calling you out by name. The very nature of a call is present tense indicative of a future event. At supper time, when Mom calls out to her children playing upstairs or outside, somewhere down the street (for those with ears to hear), she understands and anticipates it will take some time for them to *get from there to here.*

In our case, Mom called us three boys to the house, and dinner table, in succession. She did so by order of age, in order to ensure compliance and accountability. This is leadership modeling for succession planning at its natural best. The baton is openly passed down the line. God operates in similar fashion. When it comes to life, it is true, we are to run our own race. When it comes to leadership, it also holds true that God runs our lives like a relay race.

> *"Do you not know that in a race all the runners run, but only one gets the prize? Run in such a way as to get the prize. Everyone who competes in the games goes into strict training. They do it to get a crown that will not last, but we do it to get a crown that will last forever. Therefore, I do not run like someone running aimlessly; I do not fight like a boxer beating the air. No, I strike a blow to my body and make it my slave so that after I have preached to others, I myself will not be disqualified for the prize."*

> *1 Corinthians 9:24-27 (NIV)*

Whenever God is preparing a paradigm shift, He calls for the next leader to step up and step out on faith while simultaneously raising up their successor. He also encourages them along, to be of good courage. Man down. Man up. When it comes to high performance, at the end of the day, like a good chief executive or head coach, God shows himself to be no no respecter of persons.

> *"For God shows no partiality [no arbitrary favoritism; with Him one person is not more important than another]."*

> *Romans 2:11 (AMP)*

85

Spotlight On 💡 Delegation

"But how can I bear your problems and your burdens and your disputes all by myself? Choose some wise, understanding and respected men from each of your tribes, and I will set them over you." You answered me, "What you propose to do is good." So I took the leading men of your tribes, wise and respected men, and appointed them to have authority over you—as commanders of thousands, of hundreds, of fifties and of tens and as tribal officials."

Deuteronomy 1:12-15 (NIV)

While it is certainly true that God shows no partiality when it comes to getting the job done, this is not to suggest God is oblivious to the need of putting the proper support mechanisms in place to balance out the workload and accomplish the task at hand. Whereas, even the most accomplished leader struggles in this area, God inspires us to higher levels of mastery when it comes to the fundamental notion of delegating.

In fact, as Moses is our witness in the above, opening verses in the Book of Deuteronomy, we advance our position further to suggest that ***effective*** delegation and empowerment is fundamentally, inextricably linked to ***efficient*** succession planning. In order to be successful at succession planning, leaders must equip other leaders. It's that simple, but complicated.

These days, leaders are being asked to identify, plan and prepare their cross-functional teams to function in leadership capacities within vertical silos. Meanwhile, failing to adequately empower them with sufficient authority or unleash them with the suitable (peripheral) vison required to navigate and impact the business horizontally.

This process of delegation within succession planning does not occur by osmosis. It must be placed into best practices. God left no doubt about how Moses would train and equip the inner circle, formed around the tabernacle. According to The Maxwell

Leadership Bible's Law of Empowerment, referencing Numbers 11:16-30, God says potential leaders need 7 things:

1.) *They need authority* (v.16, "bring them...that they may stand there with you").
2.) *They need anointing* (v.17, "I will take of the Spirit...and will put the same upon them").
3.) *They need ownership of the vision* (v.17, "the Spirit that is upon you...upon them").
4.) *They need responsibility* (v. 17, "they shall bear the burden of the people with you").
5.) *They need specific ministry roles* (v. 24, "placed them around the tabernacle").
6.) *They need to express their gifts* (v.25, "when the Spirit rested upon them...they prophesied").
7.) *They need a secure shepherd who will release them to succeed* (vv. 26-30, Moses).

Specifically, in times of transition, delegation for God's anointed leaders becomes embedded in both process orientation and spiritual formation. For instance, we don't know a lot about these seventy elders God instructed Moses to gather and aid him when his burdens back in the Book of Numbers had reached a breaking point. However, in rightfully dividing the following passage with the above scripture in Deuteronomy 1:12-15, we witness the establishment of an undeniable, consistent pattern of God's methods for delegation and succession planning.

> *"I cannot carry all these people by myself; the burden is too heavy for me. If this is how you are going to treat me, please go ahead and kill me—if I have found favor in your eyes—and do not let me face my own ruin." The Lord said to Moses: "Bring me seventy of Israel's elders who are known to you as leaders and officials among the people. Have them come to the tent of meeting, that they may stand there with you. I will come down and speak with you there, and I will take some of the power of the Spirit that is on*

*you and put it on them. They will share the burden of the
people with you so that you will not have to carry it alone."*

Numbers 11:14-17 (NIV)

It goes without saying, these elders and officers had gained influence and respect among the people. Most likely, they were among the rulers of thousands, hundreds, fifties and tens previously selected by Moses to judge the people (Exodus 18:25). The Old Testament mentions the seventy elders twice, both times to witness God's presence, power and glory.

Clearly, they are there for a reason. Like an Advisory Board, somewhere in the shadows, ready to be disposed and unleashed on behalf of a fledgling start-up or non-profit. But, for what reason, or task? For certain, we know the seventy elders were not assigned the more menial task at hand which was ticking the box for the hunger pains of the children of Israel as they grumbled and growled over the manna they were being fed.

Instead, in the last verse, we see that God has since expanded their role from witnesses, to participants. From passive governance to active stewardship. As God tells Moses, *"I will take of the Spirit that is upon you, and will put the same upon them; and they shall bear the burden of the people with you."* Not only does God provide His anointed leaders with extra arms, legs and hands on deck, to help share the load, He anoints them with the same power.

Moving further along a few verses later, we see that the Spirit has rested upon the seventy elders and they began to prophesy around the tabernacle (Numbers 11:24-25). We bookmark our text here, to underscore the main variables delineating the difference between how mankind delegates and how God delegates. It lies in the mechanics, timing and techniques being employed.

Like all things, there is calculated divine purpose in God's routine delegation. He doesn't delegate tasks for the sake of ticking boxes and lifting the leader's burdens. He delegates tasks for the sake of lifting the people's present burdens but also delegates tasks in such a way that ticks the bigger box next to His future succession plan.

In that regard, it is Moses' assistant Joshua, "one of his choice men," who God delegated the task of spying out and warning Moses against two other men in the camp named Eldad and Medad who were also prophesying but had not gone out to the tabernacle. Within the execution of this task of surveillance, we catch a glimpse of God's succession plans for Joshua to be included among the 12 spies. The successful completion of that task, leading to Joshua assuming the reigns form Moses and leading the children of Israel into the Promised Land.

Joshua's keen observation skills also detected something Moses must have overlooked. *God didn't so much call Moses to the task of getting the people to the Promised Land as much as he called Moses to the people*. During his 360 panoramic exit interview, God didn't judge and call Moses "to task" for his inability to *get them there physically or logistically* but for his inability to *get them there emotionally and spiritually*.

> *"And the Lord said to Moses that very same day, Go up to this mountain of the Abarim, Mount Nebo, which is in the land of Moab opposite Jericho, and look at the land of Canaan, which I am giving to the sons of Israel as a possession. Then die on the mountain you climb, and be gathered to your people [in death], just as Aaron your brother died on Mount Hor and was gathered to his people, because you broke faith with Me among the sons of Israel at the waters of Meribah-kadesh, in the Wilderness of Zin, and because you did not treat Me as holy among of the sons of Israel. For you shall see the land opposite you from a distance, but you shall not go there, into the land which I am giving to the children of Israel."*
>
> *Deuteronomy 32:48-51 (AMP)*

God didn't want the children of Israel to make a mass exodus to freedom, He needed them to know *He* was the one delivering them from bondage. Thus, it was still **Him** that was removing their wilderness burdens. While he had entrusted them into Moses' care, God was needing Moses to let the Hebrews know it was in God in whom they needed to trust. *This* was the task at hand.

> *"But you are a CHOSEN RACE, A ROYAL PRIESTHOOD, A CONSECRATED NATION, A [special] PEOPLE FOR God's OWN POSSESSION, so that you may proclaim the excellencies [the wonderful deeds and virtues and perfections] of Him who called you out of darkness into His marvelous light. Once you were NOT A PEOPLE [at all], but now you are God's PEOPLE, once you had NOT RECEIVED MERCY, but now you have RECEIVED MERCY."*

> *1 Peter 2:9-10 (AMP)*

This was not because God needed the credit, but because they needed to learn how to praise Him. This was not for now, but because they would need it later. They needed to see the big picture Peter paints for us. For so many of us leading others through wilderness experiences, be it in transition and acquisition or seasons and quarters, it gets difficult to see the proverbial forest for the trees. The trees represent the tasks and obstacles that are before us and appear to be in the way. The Israelites couldn't see the Promised Land for the commands and manna in their midst.

They couldn't see that the forest and the trees were both designed by God. They were the designated place and unfamiliar confines that would turn them from rebels into a royal priesthood. Likewise, God is wanting us to help those entrusted to our care to see themselves and the things going on around them for what (and who) they really are.

He wants to help us help them by recognizing we are in the forest, itself. For a season. And the trees are there for a reason. They are not there to be removed, but to be reckoned with. They are part of our current environment or new surroundings. Get over it. Go under it. Go around it. No matter what, get used to it. Get accustomed to being burdened. Get acclimated to conflict.

Times are lean, so get used to leaning in on that manna. Eat to live, don't live to eat. After all, it's an eternal lifetime's worth of angel food that is falling down from Heaven. Hallelujah! Indeed, manna should be something to shout about because it should tell you something about who you *really are*.

Upon completing the task of alleviating obstacles and reckoning with the trees in our midst, we can make progress. Sounds good, right? If only we knew how many trees are in your forest right now. If Paul Bunyan were CEO, he could resign with a lifetime of axes to grind. We get it. Fortunately, God does too. He knows the most challenging thing for leaders with broad shoulders to admit is when too much is much too much. He knows the most difficult thing for a leader accustomed to doing more with less to grapple with is realizing just enough is no longer enough.

We've articulated the fact that God uses delegation to offer glimpses into his succession plan. In order to properly frame the practice for our organizations, we now pedagogically establish the following as guiding Kingdom principles for succession planning:

Succession Planning Guiding Principles

1.) Don't get it twisted. God wants to establish his purpose through leadership succession planning, not your agenda. As the Bible says, He will establish you and "your thoughts" once you and your organization are aligned with this way of thinking.
2.) Because He uses who He pleases unto his perfect pattern, God's work and divine plan for the ages is never void of a representative. No need to call the bullpen. The ace is already somewhere working his way to the mound.
3.) Lest we think too highly of ourselves or start believing our own hype that nobody can preach, teach or outreach the way we do, God will call up a minor shepherd boy figure to

the palace or take a sheepish, unskilled minor leaguer and turn him back into a GOAT.

4.) Succession is ongoing but the transfer of power and authority occurs in an instant, at the pinnacle of God's timing, not the prime of our lives or careers. Surely, AARP can delight in the stats that Moses was 80 and Aaron 83 when they stepped to Pharaoh. Denny's would be anatomically correct by naming a meal after Joshua who was just north of retirement age, between 68-78 years old, when he entered the Promised Land.

5.) Servitude determines altitude. There is simply no way around it and no short cuts to take. Servant Leadership goes hand in hand with God's succession plan. *To lead* and succeed, is to have first successfully served others. *To serve*, is to have last succeeded in the task of leading others successfully into service.

Spotlight On ● Servant Leadership

In other words, servant leadership is not just *showing your commitment* by volunteering during your annual community or giving day. Servant Leadership is *demonstrating your commitment* by showing others how to serve. Like Christ.

> *"Then He poured water into the basin and began washing the disciples' feet and wiping them with the towel which was tied around His waist. When He came to Simon Peter, he said to Him, "Lord, are You going to wash my feet?" Jesus replied to him, "You do not realize now what I am doing, but you will [fully] understand it later." Peter said to Him, "You will never wash my feet!" Jesus answered, "Unless I wash you, you have no part with Me [we can have nothing to do with each other]."*
>
> *John 13:5-8 (AMP)*

Wait a minute. Why is Jesus so emphatic about this? That's pretty strong language, is it not? Preparing to distance Himself, and cut off His right hand man, in a dispute over who would wash each other's feet! That's a departure and pretty far cry from Philippi and the Book of Matthew where we find Jesus calling Peter by name, as the rock He would build his church upon.

Or, perhaps, is this foundational illustration of servant leadership also teaching us something not so fundamental about how we are to perceive and approach succession planning? Indeed, Christ was probably thinking: "Peter, if you see *Me* washing your dusty feet and the downtrodden dogs of the others, how much more should I expect from *you*."

In order to be effective, Christ knew His disciples needed to shift their mental model, change their thinking around succession and rearrange their idea of what it meant to serve as a Messiah. It was their servitude that would determine their altitude. This elevated thinking would not come to them or flow through them for others to follow, merely by sitting "in glory" to the right and left of Christ as John and James so desired (Mark 10:37).

Instead, it would come through the sacrifice of ego and pride made from getting into a lowly position and humble posture of true servitude.

> *"So when He had washed their feet and put on His [outer] robe and reclined at the table again, He said to them, "Do you understand what I have done for you? You call Me Teacher and Lord, and you are right in doing so, for that is who I am. So if I, the Lord and the Teacher, washed your feet, you ought to wash one another's feet as well. For I gave you [this as] an example, so that you should do [in turn] as I did to you. I assure you and most solemnly say to you, a slave is not greater than his master, nor is one who is sent greater than the one who sent him. If you know these things, you are blessed [happy and favored by God] if you put them into practice [and faithfully do them]."*

> *John 13:12-17 (AMP)*

What is Christ doing?

Yes, He is teaching. But, *what* is He teaching? Servant Leadership 101? Without a doubt. But there's more. Catch this. Upon taking a deeper dive, we see Jesus is actually reeling Peter in to what it *really* means to be a "Fisher of Men" during the last supper with His. Inside of this defining moment in the upper room, before making His transition from office, Christ is having a meeting of the minds with His disciples to *demonstrate* His plans for succession planning.

And it's a tad bit different from what James and John had in mind. The purpose of the meeting is to totally change and reframe their perspective. Before they could "go out" externally and make disciples of the nations, Christ was aligning their internal company mission, vision and values around discipleship. He was recasting their image of what it *meant* to be a disciple, and what it *took* to be a Messiah. Christ was refocusing their mindset on succession planning by demonstrating it *himself* through servant leadership.

Jesus is making it plain to the disciples that there can be no succession without sacrifice. His example, serving as living proof there will be no succession going on *up there*, without some suffering taking place *down here*. The Lord is telling his anointed leaders to plan on sacrificing something back there in that cubicle, before you get up here to the C+Suite. As the saying goes, it costs to be the boss.

In the end, that all sounds good, and looks good externally. Especially, when you're on the outside looking in. What Christ is really after, and what he's really wanting to know from his executive team is if they have exercised proper accounting for all the internal costs? We can hear Christ saying, "I get that everyone wants to be the CEO, but is there a CFO in the house?"

> *"If one of you wanted to build a tower, wouldn't you first sit down and calculate the cost, to determine whether you have enough money to complete it? Otherwise, when you have*

laid the foundation but couldn't finish the tower, all who see it will begin to belittle you. They will say, 'Here's the person who began construction and couldn't complete it!"

Luke 14:28-29 (CEB)

The teacher in Him wants to know that his MBA students are employing the correct method of accounting. Let's go there for a brief moment, for the sake of hammering home the point. Financial Accounting deals with the reports that analysts, creditors, third-parties and Pharisees haggle over. These external users and commentators rarely have access to the exact, specific information that is internal to the organization.

As a result, they must rely upon heresy, general reports and the results presented by the company. Which is fine by them. In effect, when it comes to going inside the numbers, they are remotely interested in which particular department office paid for stuff. Depending upon how much skin they have in the game, they are mainly interested in the bottom line. Overall, they are concerned with overall costs. Net-net, they want to know the profit margin, yield or gain.

Essentially, these external players want to know what value was extracted from the project.

Conversely, managerial accounting deals with house business. It provides internal managers with itemized views into personnel matters and resource constraints. Unlike external users, the managers of a business have a need to know and desire to have access to far more detailed information. As such, managerial accounting information tends to be focused on products, departments and activities. Great care is taken to ensure that the resulting reports which are made public stem from and enable good, informed decision making. Both seasonally and in real-time.

Lastly, cost information is disseminated in such a way that managers can focus on and be held accountable for their specific segment of the business. It's little wonder CFO's often make for great successors and are typically the most likely to be chosen or named as interim CEOs.

In either event, viewing discipleship activity within the context of Father's housekeeping, we see why the nature of Christ's concerns in the upper room go beyond toe jams. For what it's worth, we're beginning to catch Christ's drift. In the final analysis, Jesus is not merely addressing the accrued costs of being a disciple. That's where the carrying of the cross comes in.

What Christ is really trying to do is bring us around to observing the fixed costs. Beyond the variable sacrificing and suffering that comes with waiting *until* it's your turn, the upper room points us to the sacrificing and suffering required *when* it's your turn. This is the fixed, eternal posture referenced above. Before handing over the Kingdom keys, Christ is showing His disciples they can't succeed Him until they've sacrificed like Him and served like Him.

Jesus could not depart from them until they got the message we received from the earlier scripture in the Book of John where Christ says, *"nor is one who is sent greater than the one who sent him."* This is succession planning in perpetuity.

Peter's natural train of thought on succession was for him to wash the feet of the Messiah. No doubt, humbly accepting the ritual as being ceremoniously attached to it. Just as he would expect of those who would, in turn, wash his. However, he had yet to grasp the Kingdom lesson Christ was teaching referenced above, and now further established here.

Peter didn't realize that *to lead and succeed, is to have **first** successfully served others*. Up until now, Peter didn't understand that *to serve and succeed, is to have **last** succeeded at leading others* successfully into service. Like Christ.

Jesus successfully led by first serving others. Jesus was adamant with Peter because He knew He was in the correct posture in the upper room. Christ was successfully serving by leading His disciples successfully into service. Therefore, He now sits and serves forevermore at the right hand of the Father. In God's eyes, this is what it means to say servant leadership goes hand in hand with succession planning.

What does this mean for your enterprise? It means you must come to grips with how your organization grasps this concept, or not. It means that shifting, engaging and converting the mental models of your leadership team around the "service of succession" must be as intrinsic to your business model as engagement, conversion and customer service. It means your entire C+Suite must be first adopters when it comes to fostering a culture of servitude.

If your leadership demonstrates a life and commitment to the service of others, it only makes sense that others will model that same behavior. In order to transform the way people throughout your organization think, it begins with transformative, corrective action at the top. As a wise person once said: *"You might not always think your way into right acting, but you sure can act your way into right thinking."*

Take a look around. Who do you see right acting, in the eternal posture of servitude? Not in the usual "CYA" stance. Not putting on a show for clients and investors. Not at their annual review, or when a new position opens up. Not when they show up for credit, to their aforementioned volunteer commitment. Not those at the entry-level who are always looking to *serve up* to those in higher positions, but those in higher up positions who are willing to *serve down*.

Do you work for your team, or does your team work for you? Bottom line, if this intangible metric of servant leadership doesn't tangibly factor into your succession planning, you're wasting precious time, money and human resources. Indeed, the harvest is plentiful but the workers are few. God is not necessarily going around asking for volunteers either. He's equipping a succession of his most capable servants to lead.

In this very moment, God is incubating some leaders and calling upon others to courageously come out from the shadows to lean in on a specific assignment. For every good work. Some jobs a lot taller. Some tasks more menial than others. All of them being of equal importance in the functioning of the corporate body during these millennium times of transition.

It bears repeating. The Holy Bible is the definitive source and blueprint for succession planning. God's mastery is self-evident, and made readily apparent, throughout. God foretells us as much. This is not a nebulous task. We serve a God who is quite thorough. When it comes to God's criteria or rubric for succession planning, scripture affords us these everlasting encounters of God passing the mantle of Leadership from one to the other and to the next.

From beginning to end...
Last to first...
In particular order...

> *"Look, I am coming soon! My reward is with me, and I will give to each person according to what they have done. I am the Alpha and the Omega, the First and the Last, the Beginning and the End."*

> *Revelation 22:12-13 (NIV)*

John to Jesus...

> *"There was a man sent from God whose name was John. He came as a witness to testify concerning that light, so that through him all might believe. He himself was not the light; he came only as a witness to the light. The true light that gives light to everyone was coming into the world. He was in the world, and though the world was made through him, the world did not recognize him."*

> *John 1:6-10 (NIV)*

Eli to Samuel...

Though the young Samuel was ministering in the tabernacle, he still didn't know the Lord, and the word of the Lord had not yet been revealed to him (1 Samuel 3:7). The first three times the Lord called Samuel, the boy responded to Eli. Eli then understood what was happening and instructed Samuel to respond to the Lord if he called again. Then, "The LORD came and stood there, calling as at the other times, 'samuel! Samuel!' Then Samuel said, 'speak, for your servant is listening'" (1 Samuel 3:10). God gave him a message of judgment to relay to Eli. The following day, Samuel took his first leap of faith, telling Eli everything, even though the message was bad news for Eli and his family (1 Samuel 3:11–18). Eli responded with acceptance. Samuel's credibility as a prophet spread throughout Israel, and God continued to reveal His Word to His people through Samuel (1 Samuel 3:20–21).

Samuel to Saul to David to Solomon...

> *"Now a day before Saul came, the Lord had informed Samuel [of this], saying, "About this time tomorrow I will send you a man from the land of Benjamin, and you shall anoint him as leader over My people Israel; and he will save My people from the hand of the Philistines. For I have looked upon [the distress of] My people, because their cry [for help] has come to Me." When Samuel saw Saul, the Lord said to him, "There is the man whom I spoke to you. This one shall rule over My people [as their king]."*

> *1 Samuel 9:15-17 (AMP)*

What a powerful illustration of the precise, divine nature of God's divine succession plan in the above passage of scripture in First Samuel. *"About this time tomorrow."* It wasn't "at some point this week," or "sometime over the weekend" that God informed Samuel of Saul's arrival to be anointed. Instead, we discern how God pre-arranges the divine appointments He makes for those He calls to leadership right up to, coming down from eternity into, the moment.

This is providentially powerful. In this moment, at the city gate, we enter into further witness and gain all access to added perspective from our earlier measuring of Peter and Cornelius' acts of divine providence. When God is preparing someone for a moment, He is quite capably, multi-tasking someone else simultaneously. Just as Abraham was preparing to sacrifice young Isaac, God was preparing a ram to come up the other side of the mountain to arrive at the same time.

It's often said, half the battle comes from our showing up on time, and coming prepared. We say, the other half is preparing to show up, *on his time*. Not ours. His comes in an instant. Are you prepared for your "this time tomorrow" moment?

Saul was certainly prepared as the one God had selected to lead the nation of Israel. Samuel had physically anointed Saul with oil when God selected him as the first king over Israel. 1 Samuel 10:1 says, *"Samuel took a flask of olive oil and poured it on Saul's head and kissed him, saying, 'Has not the Lord anointed you ruler over his inheritance?'"* The meaning of the physical anointing is found in the fact that Saul was set apart by God for leadership.

For a season.

> *"The Lord said to Samuel, "How long will you grieve for Saul, when I have rejected him as king over Israel? Fill your horn with oil and go; I will send you to Jesse the Bethelemite, for I have chosen a king for Myself among his sons."*
>
> *1 Samuel 16:1 (AMP)*

Samuel anointing David is one of the most pivotal moments in scripture. Reading and reflecting upon this passage of scripture gives depth of insight into God's sovereign sense of urgency behind the call to succession. If we were to sermonize this message as part of a series on succession, we might title it: *Part 1: "When God Says Go." Part II: "Because I Said So."*

God is telling Samuel in this moment that He must get over what was (and what was not to be) in order to go forward. In order to get from Point A to Point B, leaders must have the capability to go beyond what went wrong yesterday and get past their attachment to what they thought was to be. Ok, so this time God has found a king "*Himself.*" Why is that?

Because He is God all by *Himself.* Like a good parent, God is there. Have you ever tried working with your child to give them what they want? Even though you know it's an unreasonable request that is not going to end well. But you go along with it because you know there's an important lesson in it. Besides, you already have other plans for them so it's not really going to *change* anything in the grand scheme of things. Except their feelings, at the moment.

In Israel's case, they wanted a king. Complete with horses, chariots and the chance to play dress up like the other nations. God heard their whining. And allowed it. Up to a certain point. The point where unreasonableness starts to interfere with progress. Like the parent trying to excuse themselves from the play date early because of the other birthday party that awaits their child.

Until their child nags, whines and negotiates their way into 10 more minutes in the bounce house. After all, they've never experienced a bounce house in the backyard with a pool and tree house too, which is now looming so much larger than their own house. Less than 15 minutes later, same child is sprawled out on the bounce house floor crying over having to leave.

Those extra 10 minutes of happiness now morphing into sheer and utter embarrassment. "*One more jump*, pleeeaasseeee." That's the point just past reasonableness where you tell your child, as God did Samuel. "Time to go....*it is what it is.*" Point being, far too often, we hold on far too long to what God is telling us to let go of. We hold on to what didn't work instead of trusting that God has already worked out what's next. The next big event and major milestone is right around the corner. Something exceedingly, abundantly above what we can ask or think is in the works, while we're still caught up in the moment.

Isn't it comforting to know that God is the type of leader that acts like a good parent. He's not winging our weekend plans, or making this thing called life up on the day-to-day basis as we go along. If only we could blindly trust him to order our steps in his succession. God tells Samuel *"I will make clear to you what to do."* Our Father's sense of urgency always comes with the assurance and encouragement that He will take care of us, address our concerns and properly guide us. Without fail, or need of falling out.

As leaders and future masters of succession planning, we are becoming more cognizant of the fact that we may be carrying someone else's anointing as much as someone may be carrying ours. Both roles are pivotal in the process of divine alignment. Human Resource practitioners and Executive Recruiters play a vital, often unsung, role in such a way. In fact, we might argue that the best of them come into an organization or search with their horns full of oil.

And they know it.

Because of this, they also know an anointing flows back and forth, to and from the source. From one day to the next, one search to the other. At the end of the day, it's not about *who* they *have* in mind. It's about *what* the client *has* in mind. To that end, it's about the bigger picture that is always bigger than them. Saul was the people's choice, but David was God's decision.

For example, you may be assigned to support a business unit or lead a search that gives you much consternation, or causes you to question an unpopular personnel decision made "above your pay grade" and outside of your consideration set. That's until realizing the move opened up the opportunity for you to fill your horn back up with oil to go and anoint the C+Suite with the chosen one God is sending your way or get ready for the search assignment that will show up on your radar "this time tomorrow."

Having tangible experience managing someone else's anointing and knowing where to find the anointed one is to be a power broker among searchers. Possessing the uncanny ability to let go of preconceived notions is invaluable. Learning how to respect the choice and trust the process (despite the events) is a crucial management skill for HR leaders to hone and develop in order to become trusted advisors to the business.

Furthermore, it's downright critical in family-owned businesses for all parties involved to show proper respect downstream for choice, cadence and sequence. Indeed, it comes by Executive order to gain access to and be granted a seat at the table in the King's court of succession planning. You might say, David's grace was in the past. But his favor was in the future.

> *"Because David respected God's choices and readily accepted God's will in the past, the young David had already been anointed as the future king of Israel. First Samuel 16:13 records, "Samuel took the horn of oil and anointed him in the presence of his brothers, and from that day on the Spirit of the Lord came powerfully upon David." It would be many years before God would place him as the official king of the nation, but David knew from experience what it meant to be the Lord's anointed. King David answered, "Call Bathsheba to me." And she came into the king's presence and said, "As the LORD lives, who has redeemed my soul from all distress, even as I swore to you by the LORD, the God of Israel, saying, 'Solomon your son shall certainly be king after me, and he shall sit on my throne in my place'; I will indeed do so this very day."*
>
> *Bathsheba bowed down with her fact to the ground, and laid herself face down before the king and said, "May my lord King David live forever!"*
>
> *1 Kings 1:28-31 (AMP)*

Solomon was the third and last king of the united kingdom of Israel, following King Saul and King David. He was the son of David and Bathsheba, the former wife of Uriah the Hittite whom David had killed to hide his adultery with Bathsheba while her husband was on the battle front. Solomon wrote the Song of Solomon, the book of Ecclesiastes, and much of the book of Proverbs. His authorship of Ecclesiastes is contested by some, but Solomon is the only "son of David" to be "king over Israel" (not just Judah) "in Jerusalem" (Ecclesiastes 1:1, 12), and many of the descriptions of the author fit Solomon perfectly. Solomon reigned for 40 years (1 Kings 11:42). We will revisit the tragic story of Solomon in a later chapter.

Elijah to Elisha...

As we will also dig deeper into shortly during the discussion on mentorship, and exploration of 2 Kings 2, Elijah and Elisha crossed the Jordan River on dry land. Elisha, knowing that Elijah would not be with him much longer, asked to be blessed with a double portion of Elijah's spirit. Elijah was taken directly into heaven by a chariot of fire. Elisha picked up Elijah's mantle and used it to cross the Jordan again on dry land. He received the double portion he had asked for and performed many miracles in Israel.

> *"When the LORD was about to take Elijah up to heaven by a whirlwind, Elijah and Elisha were traveling from Gilgal. And Elijah said to Elisha, "Please stay here, for the LORD has sent me to Bethel." But Elisha replied, "As the LORD lives and as your soul lives, I will not leave you."*
>
> *So they went down to Bethel. Now the sons of the prophets who were at Bethel came out to Elisha and said to him, "Do you know that the LORD will take your master away from you today?" He said, "Yes, I know it; be quiet [about it]."*
>
> *2 Kings 21-3 (AMP)*

Naomi to Ruth...

"Then Naomi said, "Look, your sister-in-law has gone back to her people and to her gods; turn back and follow your sister-in-law." But Ruth said, "Do not urge me to leave you or to turn back from following you; for where you go, I will go, and where you lodge, I will lodge. Your people will be my people, and your God, my God. Where you die, I will die, and there I will be buried. May the Lord do the same to me [as He has done to you], and more also, if anything but death separates me from you." When Naomi saw that Ruth was determined to go with her, she said nothing more."

Ruth 1:15-18 (AMP)

Ruth was "of the women of Moab," which was a pagan culture, but was genetically linked to Israel through Lot, the nephew of Abraham. She had married the son of an Israelite family while they were living in Moab, but at some point her father-in-law, her husband, and her husband's only brother died. Ruth had to make a decision whether to stay in Moab, her home, or to go with her mother-in-law, Naomi, to a land she had never known—Judah. Ruth identified herself completely and totally with Naomi. Scripture says, "Ruth clung to her" (Ruth 1:14). The verb translated "clung to" is the same term used in Genesis 2:24 to define the "cleaving, uniting, or holding fast" of a man and woman in marriage.

Needless to say, Ruth's identity was now inextricably linked to Naomi's. She had made a radical and absolute dedication to Naomi, her people, and her God. Ruth surrendered every aspect of her life into Naomi's hands. Together, they made the journey back to Judah to the city of Bethlehem, where they decided to settle. Ruth's following of Naomi led her from Moab to Jerusalem, where she found a new beginning and also discovered Boaz, her new husband and kinsman redeemer.

Ruth trusted the Lord, and He rewarded her faithfulness by giving her not only a husband but a son (Obed), a grandson (Jesse), and a great-grandson named David, the king of Israel (Ruth 4:17). Besides these gifts (Psalm 127:3), God gave Ruth the blessing of being listed in the lineage of Jesus (Matthew 1:5). The lives of these, two matriarchal women from different cultures underscore the significant role women would play – leading up to Mary and Elizabeth - in God's Messianic succession plan from umbilical cord to umbilical cord. Ruth shows how God can change a life and take redemption and succession in a direction He has preordained.

Spotlight On ♀ Next Gen Leadership

Moses to Joshua...

As much as we tend to focus on the defining moment of Moses' failure to obey God which cost the Promised Land, his transgression is only half the battle. Literally. In God's grand scheme of things, Moses wasn't supposed to go. Joshua was better suited for the next phase of the assignment. God knew what was around the corner and waiting for the children of Israel on the other side. He knew the competition was going to be more hostile toward them.

He knew the battle was shifting from managing the internal drama to responding to the external theatre. He knew they were moving past Egypt, but traveling behind enemy lines. He knew the Canaanites were waiting in the south. And the Amalekites were camped out in the mountains. And Moses was getting up there in years. Knowing all of this, God was already preparing a more skillful warrior in Joshua, in advance. God knew He needed someone of good courage with both a brave and loyal heart for the fight. More importantly, He knew *the people* would need Joshua.

God has patterned and optimized succession planning at its absolute best for us. Unlike us, God is not reacting to current events, but anticipating future events. When God knows it's time to change the course and direction of leadership in the C+Suite, He will not overreact or overreach by pulling an "outsider" in for the sake of shaking things up. God is not going to deploy Kingdom capital for the purpose of neutralizing or appeasing the board. Although he most certainly has authorization and unilateral approval to do so.

"But who [among them] has stood in the council of the Lord, That he would perceive and hear His word? Who has marked His word [noticing and observing and paying attention to it] and has [actually] heard it?"

Jeremiah 23:18 (AMP)

Still, time and time again, God proves himself to be the fair and righteous judge. And deliberate decision maker. God can ALWAYS be found in the continuous process of success planning. Not for one fiscal year. Not for an election cycle, or two. You most certainly won't find Him outsourcing His divine appointments to a search committee, on an exclusive basis. Regardless of circumstance, God will be *"in-sourcing"* the overall process to ensure proper divine alignment.

Which brings us to fit.

Being no respecter of persons, the succession plan that God puts in place will cast the right leader in the right role, at the right place, at the right time. As the word says, *"God doesn't call the qualified, He qualifies the called."* How often does our succession planning juxtapose the position and nullify such order? Far too often, we find the right person, in the wrong place, at the right time. In other instances, we have a tendency to place the wrong person, in the right place, at the wrong time. Or, some muddled sequence thereof. If only we could see beyond our own bias and get past the perceptions and opinions of others to see the way God levels the field.

"For when God made the promise to Abraham, He swore [an oath] by Himself, since He had no one greater by whom to swear, saying, "I will surely bless you and I will surely multiply you." And so, having patiently waited, he realized the promise [in the miraculous birth of Isaac, as a pledge of what was to come from God].

Indeed, men swear [an oath] by one greater than themselves, and with them [in all disputes] the oath serves as confirmation [of what has been said] and is an end of the dispute. In the same way God, in His desire to show to the heirs of the promise the unchangeable nature of His purpose, intervened and guaranteed it with an oath, so that by two unchangeable things [His promise and His oath] in which it is impossible for God to lie, we who have fled [to Him] for refuge would have strong encouragement and indwelling strength to hold tightly to the hope set before us."

Hebrews 6:13-18 (AMP)

If only we could get with the fact that God is not a man that he should lie when He provides encouragement with His marching orders and strength in His changing of the guard.

"Only be strong and very courageous; be careful to do [everything] in accordance with the entire law which Moses My servant commanded you; do not turn from it to the right or to the left, so that you may prosper and be successful wherever you go."

Joshua 1:7 (AMP)

If only we could let go of our ego long enough to grab hold of the way God leads and realize *we* don't always have to be in command to be in control.

"Have I not commanded you? Be strong and courageous! Do not be terrified or dismayed (intimidated), for the Lord your God is with you wherever you go."

Joshua 1:9 (AMP)

If only we could pledge our allegiance the same way God serves up the same oath and pledges the same promise to support the successor, as He did for the outgoing leader. God's word is bond.

His offer is not mere lip service. Can we boast the same? Show of hands, quickly.

How many leaders have come into the C+Suite, been promoted to an interim position, given an appointment to replace an executive director or supplant a new management team and been told *"we're here for you, we've got your back, whatever you need!"* or some affirmative composite of that hollow promise? Only to have that promissory note return null and void when you looked to cash it in. Only to find the location of the knife in your back was precisely targeted and exacted by the same source of your affirmation or consecration. Only to have the knife pulled out by your successor.

Verily, verily, I say to you. God's ways are not our ways, when it comes to succession planning.

> *"No man will [be able to] stand before you [to oppose you] as long as you live. Just as I was [present] with Moses, so will I be with you; I will not fail you or abandon you."*
>
> *Joshua 1:5 (AMP)*

With God giving Joshua the same oath and promise of his predecessor Moses, God is showing his leaders that succession planning is not only a *continual process* but a *continuous covenant.*

> *"Now it happened after the death of Moses the servant of the Lord, that the Lord spoke to Joshua the son of Nun, Moses' servant (attendant), saying, "Moses My servant is dead; now therefore arise [to take his place], cross over this Jordan, you and all this people, into the land which I am giving to them, to the sons of Israel. I have given you every place on which the sole of your foot treads, just as I promised to Moses."*
>
> *Joshua 1:1-3 (AMP)*

Precisely.

"Then God said, "Do not come near; take your sandals off your feet [out of respect], because the place on which you are standing is holy ground." Then He said, "I am the God of your father, the God of Abraham, the God of Isaac, and the God of Jacob." Then Moses hid his face, because he was afraid to look at God."

Exodus 3:5-6 (AMP)

Right down to the consecutive ground the leaders stand on.

"The captain of the Lord's army said to Joshua, "Remove your sandals from your feet, because the place where you are standing is holy (set apart to the Lord)." And Joshua did so."

Joshua 5:15 (AMP)

So it ends, and begins. Then ends. In the exact, same spot. Only to begin again. Joshua gets laid to rest at Shechem. The site of Abraham's covenant. In the same portion of field Jacob purchased for the descendants of Joseph. All, in God's succession plan.

"On that day Joshua made a covenant for the people and established just rule for them at Shechem. Joshua wrote these words in God's Instruction scroll. Then he took a large stone and put it up there under the oak in the sanctuary of the LORD. Joshua said to all the people, "This stone will serve here as a witness against us, because it has heard all the LORD's words that he spoke to us. It will serve as a witness against you in case you aren't true to your God." Then Joshua sent the people away to each one's legacy. After these events, Joshua, Nun's son, the LORD's servant, died. He was 110. They buried him within the border of his own legacy, in Timnath-serah in the highlands of Ephraim north of Mount Gaash. Israel served the LORD all the days of Joshua and all the days of the elders who outlived Joshua. They had known every act the LORD had done for Israel. The Israelites had brought up the bones of Joseph

*from Egypt. They buried them at Shechem in the portion
of field that Jacob had purchased for one hundred qesitahs
from the descendants of Hamor the father of Shechem. They
became a legacy of the descendants of Joseph."*

Joshua 24:25-32 (CEB)

God has a 100% retention rate for this reason. He keeps His word.
You can count on it. You can take His promises to your treasury
department and seal it with a covenant. For this reason, leadership
continuity is paramount toward achieving *His* ongoing concern and
organizational success in perpetuity. This is simply not possible to
achieve without succession planning rooted in the Kingdom principles we are espousing here.

Let's proceed further into the succession plan of this next-gener-
ation leader to observe another clear distinction. Joshua was the
right *type* of leader, at the right *pace*, at the *ripe* time.

Not because he somehow arrived at the pivotal, inflection point
in response to a leadership crisis, or thrust himself into a leadership vacuum. It was because God put him there. And knew exactly
where He wanted Joshua to be placed. And when He wanted Moses
to be replaced. And not by happenstance. There is no succession
of accidents when you plan on (and with) God's purpose. In that
regard, Joshua assumed the leadership mantle from Moses in a
season where Israel needed military *leadership might*, not diplomatic *leadership finesse*.

Think about that for a minute. While Moses was fighting the children of Israel in the wilderness with internal finesse, God was really
building up their stamina and resistance in preparation for their
fight with the "ites" that lied ahead of them. A fight for which,
diplomacy was ill gotten gain. In Moses' stead, they would need a
leader of military might.

Like Joshua.

✎ *Leadership Key of Joshua*

"Who Got Next"

Inquiring minds always want to know, but often can't handle the truth. Like the Israelites, the answers come with weeping and mourning. And much travails. After traveling so far, and coming so close to victory. Coach, how do we game plan after Vince Lombardi?

When Joshua's time came, he succeeded Moses carefully, respectfully and naturally. He didn't reinvent the wheel. He finished the work *of* Moses, not *for* Moses. He led the people of Israel to victory into the Promised Land.

In doing so, the former assistant coach, winning one for the Gipper.

As you look into your five-year business plan and succession plan, are they synchronized operationally? Or, compartmentalized dysfunctionally? Are these plans united in the C+Suite, or housed within separate divisions and business units? Are you preparing your next cadre of managers and leaders to assume the next stage of growth and phase of competition? Or, are you assuming they will have the right skill set for the task? Or, worse still, will you simply be hoping and praying everything adapts and adjusts when the time comes?

No doubt, when Joshua's time came, he was coming into some pretty big shoes to fill.

> *"Now Joshua the son of Nun was filled with the spirit of wisdom, for Moses had laid his hands on him; so the sons of Israel listened to him and did as the Lord commanded Moses. Since that time no prophet has risen in Israel like Moses, whom the Lord knew face to face, [none equal to him] in all the signs and wonders which the Lord sent him to perform in the land of Egypt against Pharaoh, all his servants, and all his land, and in all the mighty power and*

*all the great and terrible deeds which Moses performed in
the sight of all Israel."*

Deuteronomy 34:9-12 (AMP)

Earlier, in the opening chapter of Deuteronomy 31, we were
afforded an internal seat and birds-eye view into a momentous
corporate event. It is the 120th birthday for Moses. And he has
chosen to mark the occasion by naming his successor. We've all
been there before.

Perhaps, you worked for a family-owned business where the patriarch was the only leader anyone ever knew. Maybe you were part
of a privately-held enterprise where the founder kept ticking well
past retirement. Could be, the owner of your previous company
kept coming to the office bright and early every day, as if it were
the last. Like the Energizer Bunny, they all kept lasting. Growing
old, but staying longer and going home later than the company's
new jacks.

Then, suddenly you heard the news.

The founder was stepping down, or falling back. The day everyone
quietly speculated and not so quietly murmured about, has finally
arrived. The moment some silently and others openly wished for,
was there. Cause for celebration, or consternation? Isn't it ironic,
the one leadership change we think we want the most, is the one
thing we are the least prepared to handle when the actual time
comes. Once they are no longer with us.

> *"So Moses the servant of the Lord died there in the land of
> Moab, according to the word of the Lord. And He buried
> him in the valley in the land of Moab, opposite Beth-peor;
> but no man knows where his burial place is to this day.
> Although Moses was a hundred and twenty years old when
> he died, his eyesight was not dim, nor his natural strength
> abated. So the sons of Israel wept for Moses in the plains*

of Moab for thirty days; then the days of weeping and mourning for Moses were ended."

Deuteronomy 34:5-8 (AMP)

Once the patriarch has passed, or the matriarch moves on, there really is one question on the minds of those that matter, and the rest really don't mind either way. Before the people could ask, Joshua made it perfectly clear who was in command now. And exactly who had next.

"Then Joshua commanded the officers of the people, saying, "Go throughout the camp and command the people, saying, 'Prepare your provisions, for within three days you are to cross this [river] Jordan, to go in to take possession of the land which the Lord your God is giving you to possess [as an inheritance]."

Joshua 1:10-11 (AMP)

To which, the people responded:

"They answered Joshua, saying, "All that you have commanded us we will do, and wherever you send us we will go. Just as we obeyed Moses in all things, so will we obey you; only may the Lord your God be with you as He was with Moses. Any man who rebels against your command and does not obey everything that you command him, shall be put to death; only be strong and courageous."

Joshua 1:16-18 (AMP)

Did anyone just catch that?

Are these *not* the same disobedient rebels who made Moses yell? Are these *not* the same Hebrew children who essentially told Moses, "I would rather go my way than your "high way," now expressing their willingness to go the distance for Joshua? Is this *not* the same wishy washy *"Yes, Lord* we shall follow all of your commands today but not so sure what tomorrow brings" generation now responding back to Joshua with the *very same* command God have to Joshua???

"Only be strong and courageous."

The answer is, Yes and No.

You can file this under different times calling for different leadership measures. You can place it under the header of God's rule being sovereign, and moving unilaterally, but His leadership style showing itself to be far from monolithic. During Moses' tenure, God maintained a role of governance. He played the role of mentor, and stern but loving Father, allowing His children to mature from nursing on milk to digesting the meat and potatoes of their circumstances.

By the time Joshua takes command, God assumes a different posture altogether. He negotiated, as much as navigated, Moses and the Israelites through the Wilderness. Not negotiating in the passive-aggressive sense, or flip flopping on his laws or precepts. That much was clear. However, bringing them all under subjection to His will and Moses' direction required more finesse. And flexibility.

> *"The Lord said to Moses, "I will also do this thing that you have asked; for you have found favor (lovingkindness, mercy) in My sight and I have known you [personally] by name.""*

> *Exodus 33:17 (AMP)*

In God's Human Resources manual, the most effective succession planning involves more than just the leaders themselves. It must involve the people power. After all, who powers the business, the leaders or the people? God says both. Especially, when the company is turning the corner from transition, into turmoil. From inoculating the team from external conditions, to having to face them together. Assuredly, growing and moving the cultural and operational mindset from stewardship and management to actual ownership.

What we are suggesting here is that organizations must purge itself of its "stinking thinking" in order to successfully navigate its succession planning through times of transition. Not everyone is fit for the next phase of the plan. There will be losses. Perhaps, like the Israelites, there will be a generation that gets lost in the pivot, losing their way and sense of direction in the wilderness.

> *"For the Israelites walked forty years in the wilderness, until all the nation, that is, the men of war who came out of Egypt, died because they did not listen to the voice of the Lord; to them the Lord had sworn [an oath] that He would not let them see the land which He had promised to their fathers to give us, a land [of abundance] flowing with milk and honey."*

> *Joshua 5:6 (AMP)*

Maybe, just maybe, their slave mentality is preventing them from pivoting, and thinking more like an owner. After 400 years of generational bondage, it's difficult to get their collective minds right when they've been conditioned to think wrong, for so long. More than likely, it's inevitable there will need to be some cutting or rolling away. Sometimes, less is more, good and plenty.

> *"Then, when they had finished circumcising all [the males of] the nation, they stayed in their places in the camp until they were healed. Then the Lord said to Joshua, "This day I have rolled away the reproach (derision, ridicule) of Egypt from you." So the name of that place is called Gilgal (rolling) to this day."*

> *Joshua 5:8-9 (AMP)*

Moreover, getting the team up for the task *must* be interwoven into the process and very fabric of succession planning *from the top down AND bottom up*. Personnel decisions at the officer level must mirror those at the director level, which must reflect those being made at the manager level to the entry level, and so on. This is *not* to suggest we go to the extreme of populating teams, organizations, staff plans and board composition to become a sea of succession sameness or, otherwise, *"holier than thou"* version of the good old boy network.

That doesn't bode well for these days and times. It naturally defies the logic behind diversity and inclusion which is a separate discussion altogether and not our objective here. Rather, the leadership key we are unlocking for the Book of Joshua is less about demographics and more about "psychographics." It's about the congruence between the values and personality profile of your leadership with the composition of your rank and file.

This blind spot is what prompted the development of our proprietary Christ-centric personality profile and leadership quotient. These tools are designed to embed this level of actionable data and insights into the theory and process of succession planning which allows for more informed decision making throughout the organization. Our platform is designed to help you build your team for the task by objectively and subjectively curating and calibrating them.

Thus, as you go about determining "Who Got Next," the weighted HR decisions you make should be just as bottom heavy as they are top heavy. Your best assets should be equally distributed and representative in the C+Suite as the reception area.

In fact, designing the team for the task actually begins *before* Day 1. We've developed and implemented a creative exercise for clients and partners to illustrate this.

It's called "In for a Treat."

And it goes like this.

As a rule of thumb for proper courting, if you really want to know the true measure and character of a man or woman, you should ask to meet *them* before meeting their "*representative*." As it follows, whenever we would open up an RFP for an outside agency and bring the finalists in to pitch their capabilities, we would be sure to observe their interactions with *everyone* on our team, not just the decision makers.

After tending to the business at hand, and hosting our guests for dinner at a local restaurant, we paid attention to how they treated the hostess, for sure. Just as important, was how they treated the server replenishing the water for the table. Or, how engaging and generous they were to the young person trying to make a humble living putting themselves through school while hustling cars for tips at the Valet Stand.

This speaks volumes. It tells us loud and clear *what* and *who* people value. And what lies beneath the surface when God searches the heart. It has reverberating impact on selfish motives and individual striving versus group interests and collective gain. It indicates how one part will function together (or not) as part of the whole body. It also naturally begs the answer to the proverbial question *"What Would Jesus Do?"*

As an organization or enterprise, it is imperative you get to know the *authenticity* behind the group, partner or person you are considering *before* you interview them for the role. Well in advance of making them an offer you may end up wishing they had refused.

How do we go about doing this?

Reviewing their resume or CV? Think again. At least not exclusively. Studies have shown that rarely ever tells the real story.

Besides, on some level, everyone looks pretty good and roughly the same on paper when you get to the point of the interview.

How about that criminal background check and credit report? Sure thing. But that only amounts to half of the story. And, it may actually rule out the most important half for consideration and contains their critical narrative of redemption.

How about watching how they treat the people they encounter along the way to the interview or leading up to the meeting? The janitor or cleaning crew in the conference room. The raw, introverted intern on the elevator or extroverted tenant who strikes up a conversation on the way up, before going separate ways, to separate floors.

Something like *"secret enterprise shopping."*

We call the exercise *"In for a Treat"* for that very reason. As a decision maker, it gives you an opportunity to see how someone treats the otherwise "insignificant" others subtly and organically placed in their path, just as they would encounter them in the course of daily interaction. We do this without the client even knowing. Without giving away the secret sauce, you can trust when we say the objectives are met and desired outcomes satisfied every time.

What's the point of this exercise?

When it comes to building the team for the task in perilous times of transition, there simply is no room for "faking it until you make it." When preparing to go to war, or in the heat of the battle for market share, you want to know the shaky ground and principles your people are standing on. And if, like Moses and Joshua, they are able to ascertain and discern it to be hallowed ground they are actually defending.

You want to know beyond a shadow of a doubt, when they say they are putting on the full armor of God, they are not putting on a show.

Verily, verily we say to you it is comforting to know that your new hires are wearing their faith on their sleeves before rolling them up.

By taking such such a deliberate, philosophical approach to HR and succession planning, implemented from top to bottom and bottom up, your organization will effectively begin building the team for the task. As opposed to on-boarding remedial "task masters," you will begin to populate teams layered with what Bishop T.D. Jakes calls "instincts to increase."

In other words, increase becomes the task. To be certain, it becomes the shared task. And it is their individual instincts to increase that makes them up for the group task. Indeed, *instincts and increase are both "it" factors for succession planning.*

Which, is to say...Like attracts like.

Like Christ.

Christ ↑ Type

Joshua

> *"These are the names of the men who Moses sent to spy out the land; but Moses called Hoshea the son of Nun, Joshua (the Lord is salvation)."*
>
> *Numbers 13:16 (AMP)*

What is it? It's something about that name. Let Joshua tell it; *it* is *in* the name.

Phonetically speaking, *"it"* is what makes Joshua a sure fire type of Christ.

When it comes to the family office, succession starts with the name. When it comes to family owned and operated businesses, the namesake indicates who's got next. And who's coming further down the line. And so it is, as it was.

As it were, Hebrew 101 teaches us the Hebrew name for Jesus is *Yeshua.* In fact, Yeshua is mentioned 27 times in the Hebrew Bible, leaving no doubt as to what his name is. Yeshua is also short for *Yehoshua,* or "Joshua," which means *"Yahweh is salvation."* Or, according to some translations, *Yahweh's savior."*

Through parenthetical biblical study, we also learn the first trace of the name for the savior is found in connection with Joshua, the son of Nun, Moses' assistant. Tracing back to the Book of Numbers, we find Joshua descends from the tribe of Benjamin and his original name was Hosea (Numbers 13:6-8).

The name *Hoshea* is derived from the Hebrew verb *"yasha,"* which means *"he saves, delivers."* The scripture above informs us that Moses changed his original name in Hebrew to "Yehoshua" (Joshua in English). Moses coined this name by merging Hosea with the prefix abbreviation "Yeho" of the divine name "YHWH." Thus, changing the meaning to "YHWH is salvation" or "YHWH saves, delivers." God himself indicating through His angel that Jesus' name and meaning was to be a savior.

> *"She will give birth to a Son, and you shall name Him Jesus (The Lord is salvation), for He will save His people from their sins."*

Matthew 1:20 (AMP)

But wait, there's so much more to this name. For further witness, we discover there is also a high priest named Jeshua in the Book of Ezra (Ezra 3:9). This same high priest is called Yehoshua ("Joshua') in Zechariah 3 and 6, further establishing the name Yeshua as the abbreviation and translation of this very same name.

Ok, so what's the point? Glad you asked. We place an emphatic bookmark on the aforementioned text in Zechariah as we are now offered an exclusive, secretarial invitation behind the scenes to record the minutes of God's offsite meeting with the high priest Joshua and his colleagues in the inner sanctum. This is no ordinary executive session. Seriously. In this virtuous moment, we find God boldly declaring His intentions and announcing his succession plan to fill **both** of his vacant offices.

The office of Priest **and** the office of King.

This is *it*. The moment none of them were waiting for, hoping for, or even Joshua as high priest was expecting for. Still, it was a watershed moment that each of them was being prepared for. This is a defining moment which characterizes the prophetic nature and aspect of God's succession planning. God reveals to Joshua, that the branch is *it*.

> *"Now listen, Joshua, the high priest, you and your colleagues who are sitting in front of you - indeed they are men who are a symbol [of what is to come] – for behold, I am going to bring in My servant the Branch [in Messianic glory].*
>
> *Zechariah 3:8 (AMP)*

Notice how God says each of these men are a "symbol" of **what is** to come. This is one of the finest insights and granular nuances behind God's methodology for succession planning we can ever hope to receive if we truly desire to grasp this concept for our organization. *God establishes what* is coming, *before he decides who* is coming. This is why God is able to use anybody. This is why God is no respecter of persons.

This is why God is able to remain just in his decision making process. He's really just being true to *himself*. We've got it backwards. We look to the who, to fill the what. If we can't find the who, we don't quite know what to do.

Because God knows exactly *what it is* that he is looking for in a Messiah, he knows *who* will ultimately spring forth like a branch from *within* (Isaiah 11:1). Likewise, if we are cultivating a leadership culture of this type, our succession plans will naturally begin to focus on the what type, not the who type.

As we move further along with God's prophetic vision and instructions to Zechariah, he is providing Joshua with every detail about how to prepare the organization for the onboarding of the man, the Son of Man, who will sit in succession next to the Father. The man who will hold both offices, and two enormous titles of Priest and King. His name? Branch.

> *"Then say to Joshua, 'Thus says the Lord of hosts, "Behold (look, keep in sight, watch), a Man (Messiah) whose name is Branch, for He shall branch out from His place (Isarel, the Davidic line); and He shall build the [ultimate] temple of the Lord. Yes, [you are to build a temple of the Lord, but] it is He who shall build the [ultimate] temple of the Lord, and He shall bear the honor and majesty [as the only begotten of the Father] and sit and rule on His throne. And He shall be a Priest on His throne, and the counsel of peace shall be between the two offices [Priest and King].*
>
> *Zechariah 6:12-13 (AMP)*

How fascinating to see God's High Priest succession order from Joshua to Yeshua. How magnanimous to see God reconstitute the King line with the Priest line through Christ. How interesting it is to witness Moses choose the occasion of naming the representative leaders of the 12 tribes that would spy out the land of Canaan to change the meaning and mantle of his assistant's namesake from Hosea to Joshua.

What was Moses foretelling us? More importantly, how telling is this with regard to how and where Joshua was to fit within God's succession plan for the ages? As a type of savior.

Like Christ, Joshua came to succeed, and fulfill the work Moses could not complete. He did so, by remaining obedient to God's order of succession. As a young, dynamic leader he wasn't gunning for Moses' leadership position and mantle. Even as Moses grew older and unable to do what he was always capable of doing, Joshua maintained respect for his mentor and never overstepped God's sequence of events. Joshua waited until his time came, just as David waited for King Saul's reign to come to an end.

Consider this a tried and true lesson for the next generation of leaders reading this. Always recognize the process involved in God's plans for succession and leadership can never be bypassed, for good reason. God is not preparing the opportunity for you, He is preparing *you* for the opportunity. And it takes time. Succession is a seasonal business. Measured by time horizons, not new hire dates.

Being prepared means knowing how to wait your turn, for your season. Getting prepared means, instead of looking dismissively past those ahead of you or above you, in age, rank, or title, take a moment to observe them and see where things are going so you can fully appreciate it as you get there. Like Christ, Joshua was also the type of leader who was strong and courageous in his leadership. And with it, an understanding of the type of leader God was calling him to be at that particular time. And it couldn't be what everyone else thought, or expected.

Everyone assumed Christ was coming to conquer the Romans as a Lion, but God needed him (first) to be a lamb. In similar fashion, but opposite effect, Joshua recognized he was not to imitate Moses' brand of diplomatic leadership as he was coming into leadership during a time and season where Israel needed military might. Not diplomatic efforts. When God tells you to go take, and possess something, you better handle your business.

Quite simply, Joshua had it.

This symbolic "it" factor is also what made up the difference between one generation of Israelites (ages 20+) who died in the wilderness while turning their backs on God (Moses and Aaron) and the next generation that went into the Promised Land to acquire the promise of increase - with Joshua's back.

Now, if you don't unlock anything else from the leadership key for Joshua, hold on to this one for the dear life of your succession plans to succeed. Ready? Here, we go. The next generation of Israelites followed Joshua's commands into the Promised Land with the *very same* instincts to increase that Caleb and Joshua had demonstrated while under Moses' command.

> *"The Lord spoke to Moses and Aaron, saying, "How long shall I put up with this evil congregation who murmur [in discontent] against Me? I have heard the complaints of the Israelites, which they are making against Me. Say to them, 'As I live,' says the Lord, 'just what you have spoken in My hearing I will most certainly do to you; your dead bodies will fall in this wilderness, even all who were numbered of you, your entire number from twenty years old and upward, who have murmured against Me. Except for Caleb the son of Jephunneh and Joshua the son of Nun, not one of you shall enter the land in which I swore [an oath] to settle you."*
>
> *Numbers 14:26-30 (AMP)*

They did so by exhibiting and voicing the *very same* leadership attribute that God commanded of Moses and Joshua. Themselves, living proof of Joshua's good courage. Generationally speaking, when it comes to legacy, when it comes to promises, when it comes to covenant, when it comes to ***courage***, you can take God's word for it.

Measuring The Christ Quotient (CQ)

♛ C+Instincts
"Going The Distance"
Joshua & Caleb

> *"Then Moses called to Joshua and said to him in the sight of all [the people of] Israel, "Be strong and courageous, for you will go with this people into the land which the Lord has sworn to their fathers to give them, and you will give it to them as an inheritance. It is the Lord who goes before you; He will be with you. He will not fail you or abandon you. Do not fear or be dismayed."*

> *Deuteronomy 31:7-8 (AMP)*

What made the measure of the men Caleb and Joshua so special? Let's look at their resume. It's not their job qualifications, though. Remember, at a certain level, we all look pretty good on paper. In that regard, although Joshua and Caleb were both qualified for the position, it is their career highlights that we are drawn to. It is within that sphere we can reveal something much more intangible.

> *"As for the men whom Moses sent to spy out the land, and who returned and made all the congregation murmur and complain against him by bringing back a bad report concerning the land, even those [ten] men who brought back the very bad report of the land died by a plague before the Lord. But Joshua the son of Nun and Caleb the son of Jephunneh remained alive out of those men who went to spy out the land."*

> *Numbers 14:36-38 (AMP)*

How did Caleb and Joshua survive? Why did they stay alive, while the other spies met their demise? The answer is simple. Good instincts. And faith. Though complicated by the fears of others. In

126

spite of that, Caleb and Joshua simply had "it." They had presence of mind. And enough sixth sense to follow their instincts. Not just the basic instincts that informed them they were tasked to perform the role and responsibilities of one of the twelve Moses designated as spies. No, Joshua and Caleb followed their instincts to seize a much bigger moment. By *seeing* a much bigger picture. Not only did they see the opportunity to earn their stripes, they saw the land flowing with milk and honey as an opportunity to collectively advance their *next generation* toward the increase that God promised and awaited them on the other side.

And they were right.
And here's the shout…

They came back with a good report *despite* the bad report given by the other ten. In spite of the fact, and in the face of much larger competition. In fact, according to the report, the Israelites were like "grasshoppers" in the sight of these giants. The Canaanites were so large, they devoured their enemies. Conversely, the grapes in the were so big, it took two men to carry one cluster. Big challenge, or greater opportunity?

The bigger the risk, the bigger the reward. If you're in the precarious position of feeling overwhelmed, outmanned and a bit undersized for the opportunity in front of you, this vine is for you. If you're in the middle of due diligence in the midst of fear, this report contains classified information for you.

> *"They reported to Moses and said, "We went in to the land where you sent us; and it certainly does flow with milk and honey, and this is its fruit. But the people who live in the land are strong, and the cities are fortified (walled) and very large; moreover, we saw there the descendants of Anak [people of great stature and courage]. [The people descended from] Amalek live in the land of the Negev (South country); the Hittite, the Jebusite, and the Amorite live in the hill country; and the Canaanites live by the [Dead] Sea and along the side of the Jordan." Then Caleb quieted the*

people before Moses, and said, "Let us go up at once and take possession of it; for we will certainly conquer it." But the men who had gone up with him said, "We are not able to go up against the people [of Canaan], for they are too strong for us." So they gave the Israelites a bad report about the land which they had spied out, saying, "The land through which we went, in spying it out, is a land that devours its inhabitants. And all the people that we saw in it are men of great stature. There we saw the Nephilim (the sons of Anak are part of the Nephilim); and we were like grasshoppers in our own sight, and so we were in their sight."

Numbers 13:27-33 (AMP)

While the Israelites voted to turn back after hearing the report, Joshua and Caleb instinctively knew the distance required to meet the scope of this generational challenge and grand opportunity descending upon them was far beyond what *human eyes could see.* They realized it would take them having to go much further than half way. Joshua and Caleb had the foresight to close the gap with the substance of things they couldn't see. They faithfully believed God would meet them the rest of the way. Indeed, the delta between instincts to increase and opportunity lies somewhere between faith and courage.

"Joshua the son of Nun and Caleb the son of Jephunneh, who were among those who had spied out the land, tore their clothes [as a sign of grief], and they spoke to all the congregation of the sons of Israel, saying, "The land through which we passed as spies is an exceedingly good land. If the Lord delights in us, then He will bring us into this land and give it to us, a land which flows with milk and honey. Only do not rebel against the Lord; and do not fear the people of the land, for they will be our prey. Their protection has been removed from them, and the Lord is with us. Do not fear them."

Numbers 14:6-9 (AMP)

When it comes to measuring the Christ Quotient (CQ) for Joshua, the moral of the story and title of the namesake song makes it self-evidently clear. Because he had the "it" factor and knew only how to be of good courage, not only was Joshua fit *for* battle, God knew Joshua fit *the* battle.

Joshua fit the battle of Jericho
Jericho, Jericho
Joshua fit the battle of Jericho
The walls come tumblin' down, Hallelujah
Joshua fit the battle of Jericho
Jericho, Jericho
Joshua fit the battle of Jericho
And the walls come tumblin' down
You may talk about the men of Gideon
You may talk about the men of Saul
But there're none like good old Joshua
At the battle of Jericho
Joshua fit the battle of Jericho
Jericho, Jericho
Joshua fit the battle of Jericho
And the walls come tumblin' down, Hallelujah

Succession Planning

Leadership Summary

• **Discipleship in theory is a necessary byproduct and inherent function of systemic succession planning.** "Therefore go and make disciples of all nations." Matthew 28:19-20 brings us into this symbolic, emblematic nature of Christianity and the fundamental life and teachings of Jesus Christ.

•**There is no more definitive text, guide or authority on succession planning than the Bible**. Throughout scripture, we see God's divine succession plan being carefully orchestrated and executed from Alpha to Omega, beginning to end. In no particular order, our examples include John to Jesus, Saul to David to Solomon, Eli to Samuel, Elijah to Elisha, Naomi to Ruth and Moses to Joshua.

• **Whenever God is preparing a generational paradigm shift, He simultaneously begins raising up their successor.** Man up, man down. Man down, Man up. At the end of the day, like a good chief executive or head coach, God shows no partiality, revealing himself to be no respecter of persons.

• **God is not oblivious to the need for putting proper support mechanisms in place to balance the workload.** Whereas, all leaders struggle in this area, God inspires us to higher levels of mastery when it comes to delegating. Effective delegation is inextricably linked to efficient succession planning.

• **God doesn't delegate tasks for the sake of ticking boxes. He delegates tasks for the sake of lifting burdens.** God didn't call Moses to the task of getting the children of Israel to the Promised Land as much as he called Moses to the people.

• **God establishes sound, guiding principles for succession planning.** He establishes his purpose, not individual agendas. God uses whomever He pleases unto His perfect pattern, lest we think too highly of ourselves. Succession planning is an ongoing process but the transfer of power occurs instantaneously. Lastly, "servitude determines altitude." To lead, is to first have successfully served others. To serve, is to have first succeeded at leading others into service.

• **Through Moses and Joshua, God patterned, modeled and optimized succession planning for us.** Unlike man, God does not react to current events, but anticipates future events. In the grand scheme of things, Joshua was better suited to take the Israelites into the Promised Land than Moses because they were going behind enemy lines into conflict and stiff opposition. God knew they needed a skillful warrior.

• **When it comes to determining fit in the process of succession planning, we are reminded that "God doesn't call the qualified, he qualifies the called."** Our organizational behavior in this regard has a tendency to juxtapose the position. For example, placing the wrong person, in the right place, at the wrong time.

• **By pledging the same oath and promise to Joshua as his predecessor, God is showing His leaders that succession planning is not only a continual process but a continuous covenant.** Right down to the consecutive holy ground the leaders stand on. (Exodus 3:5-6) (Joshua 5:15).

• **Looking into our 5-year business plan and succession plan, we must ask ourselves some fundamentally tough questions.** Do we find them to be synchronized operationally? Or, are they compartmentalized in a dysfunctional process. Are these plans united from the C+Suite, or housed within separate divisions and business units? Is our leadership prepared for the next phase of growth and competition? Or, are we assuming they will have the right set of tangible and intangible skills, while hoping everyone else adapts and adjusts when the time comes?

• **Different leadership times call for different leadership measures from God.** God moves unilaterally but his leadership is far from monolithic. During Moses' tenure, God was firm but negotiable. By the time Joshua takes command, God assumes a different posture. He speaks in a straightforward manner. He has grown weary of the people's disobedience, murmuring and complaining against His leadership. The children of Israel were coming into a season of intense, constant conflict for which they needed to act and think like a military unit. Therefore, both God and Joshua provided leadership and direction with a militaristic style and overtones.

• **Getting the team up for the task must be interwoven into the very fabric of succession planning from the top down AND bottom up. Personnel and personality decisions must reflect one level to / from the next.** Permeating a culture of servitude does not begin at the entry-level with those who are always looking to *serve up* to those in higher positions, but starts from those in higher up positions who are willing to *serve down*. This is also not to suggest creating a sea of succession sameness, which goes against the sound wisdom behind diversity and inclusion.

- **Instincts to increase are the "it" factors for succession planning.** Like attracts like. Lack attracts lack. This "it" factor is what made up the difference between one generation of Israelites (ages 20+) who died in the wilderness and the next generation that went into the Promised Land. This leadership key for Joshua informs us that the next generation of Israelites followed Joshua's commands to possess the land with the exact same courageous instincts to increase that Joshua demonstrated while under Moses' command (Numbers 14:26-30).

- **What makes the measure of the men in Caleb and Joshua special is their career highlight**. This is not to be found in quickly scanning their professional experience. There were 10 others who could boast the same. Their finest measure is taken by an intangible skill set. Their instincts to increase led them to come back with a good report. Joshua and Caleb instinctively knew the distance required to meet the scope of this generational challenge was beyond what human eyes could see. They had the foresight and insight to close the gap with the substance of things they could not see. Faithfully, they believed God to get them the rest of the way.

- **In order to function effectively in your calling and assignment, next generation leaders recognize that the process involved in God's succession and leadership plans can never be bypassed**. And for good reason. God is not preparing the opportunity for you, He is preparing *you* for the opportunity. And it takes time. Succession is a seasonal business.

- **When it comes to the family office, succession starts with the name.** When it comes to family owned and operated businesses, the namesake indicates who's got next. And who's coming further down the line.

• **How fascinating to see God's High Priest succession order from Joshua to Yeshua**. How interesting, and perhaps more than a coincidence, Moses chose the occasion of naming the representative leaders of the 12 tribes that would spy out the land of Canaan to change the meaning and mantle of his assistant's namesake from Hosea to Joshua.

• **Christ knew that the Disciples had to shift and rearrange their mental model around succession, and what it meant to serve as a Messiah, to be effective as disciples**. This elevated thinking would not come to them or through them, for others to follow, by sitting "in glory" to the right and left of Christ as John and James envisioned (Mark 10:37). Instead, it would come through the sacrifice of ego from the lowly position, and humble posture of true servitude. In the upper room, Jesus teaches His disciples they couldn't succeed Him until they sacrificed like Him, *and served* like Him.

• **In the final analysis, Jesus is teaching us to use the managerial accounting method when it comes to managing the Kingdom's family business**. The accrued costs are where the carrying of our cross comes in. Christ is trying to bring us around to observing the fixed costs. He wants to lead us into informed decision making by counting up the costs for the office of discipleship and its ramifications on our succession planning activities. Beyond the variable costs of sacrificing and suffering *until* it's our turn, He's pointing us in the upper room to the sacrificing and suffering that is required *when* it's your turn. This is succession planning in perpetuity.

Chapter 4:
Mentorship

"As iron sharpens iron,
so one person sharpens another."
Proverbs 27:17(NIV)

Joshua is a prime example of the sharpening benefits and redeeming qualities of having a worthy mentor. For years he remained close to Moses. As his able bodied, young assistant, he watched intently as Moses followed God to the letter of each commandment. He learned about obedience throughout Moses' fights with frustration, closed veil sessions and confessions with God.

He learned how to command courage from God, but learned how to develop it from Moses. He was a man after Moses' heart, but never patterned his leadership style after him. Like any mentor-mentee relationship worth its salt of the earth, Joshua learned as much from what his mentor *didn't do,* then what he *did do.* He acquired far more from the mistaken example costing Moses the personal satisfaction of a "job well done" and "atta boy" upon entering the Promised Land as he did his successful examples preparing him to subsequently take the reins from his mentor and enter into the land of Canaan (Joshua 1:5-11).

Joshua learned how to become a servant of God by watching and serving Moses. Obedience is as much an observed behavior as it is a learned one. And it's one that is best modeled by a yielded mentor. Regardless of your future caseload or current volunteer commitment, if you are called by God into leadership, you are a mentor. That means that someone, somewhere, is always watching you. Because God placed them there. And He is entrusting them to your care. And it's not about you. Or him. Or her. It's about them. And who's coming after them. And so on.

It's about everything, and everyone going on around you. Watching them, watching you. Make no mistake, some younger person or someone you are influencing is looking at how you live and watching how you react. In your house, on the job, or pulling up to carpool. Whether you are too self-absorbed to notice it or not. Someone is learning from you. Good, bad or indifferent. Whether you know it, like it or not. Someone is following your example. Whether you are moving in righteous fashion and living self-righteously at the moment. Or not.

Either way, your life is on full display.
Whether you are highly visible, or not.

For this reason, mentorship is an active call to discipleship duty. Sounds pretty basic, but talk to anyone dedicated to serving any mission that involves mentorship (particularly targeting youth), and you will hear a familiar refrain of the fundamentals of mentorship. Mentorship must be sustainable. Sustainable enough to produce the desired outcome over time. Not in blocks of it. Mentorship must be consistent. Consistent enough to shape and mold new behaviors that break old thought patterns. Far more than the words that are spoken by the mentor, his or her actions speak much louder than words.

In the apostle Paul's case, whether the church liked it or not.

Spotlight On 💡 Mentorship Mastery

Paul sets the definitive standard for secular and non-secular mentorship. Hands down, or hands up high. Paul was a master mentor. Case, and case study closed. He was a master of attracting and equipping others for explosive growth and development. Inside, and outside of the church. He dedicated his vocation to people and activities that would impact the world for generations upon generations upon future generations to come. His precise, tactical approach to his craft remains as relevant and effective today as it was thousands of years ago.

Why?

Paul saw mentorship as a process of continuous innovation. No matter where he went, he gathered and captured his audience of listeners by teaching and finding new ways to reach them. Even tough loving them from a distance. When Paul showed up in a town, he planted himself and the word, with his works and the workers, for days, months and years.

Paul knew how to find, equip and mentor emerging leaders. Paul's brilliance didn't bedazzle himself out of the realization that leaders quantify themselves and multiply their impact developing other leaders. Early and often. Paul knew the power of ten. He sought younger leaders out for this reason.

Paul mentored too many leaders to count. Some, like Silas already possessed natural influence and leadership skills (Acts 15:22). Others, like Timothy, were handmade and homegrown. In either event, Paul raised them up, and turned them loose to spread the gospel. He knew the best way to keep what he had was to give it away freely.

Paul was a planter. He planted churches. He planted ministries. He planted leaders to carry on the ministry and *co-labor* together. To be real, Paul was a master mentor because he was a true *co-worker* in the field. Unlike our primary mental model around mentorship as "Big Brother, Big Sister," which does hold some redeeming value, Paul understood the even bigger dichotomy in the relationship between those entrusted to his care and the one who was doing the entrusting and giving the increase.

"What, after all, is Apollos? And what is Paul? Only servants, through whom you came to believe – as the Lord has assigned to each his task. I planted the seed, Apollos

watered it, but God has been making it grow. So neither the one who plants nor the one who waters is anything, but only God who makes things grow. The one who plants and the one who waters have one purpose, and they will each be rewarded according to their own labor. For we are co-workers in God's service; you are God's field, God's building."

1 Corinthians 3:5-9 (NIV)

Paul's mentorship legacy leaves us big shoes to fill because he was comfortable in knowing "one size doesn't fit all." Whereas, most mentors short stop the function of encouragement in leadership development by focusing on the apparent weaknesses in the relationship, Paul was attracted by their strengths.

Paul had the foresight to know the best way to resolve weaknesses *and* the negative is to accentuate strengths, *in* the positive. This meant different strokes, for different folks. In similar fashion, when Paul went on a mission journey, he didn't take everyone with him. He refused to roll into town high-signing with his posse on Broadway. Nor did he give everyone equal opportunity to water the churches they planted. Not everyone made the cut, or could cut it. Instead, he played to their overall strengths, according to their gifts and callings.

Paul saw mentorship as an ongoing process, not a one shot deal. Truth be told, he popularized CRM in an analog age. Imagine that. Before digital, back-end platforms, Paul maintained constant contact and follow-up by letter. He sent messages in a bottle to Macedonia.

Paul visited his church leaders to encourage them, support them and provide good orderly direction when the church was behaving anything but that. Indeed, we could conclude this entire chapter on the travails of the church of Corinth as it relates to the mentorship shaping and molding of new ideas around old thought patterns.

"Let us now go back and visit our brethren in every city where we have preached the word of the Lord, and see how they are doing."

Acts 15:36 (NIV)

Paul knew effective mentorship goes beyond changing the way mentees work, to challenge how they think. He taught others how to think unselfishly for themselves, about others. In the above passage in the Book of Acts, Paul already has a pretty good idea how these churches are doing. In some cases, the lack of response causing much chagrin, pain and anguish. Paul shows us that mentorship is a mutual investment. The planter and the waterer must both concern themselves with the increase. And where there is no thought elevation, there is no increase.

Paul soiled the atmosphere around him to cultivate seasonal investment in return. In order for this "mentorship thing to work," Paul acknowledged and impressed upon the leaders he invested in that he needed them as much as they needed him. Paul poured water, of himself, into every one of them and received libations back, particularly when the going got tough. Especially, toward the end.

"For I am already being poured out like a drink offering, and the time for departure is near. I have fought the good fight, I have the finished the race, I have kept the faith. Now there is in store for me the crown of righteousness, which the Lord, the righteous Judge, will award to me on that day – and not only to me, but also to all who have longed for his appearing. Do your best to come to me quickly, for Demas, because he loved this world, has deserted me and has gone to Thessalonica. Crescens has gone to Galatia, and Titus to Dalmatia. Only Luke is with me. Get Mark and bring him with you, because he is helpful to me in my ministry.'

2 Timothy 4:6-11 (NIV)

Subtracting from any differences of opinion, this chapter in second Timothy also carries much weight, revealing that Paul was not only able to see beyond race, but also rose above matters of gender, when you add up his mastery of mentorship.

> *"Greet Priscilla and Aquila and the household of Onesiphorous. Erastus stayed in Corinth, and I left Trophimus sick in Miletus. Do your best to get here before winter. Eubulus greets you, and so do Pudens, Linus, Claudia and all the brothers and sisters."*

> *2 Timothy 4:19-21 (NIV)*

Priscilla is one of the few women mentioned in the New Testament whose influence can't possibly be ignored. After all, her name is loosely translated as "delightful." Aquila and Priscilla were a Jewish couple who fled persecution from Rome and converted to Christianity. They met Paul in Corinth and co-labored with him to spread the gospel. Not only did they become members of the Corinthian church, helping set it up, they also traveled with Paul to Ephesus to plant and lead that church. Which, incidentally, Apollos also watered.

Under Paul's teaching, Priscilla became passionate about Christ, hungering and thirsting for Him. Like a good mentee should, she listened intently to Paul's teaching and inquired much so she could understand everything he knew. She was absolutely keen on learning about the man, not having his mantle. Too often, we muddy the waters of mentorship beneath a thick cloud of titles, professions and "if you want to be successful like me" canned speeches.

As opposed to preaching the self-righteous, stale standard of "looking up to me," how about we start talking about looking up to the fixer upper, our redeemer who saved the wretch behind the real you and me. Priscilla was bold and vulnerable in that way. As were the times they were living in. It was treacherous having to live among pagans. It took real courage because the gospel didn't preach well and they knew it would potentially lead to their eventual demise. They were right. Like Paul, Priscilla and Aquila were devoted to spreading the gospel up until death.

Therein lies the rub.

Paul's greatest mastery lies in defining the mentor-mentee relationship. Which is to say, *mentorship is a mutual investment that breeds shared sacrifice.*

Therein lies the thorn.

> *"If I wish to boast, I will not be foolish, because I will be speaking the truth. But I abstain [from it], so that no one will credit me with more than [is justified by what] he sees in me or hears from me. Because of the surpassing greatness and extraordinary nature of the revelations [which I received from God], for this reason, to keep me from thinking of myself as important, a thorn in the flesh was given to me, a messenger of Satan, to torment and harass me- to keep me from exalting myself! Concerning this I pleaded with the Lord three times that it might leave me;*
>
> *2 Corinthians 12:6-8 (AMP)*

Paul's greatest legacy he leaves us with, and most painful lesson he gives us to grown on, lies not so much in *what he taught* as a mentor. But *who taught him.*

And, more importantly, *what mentored him*. Pastor Steven Furtick of Elevation Church preached a powerful message on this, titled *"The Mentor You Didn't Ask For."* We will not attempt to do it injustice by summarizing his text, or preempting it here, by going much further beyond the title. You should do your team a favor and watch it for yourself. If you are mentoring someone, you might consider asking them to join you.

The Bible makes it clear Paul didn't ask for this particular thorn in his flesh. In fact, in the scripture above, he asks God to remove it at least three times that he readily admits. Albeit excruciatingly. *Pleading* with God. What have you been pleading with God to remove from your life, to no avail? There's a reason for it. Further along in the verse, Paul speaks of this thorn in his flesh as being a "messenger of Satan" with a purpose of "torment." The type of torment, anguish and longsuffering our brother Job can most certainly relate to.

> *"Now there was a day when the sons of God (angels) came to present themselves before the Lord, and Satan (adversary, accuser) also came among them. The Lord said to Satan, "From where have you come?" Then Satan answered the Lord, "From roaming around on the earth and from walking around on it." The Lord said to Satan, "Have you considered and reflected on My servant Job? For there is none like him on the earth, a blameless and upright man, one who fears God [with reverence] and abstains from and turns away from evil [because he honors God]*

> *Job 1:6-9 (AMP)*

Here comes the thorn, and mentor Job didn't ask for.

> *"While he was still speaking, another [messenger] also came and said, "Your sons and your daughters were eating and drinking wine in their oldest brother's house, and suddenly, a great wind came from across the desert, and struck the four corners of the house, and it fell on the young people and they died, and I alone have escaped to tell you." Then Job got up and tore his robe and shaved his head [in mourning for the children], and he fell to the ground and worshiped [God]. He said, "Naked (without possessions) I came [into this world] from my mother's womb, And naked I will return there. The Lord gave and the Lord has taken away; Blessed be the name of the Lord." Through all this Job did not sin nor did he blame God."*

> *Job 1:6-22 (AMP)*

In fact, God leaves our thorn there, intact, to make sure we don't come down with a case of "Amazing Grace" amnesia. He is leaving it there to make sure we remember not to forget that it is *his grace* that is sufficient, not our capabilities deck. And it *his power* that is being made perfect in our weakness, not our power trip going the wrong *way* down the road to Damascus.

He places our thorn at the mark of conversion, just in case we suddenly decide to change course, and go back to our old ways. Just as he did for Paul. Don't trip, God will not be mocked. Many explanations have gone forth, as to whether Paul is referring to a physical weakness, spiritual malady, emotional affliction – or something else entirely.

Alter-ego aside, we do know this. Anyone who had a personal encounter with Jesus and was personally commissioned by Him would, in his carnal state of mind, be prone to puffing their chest out a bit. Add that to the fact that Paul penned much of the New Testament, and it is easy to see how Paul might find occasion to think himself mightier than his Holy Ghost writer.

There is no definitive answer to the question. Truth be told, only Paul really knows exactly what was tormenting his flesh. That said, we are able to surmise that Paul was not referring to a physical thorn and was speaking metaphorically. As Pastor Furtick brilliantly ascribes, Paul is referring to his torMENT as being his MENTor.

Metaphorically speaking, Paul's thorn in his flesh reminds us that the best mentors stick around. Paul's thorn became his lifelong, life changing mentor on the road to Damascus. As you're reading this, what is your thorn? What, and who is your mentor tormenting you to be?

Paul continues, "but He has said to me, "My grace is sufficient for you [My lovingkindness and My mercy are more than enough - always available – regardless of the situation]; for [My] power is being perfected [and is completed and shows itself most effectively] in [your] weakness." Therefore, I will all the more gladly boast in my weaknesses, so that the power of Christ [may completely enfold me and] may dwell in me. So I am well pleased with weaknesses, with insults, with distresses, with persecutions, and with difficulties, for the sake of Christ; for when I am weak [in human strength], then I am strong [truly able, truly powerful, truly drawing from God's strength."

2 Corinthians 12:9-10 (AMP)

The mentor Paul didn't ask for is the one person, place or thing God uses to teach us about humility using the traditional definition of sacrifice, not the abridged version. The problem for us coddled students is, in the classroom of life, God is from the old school. He is a throwback teacher who knows some things are best taught through adversity. He knows we learn something new every day. And the answers are not found *in* back of the book, but *within* the book itself.

"The Problem"
Here's what I learned today.
I learned not to be deceived.
By the same ol' things.
Masked as problems,
Satan has always used to torment and deceive.
Knowledge of good and evil.
Thanks to Adam and Eve.

Facts.

And even though the Book of Genesis,
and the Garden of Eden were taught religiously at Sunday School,
Self-diagnosis was a bit of a snare for me.

Let the serpent tell it.

"And the serpent said unto the woman, Ye shall not surely die: For God doth know that in the day ye eat thereof, then

*your eyes shall be opened, and ye shall be as gods, knowing
good and evil."*

Genesis 3:4 (KJV)

*For the Life of Me, I thought I had the problem all figured out.
In my mind, I had all the answers to myself.
Never ran out of them, either.
Always looking for an escape, or short cut.
Until I found myself a prisoner of the past.
Trapped in brain cells, unable to jail break.
We all spend time in solitary confinement.
Once upon a time.
Until we're set free at last.*

*Still...
I couldn't figure out why temptation,
and choices to do certain things,
came so natural to me.
In the physical.
But thinking on things above felt so unnatural to me.
In the spiritual.
Not to mention, the toughest problems for me to wrap my
head around,
came at crucial points when my self-diagnosis seemed spot on.
Which, inevitably meant everyone else's second opinion was flawed.*

Facts.

*Looking back over the answer key, I gave a lot of wrong answers.
Based upon false positives.
And a lot of false equivalencies.
Which led me to a few, Essential Truths.
Absolute solutions I discovered when I actually did the work.
One, quite essential, in particular.*

*Self-Diagnosis and Self-Care are not mutually exclusive.
One begets the other.*

In other words,
one way or another,
"you gonna learn today."

Therein lies the sub.
Higher learning?
All depends upon which teacher we listen to that day.
Either way, we're working on the same word problem.
The Answer?
Always found inside the problem.
Only if, and while working the solution.
Subconsciously.

Therein lies the answer.

Essential Truths are universal, but not rocket science.
Not all mentors and teachers were created the same.
And there is but One, to whom there is no equal.

Think about it...
No matter which school or institution of higher learning you attended.
Anywhere on God's green earth.
Before the days of Noah.
Up until these last days and times.
This, one thing, I know for sure.

We can all recall having had that one extra special teacher.
The One who went the extra mile when you gave the extra effort.
The same One that pulled you aside, without getting extra.
As the other students ran out of class to go see their favorite teacher.

Yet, He stayed.
Because He saw you struggling.
And trying at the same time.
This time.
And, upon looking over your work,
He whispered to you.
Within ear shot.

Just over the shoulders you shrugged.
As you were ready to walk away too.

He said something that caused you to lift your head.
And perk your ears up.
To listen.
And it gave you the level of confidence that raised your grade.

He or she said...
"Just show me the work..."

This Master Teacher of one thousand years.
Didn't mind so much if you made mistakes along the way.
Thinking back on it, He was righteous about it.
Commanding us not to waste precious time lamenting over our errors.
And focusing on His corrections.
Steady trying to figure out the problem with the same mind.
Our mind.
Instead of the mind.
His mind.
That created the problem for us.
Talk about being bogged down.

But that's when He knew.
Knew that we wouldn't see the breakthrough coming.
After all, it didn't appear to be. At least not to Me.
Usually, because it wasn't right now. Yet.

Ultimately, the teacher was absolutely right about "the breakthrough."
It was staring right at me. And became so clear to me.
Once I left false pride behind.
And moved closer to the front.
So I could watch Him teach better.
And hear better.

In fact, the closer I got, the more I focused on Him.
And those same problems became less problematic.
As did my fear of taking tests.
Once I remembered what He told me.
And repeated. Over and over again.
I can still hear it, like it was yesterday.

"At the end of the day, we're here to learn...
Just show me the work..."

After stressing out.
Bugging out.
And sneaking out.
Some, eventually walking out.
Others plain flunking out.

After all of that, this is what I learned that day.
Our teacher is also a Master Mentor.
Not only was He using problems from similar tests and quizzes.
Duplicated from previous lessons and chapters.
He also included a few, new problems.

The kind we never saw before.
For extra credit.
And with a single purpose in mind.
To better prepare us.
For the Final Exam.
When we really didn't even deserve it,
He did it anyway.

He did it because He gives all of His students the opportunity
to succeed.
Remember the teacher telling us He doesn't want us to fail?
Knowing we are a reflection on Him.
He even extended the grace period to turn in our assignment.
Casting our failure to learn on the fallen ones before us.

False Teachers.
Poor substitutes.
Teaching us the fundamentals of right and wrong.
But never learning themselves.
Still, He remained determined to leave no child behind.
That's just how He is.
Which taught me to approach Him correctly.
Simply by raising my hand.
And humbling myself, was a plus.
Eventually, gaining enough faith in my walk to come to Him.
Boldly. Confidently. Never arrogantly.

That's when, like Paul, He taught me something brand new.
Life truly is a classroom.
And the Sun is still shining off the same ol' lessons.
In order to step into something bigger than ourselves.
Something outside of ourselves.
We, simply, must figure out our most difficult problem in life.
How to ask the Teacher for help.

Facts.

Indeed, our thorn is the lesson God uses to teach us about grace. Lest we think too highly of ourselves. He uses it to teach us how to love. Lest we forget *"to live is Christ, and to die is gain."* No one likes to live in pain. Paul probably had as many good reasons as his pleadings to be free of pain. That would have made him even more effective in spreading the gospel further, and building his ministry even more effectively. But, in effect, God was more concerned about building Paul's character as a mentor and preventing the type of pride that shuns people away from being right by your side. So he left it right there.

Because the pain makes it better.

And when it does come, it's always accompanied by growth. It's like the mentee you didn't ask for. But showed up in your life. At the wrong time.

Reminding you of who you once were, and where you barely made it out of. And how you had every reason in the world not to end up where you are. But for the Grace of God.

That's the *only* **reason**.

And out of the 8 million stories you tell.
Keep it 100.
Run tell that one about the Prodigal Son.
Lying in a pen, in the naked city.

Tell them that God forgave you and forever changed you.
That the last shall be first.
And you ought to know because you're one of them.
Last but not least.

And that's the *main reason* you signed up to be a mentor in the first place.

Sure, we can all dress up nice for career day or the volunteer "meet and greet" the student mentor breakfast without giving credit where credit is due. Without acknowledging the thorn that made it all possible. We can absolutely dress down, too cool for casual Friday with the best of them, but the fleshly reality is, we're still rocking a fly thorn underneath it.

But are we willing to show *it*?

As mentors, are we truly willing to show our thorn and tell it to our mentees? Not the updated bio. But the original, unedited version. Not the one with the opening line that includes the obligatory, "I came from the 'hood or rose above humble beginnings just like yours." But the authentic version that finishes with "God raised me up, brought me out this mess, so I could come back to get you."

Not the "if I made it out of here, you can do it, too." But the "truth of the matter is, I don't know what I did to deserve it, or how I even made it out, but if He did it for me, you definitely have a shot.

Now, let's go to work." That's called a shared story of experience, strength and hope.

Dr. Scott Cormode, renowned scholar and Hugh De Pree Professor of Leadership Development at Fuller Theological Seminary takes this one step further. He frames this principle of shared stories of hope in the complete context of the Christian tradition. As he writes in his book, *The Innovative Church,* "We Christians offer something more specific than future hope. We offer hope rooted in the gospel – rooted in the life, death, and resurrection of Jesus Christ. Christian hope is different from other kids of hope...Our hope is not in something (like the weather); our hope is in someone (our Savior)."

He goes on to say this shared story of hope helps us help those entrusted to our care make spiritual sense out of their longings and losses. Because the harsher truth of the matter is, not everyone makes it out with their thorn intact. For far too many, instead of carrying it and walking it out like Paul, their thorn becomes their crutch of entitlement.

It's used to lean on sympathy, instead of being emboldened by empathy. How many people are hobbling around now, wounded in your organization with an open thorn of entitlement? Not everyone turns their thorn into a cross, carries it and then crucifies it. Like Christ. Not everyone is able to sacrifice what they once believed, for who they believe in. Like Paul.

Paul's living proof leaves us with such a profound mentorship legacy. Are we vulnerable enough to get past our own insecurities to truly help others with their vulnerabilities? In order to be an effective mentor, do we have a relationship with our thorn of torment that results in a sacrifice and shared story of hope for those we mentor?

Paul's relationship with Timothy also leaves us with a wonderful example of Christian mentoring and shared sacrifice. Both Timothy and Paul had to have the right attitude for such a divine mentoring relationship to succeed. Timothy had to be humble and teachable. No doubt, it must have taken a great deal of faith and commitment on his part to submit to circumcision.

He was free in Christ. Circumcision was not necessary to have a right relationship with God (Galatians 5:6; 6:15). Yet Timothy allowed himself to be circumcised so that he could be a more effective witness for Christ. He exemplified Paul's words in 1 Corinthians 9:22: *"To the weak I became weak, to win the weak. I have become all things to all people so that by all possible means I might save some."*

Paul's role in the mentoring process was to exercise patience as young Timothy grew in wisdom and faith. He spent much time teaching him and even addressed two books of the New Testament to Timothy, who was by then pastoring the church at Ephesus (1 Timothy 1:3). Paul included Timothy in the joys as well as the difficulties of missionary life (Hebrews 13:23) while encouraging him not to allow others to disregard him because of his comparative youth (1 Timothy 4:12). Paul exhorted Timothy often to guard the truth that he had been entrusted with and to take special care not to lose his passion for ministry (1 Timothy 1:18; 4:14; 6:20).

We learn from Paul and Timothy the importance of older men providing discipline and discipleship to younger men. The relationship between Paul and Timothy grew to the extent that Paul referred to him as his "son in the faith." Timothy became a pillar in the early church due to Paul's investment in his life when he was still young. Paul did not shelter his young disciple from the realities of ministry, either, knowing that learning to suffer well was part of Timothy's preparation (2 Timothy 2:3; 4:5).

> *"To Timothy, my true child in the faith. Grace, mercy, and peace from God the Father and from Christ Jesus our Lord. When I left for Macedonia, I asked you to stay behind in Ephesus so that you could instruct certain individuals not to spread wrong teaching. They shouldn't pay attention to myths and endless genealogies. Their teaching only causes*

useless guessing games instead of faithfulness to God's way of doing things. The goal of instruction is love from a pure heart, a good conscience, and a sincere faith."

1 Timothy 1:2-5 (CEB)

For his part, Timothy received instruction and did not shy away from the unpleasant parts of true discipleship. Because of their strong relationship, both men benefited and the gospel spread. In the story of Paul and Timothy, we learn that discipleship is standing shoulder to shoulder in the work of the kingdom. Iron sharpening iron (Proverbs 27:17). Encouraging and rebuking one another when necessary, while sharing a common burden for a lost world (2 Timothy 3:10–15).

We learn from Paul that mentorship also carries its own burdens. After Paul and Barnabas parted ways, Paul chose Silas as a missionary traveling companion, picking up the young disciple Timothy along the way. In the Book of Acts, we learn from Paul, Timothy and Silas that mentorship is a three-way street when making disciples of all nations. And within organizations.

Next, we learn from Elijah and Elisha that mentorship and sacrifice also travel in both directions.

Measuring The Christ Quotient (CQ)

♔ C+Sacrifice
"Cut From The Same Cloth"
Elijah & Elisha

"So Elijah went from there and found Elisha son of Shaphat. He was plowing with twelve yoke of oxen, and he himself was driving the twelfth pair. Elijah went up to him and threw his cloak around him. Elisha then left his oxen and ran after Elijah. Let me kiss my father and mother goodbye," he said, "and then I will come with you. Go back, Elijah replied.

What have I done to you? So Elisha left him and went back.
He took his yoke of oxen and slaughtered them. He burned
the plowing equipment to cook the meat and gave it to the
people, and they ate. Then he set out to follow Elijah and
became his servant."

1 Kings 19:19-21 (NIV)

It's funny. Mentorship is a two-way street. But it usually begins with one person going the opposite way, perhaps headed in the wrong direction. With the other person, perhaps going in the right direction, but looking the other way. One is ready to follow, unprepared to lead. The other is prepared to lead, but not quite ready for the follower. One is ready to serve, and pay his or her dues. The other already serving, having paid theirs. One of them willing to give up everything. The other having nothing else to lose. Or give. But time. Elijah and Elisha met like that.

As previously stated, iron sharpens iron and like attracts like. The Law of Attraction certainly applies here. Elijah's leadership attracted people who loved God and who were also gifted in prophecy themselves. Elijah and Elisha were both strong in the Lord for the sake of Israel. And they were attracted to each other like that. Shared service breeds mutual sacrifice. Elijah and Elisha were connected like that. They were both built like that. Made to perform miracles like that. Cut from the same prophetic cloth like that. Mutual interests and mutual chemistry can also be fleeting. For Elijah and Elisha, though, the feeling was both mutually shared and lasting for several reasons.

Shared Vision – Both men shared the same vision for serving God and the people of Israel. They were seeing the people perish for lack of vision, having been blinded by Baal worship. When Elisha saw the work of the prophet among the people, he turned a blind eye toward the humble expectations and admirable vision that his family had for him to continue in their farming legacy. So, he promptly burned his plow and cooked his oxen. When it comes to someone on your team, or within your organization, expressing this type of shared vision through sacrifice you simply know it when you see it.

And you are sure to keep it. Shared vision and mutual respect go hand in hand. Word to the mentorship wise, mentees will not line up with a leader whose vision they don't respect or narrative they can't relate to.

Shared Commitment – Elisha's commitment to his mentor never waned. Without a strong, mutual commitment to sacrifice for the vision or task at hand despite the challenging circumstances, mutual goals cannot be achieved. Mentorship rarely evolves out of convenience. It is bred out of necessity. For all parties involved. Recognition of this, for the greater good, is a sacrifice. As Elijah approached the end of his leadership tenure, Elisha renewed his commitment to his mentor Elijah. Three times when Elijah offered to release his young protégé, Elisha doubled downed in response. "As the Lord lives, and as your soul lives, I will not leave you!" (2 Kings 2:2, 4, 6). In turn, Elijah's commitment to Elisha renewed each time, and grew manifold into the blessing of a double portion of his spirit. Not sharing in the man, or the mantle, but commitment of the spirit. God aligns mentorship pairs like Elijah and Elisha quite deliberately in this way.

Shared Results – Let's face it. Mentees are attracted to mentors because they see the results. And because they like what they see, they want to see similar results for themselves. And because they believe in that, they believe in that person. And because they believe in that person, they become willing to sacrifice for the results. It's that simple. Getting from A-Z is where things get complicated for organizations. The individuals within the scope of your organization will only follow your leaders as far as they believe they can take them.

If expectations are not level set, or the results down the road don't appear to lead to an expected end, you can plan on a few early exits and detours along the way. Shared results hinge upon shared expectations. Competent leaders enlist others to the vision because they understand who can get them there. And vice versa. Each contributes to the other's expectations. Elijah mentored Elisha, giving him the opportunity to learn how to be a godly leader for the people. The results, literally, prophetically speaking and sacrificing for themselves.

Ironically, Elijah and Elisha teach us to measure the Christ quotient by the standard of sacrifice. God used their sacrifice to bring forth judgment and perform miracles in the sight of the people, for the demise of the wicked. When Elijah defeated the false prophets of Baal who ate at Jezebel's table, he opened up the eyes of the people by calling down fire from heaven so even the skeptics saw the reality of the true and living God. They bore witness to exactly what it meant for God to prepare a table in the presence of Elijah's enemies. As they prepared their bull sacrifice, dancing and shouting around the altar they made for Baal, to no avail, what they saw when the fire of the Lord fell and burned up their sacrifice was merely a foreshadow of the sacrificial lamb to come!

> *"At the time of the offering of the evening sacrifice, Elijah the prophet approached [the altar] and said, "O Lord, the God of Abraham, Issac, and Isarel (Jacob), let it be known today that You are God in Israel and that I am Your servant and that I have done all these things at Your word. Answer me, O Lord, answer me, so that this people may know that You, O Lord, are God, and that You have turned their hearts back [to You]. Then the fire of the Lord fell and consumed the burnt offering and the wood, and even the stones and the dust; it also licked up the water in the trench. When all the people saw it, they fell face downward; and they said, "The Lord, He is God! The Lord, He is God!"*
>
> *1 Kings 18:36-39 (AMP)*

Another word to the mentorship wise. Miracles aren't performed overnight. And they are always preceded by some sort of sacrifice. This applies to all mentees, no matter what stage or level we are aspiring to or from, "do not despise these small beginnings, for the Lord rejoices to see the work." Be it apprentice or vir-tuoso. Account Executive or Chief Executive. Owner or oper-ator. Tenured Professor or Teacher's Assistant. Lead Pastor or Youth Pastor.

Let us also be reminded by Elijah and Elisha of the sacrifice involved in getting to the stage, or next level. Before Elijah drew crowds, he labored in relative obscurity helping out a widow and her son. God provided him with the time he needed to cultivate his gifts and vision for his life. And to make his purpose clear. As a mentor and leader, you will discover a lot about your organization's effectiveness by looking at the sacrificing going on around you.

In other words, do you see anyone who is ready to cook their ox for you? Does anyone seem to have a plough to burn? Or, are they asking you to make difficult decisions about difficult things, titles and promotions they have yet to earn? Let us then utilize Elijah, Elisha and highlighting the text below in 2 Kings to remind them of God's universal stance.

Successful succession will not happen overnight. And God must sign off on it first.

> *"And Elijah took his mantle (coat) and rolled it up and struck the waters, and they were divided this way and that, so that the two of them crossed over on dry ground. And when they had crossed over, Elijah said to Elisha, "Ask what I shall do for you before I am taken from you." And Elisha said, "Please let a double portion of your spirit be upon me." He said, "You have asked for a difficult thing. However, if you see me when I am taken from you, it shall be so for you; but if not, it shall not be so."*

> *2 Kings 2:8-10 (AMP)*

We pause the text here for a reminder and public service announce-ment addressed to all which states "never take mentorship for granted." Mentors loom large, to become paternal and maternal figures. And all of that can be taken away. Suddenly. In a traumatic instant. Becoming a distant memory. Just when you're thinking this bad boy can't stop, won't stop. Just like it happened to Elisha.

> *"As they continued along and talked, behold, a chariot of fire with horses of fire [appeared suddenly and] separated the two of them, and Elijah went up to heaven in a whirlwind. Elisha saw it and cried out, "My father, my father, the chariot of Israel and its horsemen!" And he no longer saw Elijah. Then he took hold of his own clothes and tore them into two pieces [in grief]."*

> *2 Kings 2:11-12 (AMP)*

As we measure the sacrificial Christ Quotient, let us reiterate the future point and lesson Elijah is impressing upon young Elisha that was to come through the Messiah. Which is to say, until you have suffered through the impossible like me, you cannot possibly succeed me. Until you have been my long sufferer, you cannot be my short successor. Elijah is schooling Elisha on what it means to be the people's savior. In short, saying yes to God means saying yes to sacrifice.

It means you will have to suffer something, in order to succeed someone. It means you will have to give up something in order to get something you're not even expecting in return. It means promotion will not occur, until it occurs to the student to wise up and go after the mentor who stands *behind* the man with the mantle. Bypassing the mantle itself, for now. Mantles are not passed down. Men and Women in positions of leadership are.

Until you are ready to sacrifice the mantle, and *what* comes with it, for the man or woman and double portion of *who* comes with them, nothing will happen. You will find yourself and your succession plan, like Elisha, torn to pieces. And screaming out. "WHERE NOW IS THE GOD OF ELIJAH!" WHERE NOW IS THE GOD OF ELIJAH!"

"He picked up the mantle of Elijah that fell off him, and went back and stood by the bank of the Jordan. He took the mantle of Elijah that fell from him and struck the waters and said, "Where is the Lord, the God of Elijah?" "And when he too had struck the waters, they divided this way and that, and Elisha crossed over. When the sons of the prophets who were [watching] opposite at Jericho saw him, they said, "The spirit of Elijah rests on Elisha." And they came to meet him and bowed down to the ground before him [in respect]."

2 Kings 2:14 (AMP)

As this passage of scripture and the story of Elisha can attest.

All you will receive is God's silent portion of crickets.

Until the student is ready.

Then the teacher appears.

Where did Elijah and Elisha develop such high standards of sacrifice? How did Caleb and Joshua grow their natural instincts to increase? As mentioned from the outset, leadership and discipleship are not fit, and were never intended, to be mutually exclusive. Where leadership is the art. Discipleship is the exact science.

Mentorship becomes a natural blend, or occurrence, of both.

Systemically speaking, the leadership choices you start to make, begin to reflect and constitute a broader pattern. Your Moses leads Joshua to the Jordan River, acting upon the Lord's command for the Israelites to cross it. Just so your Elijah and Elisha could eventually themselves stand together by the Jordan, then cross over on dry ground. Just so your John can prepare and pave the way for Christ to come from Galilee. And be baptized there. Just so the windows of heaven could open up. Let's go there.

Christ ↑ Type

John

> *"Then Jesus came from Galilee to John at the Jordan [River], to be baptized by him. But John tried to prevent Him [vigorously protesting], saying, "It is I who need to be baptized by You, and do You come to me?" But Jesus replied to him, "Permit it just now; for this is the fitting way for us to fulfill all righteousness." Then John permitted [it and baptized] Him. After Jesus was baptized, He came up immediately out of the water; and behold, the heavens were opened, and he (John) saw the Spirit of God descending as a dove and lighting on Him (Jesus), and behold, a voice from heaven said, "This is My beloved Son, in whom I am well-pleased and delighted!"*

> *Matthew 3:13-17 (AMP)*

Talk about having large sandals that match the job description to fill.

> *"They asked him, "Why then are you baptizing, if you are not the Christ, nor Elijah, nor the Prophet?" John answered them, "I baptize [only] in water, but among you there stands One whom you do not recognize and of whom you know nothing. It is He [the preeminent One] who comes after me, the strap of whose sandal I am not worthy to untie [even as His slave]." These things occurred in Bethany across the Jordan [at the Jordan River crossing], where John was baptizing. The next day he saw Jesus coming to him and said, "Look! The Lamb of God who takes away the sin of the world! This is He on behalf of whom I said, 'After me comes a Man who has a higher rank than I and has priority over me, for He existed before me.' I did not recognize Him [as the Messiah]; but I came baptizing in water so that He would be [publicly] revealed to Israel."*

> *John 1:25-31 (AMP)*

John is one of the most significant figures and Christ types in all of the Bible. As his name implies, John "the Baptist" made a name for himself baptizing people. Not the least of which our passage of scripture above references on the banks of the Jordan River. That would be One Jesus. God made a name for John long before, though. *His* coming prophesied some 700 years earlier. "The voice of one calling in the wilderness, make straight the way for the Lord (John 1:23).

Isaiah bringing us even closer to their share in Messianic prophecy: "Every valley shall be raised up, every mountain and hill made low; the rough ground shall become level, the rugged places plain. And the glory of the LORD will be revealed, and all mankind together will see it. For the mouth of the LORD has spoken" (Isaiah 40:3-5).

Picture that. John, carrying out God's very own succession plan. For Himself. John, his very name meaning "forerunner," named Special Ambassador for the family. John, standing in The Way of his mentor. A lone voice in the wilderness. Preparing and paving the way for the King of Kings and Lord of Lords.

John, himself a type of Christ.

> *"There came a man commissioned and sent from God, whose name was John. This man came as a witness, to testify about the Light, so that all might believe [in Christ, the Light] through him. John was not the Light, but came to testify about the Light. There it was—the true Light [the genuine, perfect, steadfast Light] which, coming into the world, enlightens everyone. He (Christ) was in the world, and though the world was made through Him, the world did not recognize Him."*
>
> *John 1:6-10 (AMP)*

John and Jesus go way back. They foreknew each other, from their Mother's wombs.

"When Elizabeth heard Mary's greeting, her baby leaped in her womb; and Elizabeth was filled with the Holy Spirit and empowered by Him. And she exclaimed loudly, "Blessed [worthy to be praised] are you among women, and blessed is the fruit of your womb! And how has it happened to me, that the mother of my Lord would come to me? For behold, when the sound of your greeting reached my ears, the baby in my womb leaped for joy."

Luke 1:41-44 (AMP)

John relates as a type of Christ, in fact, because he and Jesus were related and raised in succession. When the angel Gabriel told Mary that she would give birth to Jesus, he also told her about John. As has been shared from many a Sunday pulpit, when Mary was carrying Jesus in her womb and visited her cousin Elizabeth, the baby John leapt for joy in his mother's womb at the sound of Mary's voice. Jesus stayed quiet as kept.

That's another teaching of itself: *"Real Bad Boys Move In Silence."*

"This is the testimony of John [the Baptist] when the Jews sent priests and Levites to him from Jerusalem to ask him, "Who are you?" And he confessed [truthfully] and did not deny [that he was only a man], but acknowledged, "I am not the Christ (the Messiah, the Anointed)!" They asked him, "What then? Are you not Elijah?" And he said, "I am not." "Are you the [promised] Prophet?" And he answered, "No." Then they said to him, "Who are you? Tell us, so that we may give an answer to those who sent us. What do you say about yourself."

John 1:19-22 (AMP)

Indeed, John's teaching and ministry would speak for itself, growing in popularity from Jerusalem, Judea and the whole region of the Jordan. Like Christ, he spread the good news in the face of evil opposition. His message about kingdom succession and preparing for the Messiah's coming was simple, and way ahead of the self-righteous "vipers" of its time. In effect, "Repent, be reborn of woman (and leap for joy), for the kingdom of God is near."

By boldly declaring such stern words and warnings, the general opinion of John the Baptist was that he was a prophet of God. Indeed, many thought he was the Messiah. This, however, was not his interim intent. John knew that, once Jesus came on the scene, his work would all but be finished. In that role, he willingly gave up the spotlight to Jesus. With as much fervor.

"He must become greater; I must become less" (John 3:30).

Who among us can ascribe themselves to subscribing to promoting such a selfless brand of leadership and teamwork to "make the dream work?"

And not just to say it, but to really mean it? Like a truly "acting CEO" or any fully functioning interim leader, John said what he meant, and meant what he said. He had a clear mandate, vision and focus on what he was being called and asked to do.

No ad-libbing, stick to the Book of John script.

> *"You yourselves are my witnesses that I stated, 'I am not the Christ (the Messiah, the Anointed),' but, 'I have [only] been sent ahead of Him [as His appointed forerunner and messenger to announce and proclaim His coming].'*
>
> *John 3:28 (AMP)*

Are you the type of leader who is ahead of your time but still knows how to play your position? And wait your turn. While promoting someone else's. Faithfully. Loyally. Consistently. Publicly. Let's be honest. Who among us? Are you the type of co-founders who understand how to stand in, without letting your Egos stand in the way?

If that sounds like you and your personality, then you are a type of Christ like John. If that resonates with you and your start-up organization, then you know that humility is the determining factor for interim succession planning to succeed.

When it comes to this level of mentorship in succession, perhaps, there is no greater example of two-way humility in all of humanity than that which has been modeled for us by Jesus and John. Which brings us full circle. Crossing the chasm. Back to the River Jordan. A true "come to Jesus meeting" if ever there was one. Here comes Jesus from Galilee to be baptized by John in the Jordan.

The Jordan, symbolic in all the aforementioned ways of succession. It had to happen, here. God's way was the highway. John rightly recognized that the sinless Son of God needed no baptism of repentance and that he was qualified, though not exactly worthy, of such a mentorship credential as baptizing his own Savior.

Chalk this one up as well to God's ways simply being above our ways. Literally. His succession order descending upon John from above. Like a dove. Jesus addresses John's sequential concerns by humbling himself enough to request baptism in order to "fulfill all righteousness." Which is to say, Jesus was going with God's flow in the River Jordan by identifying Himself with sinners for whom He would ultimately sacrifice Himself. Back to Himself.

> *"But all these things are from God, who reconciled us to Himself through Christ [making us acceptable to Him] and gave us the ministry of reconciliation [so that by our example we might bring others to Him], that is, that God was in Christ reconciling the world to Himself, not counting people's sins against them [but canceling them].*
>
> *And He has committed to us the message of reconciliation [that is, restoration to favor with God]. So we are ambassadors for Christ, as though God were making His appeal through us; we [as Christ's representatives] plead with you on behalf of Christ to be reconciled to God. He*

made Christ who knew no sin to [judicially] be sin on our behalf, so that in Him we would become the righteousness of God [that is, we would be made acceptable to Him and placed in a right relationship with Him by His gracious lovingkindness]."

2 Corinthians 5:18-21 (AMP)

You will recall this being the same humble pattern and reconciliatory nature of succession planning we previously encountered with Christ and his disciples in the upper room. Just as Peter assumed himself unworthy to wash Jesus' feet, so too John felt inadequately prepared to baptize the Messiah on the lower banks of the Jordan.

John followed suit with Peter. Recognizing the supernatural order of things, he obeyed and consented to baptizing Jesus. Thus, unlocking this scriptural witness key for us as we see John's recognition opening up the windows of heaven for the Spirit of God to descend, providing a spectacular glimpse of the Holy Spirit which was to come.

After Christ.

"I did not recognize Him [as the Messiah]; but I came baptizing in water so that He would be [publicly] revealed to Israel." John gave [further] evidence [testifying officially for the record, with validity and relevance], saying, "I have seen the Spirit descending as a dove out of heaven, and He remained upon Him. I did not recognize Him [as the Messiah], but He who sent me to baptize in water said to me, 'He upon whom you see the Spirit descend and remain, this One is He who baptizes with the Holy Spirit.' I myself have [actually] seen [that happen], and my testimony is that this is the Son of God!"

John 1:31-34 (AMP)

In order for succession planning to be successful at the highest level, the actions taken by the runner are equally important to those of the forerunner. In other words, Jesus didn't go running off at the mouth about who he was, and who John wasn't. He didn't feel the need to remove any doubt over who the man next to the man was. Think about it. How many times have potential partnerships been torpedoed or new client pitches, introductions and meetings been made uncomfortable by the leader in question's overindulgence in "setting straight" who Charles in charge is?

In reality, particularly within agency environments, success from the client's perspective is strictly measured by the service provider's measurable outcomes. They more or less want to know who's on first, rather than the jockeying for positon around who (or whose idea) came first. The chicken or the egg?

When signals get scrambled, who cares!

In this light, we see Jesus as the ultimate company man. As we'll point out in the subsequent chapter, Christ is our example and ideal type who is well-suited to adjust our lens around strategic partnership. And properly frame our fellowship. Through Him, joy and sacrifice are equally measured and distributed.

Above all, what makes Christ the right type to measure leadership effectiveness by every single measure? One reason. And one reason, only. Jesus *always*, *always* gives credit to the Father, where the credit is due. Being within his full right, to keep it all to Himself. Jesus towed the party line the entire way. He never rebuked John. Never undermined his authority. Never over thought a situation by editing or pre-empting his bio for his colleague, before the meeting.

Even while John was in prison, and John doubted if Christ could stay on message.

After all, why would *He*?

Because His ways are…Loyalty. Loyalty. Loyalty.

Not like ours. Never has, never will be. He's the same yesterday, today and tomorrow. Regardless of who the audience is. His first impression, is his last impression. His community service commitment is head and shoulders above ours, and that is to be the least amongst the crowd. If you're the type of leader who gets down like that, let us put you up on the fact that you're Christ*like*.

If you're confident enough with the level of management authority given you to check your signature, Ego and name tag at the door, you'll fit right into His exclusive circle. If you're the type of individual capable of speaking about your capabilities business partner with the exact same level of respect and mutual accountability, whether they be present or absent from the room, you're probably this type of Christ.

When King Herod tossed John in prison, Jesus was free to speak out of turn, but still spoke freely about his Fam. While John was locked up, he heard of all the things Jesus was doing to keep the family business going. Perhaps, in an understandable moment of doubt, John sent *his* disciples to ask Jesus if He truly was the Messiah. *Skurr Skurr*. Come again? Did you know John had his own disciples too?

> *"When Jesus had finished giving instructions to His twelve disciples, He went on from there to teach and to preach in their [Galilean] cities. Now when John [the Baptist] in prison heard about the activities of Christ, he sent word by his disciples and asked Him, "Are You the Expected One (the Messiah), or should we look for someone else [who will be the promised One]?"*
>
> *Jesus answered, "Go and report to John what you hear and see: the blind receive [their] sight and the lame walk, the lepers are cleansed [by healing] and the deaf hear, the dead are raised, and the poor have the gospel preached to them. And blessed [joyful, favored by God] is he who does*

not take offense at Me [accepting Me as the Messiah and trusting confidently in My message of salvation]."

Matthew 11:1-6 (AMP)

Look how Jesus responds. Good God, ALMIGHTY! Jesus didn't respond with "he said, she said." Nor did he run it all down the line, all starting with the letter "I." He didn't confuse the message with the messengers. That's good. He would sow no such seed of doubt, discord or division against He and John *with them.* Instead, he responded to the men by telling them to tell John what they saw and heard – prophecies were being fulfilled. Lepers were being healed. The dead were being raised. In other words, "let John know I'm holding down the Father's family business for us until he comes home."

Just in case they walked away with any doubt as to where Jesus and John stood. He spoke up, and out, about it.

"As these men were going away, Jesus began to speak to the crowds about John: "What did you go out in the wilderness to see? A reed shaken by the wind [which is commonplace]? What did you go out to see? A man dressed in soft clothing [entirely unsuited for the harsh desert]? Those who wear soft clothing are in the palaces of kings! But what did you [really] go out to see? A prophet? Yes, I tell you, and one [more eminent, more remarkable, and] far more than a prophet [who foretells the future]. This is the one of whom it is written [by the prophet Malachi], 'Behold, I send My messenger ahead of You, Who will prepare Your way before You.'

I assure you and most solemnly say to you, among those born of women there has not risen anyone greater than John the Baptist; yet the one who is least in the kingdom of heaven is greater [in privilege] than he. From the days of John the Baptist until now the kingdom of heaven suffers violent assault, and violent men seize it by force [as a precious prize]. For all the prophets and the Law prophesied up until John. And if you are willing to accept it, John himself is [the fulfillment of] Elijah [as the messenger] who was to come [before the kingdom]. He who has ears to hear, let him hear and heed My words."

Matthew 11:7-15 (AMP)

Lord, we hear you loud and clear. When it comes to succession planning, Jesus proves He knows about sticking to the script. We could go on, travel further and unpack this text for days. No doubt, many have. However, our objective now fitting square, we humbly submit and rest our case. We aptly conclude our take on this particular subject matter on succession planning with the profound simplicity of the symbiotic relationship between Mary and Elizabeth's baby boys.

Like Love and Marriage (of the Bridegroom).

You don't get one, without the other.

Like "Game Recognize Game." Takes one to know one. You know. It's like saying, "you *already* know."

Like you can almost hear Baby John leaping in his mother's womb with excitement and full recognition saying, *"Look! The Lamb of God who takes away the sin of the world!"*

Like John ***already*** knew this was the same garment of lamb skin that God used to cover Adam and mother Eve's *nakedness* after their original sin back in the Garden of Eden.

"The Lord God made garments of skin for Adam and his wife and clothed them."

Genesis 3:21 (NIV)

169

Like John was so excited and just couldn't hide it. Mary's new-born to be was to be the same sacrificial lamb from the firstborn of Abel's flock that was pleasing to God, infuriating Cain.

> *"And Abel also brought an offering – fat portions from some of the firstborn of his flock. The Lord looked with favor on Abel and his offering, but on Cain and his offering he did not look with favor. So Cain was very angry, and his face was downcast."*
>
> *Genesis 4:3-5 (NIV)*

Like John knew his cousin was symbolic of *the* young lamb *without spot* that the Lord said to Moses and Aaron was to be sacrificed in the land of Egypt in the Book of Exodus. The blood applied to the doorposts serving as a symbolic mark of the future GOAT (greatest of all time).

> *"Your lamb or young goat shall be [perfect] without blemish or bodily defect, a male a year old; you may take it from the sheep or from the goats. You shall keep it until the fourteenth day of the same month, then the whole assembly of the congregation of Israel is to slaughter it at twilight. Moreover, they shall take some of the blood and put it on the two doorposts and on the lintel [above the door] of the houses in which they eat it."*
>
> *Exodus 12:5-7 (AMP)*

Like John already knew this was the lamb Isaiah 53 was prophesying about. Before Christ was even formed in Mary's womb.

> *"All of us like sheep have gone astray, We have turned, each one, to his own way; But the Lord has caused the wickedness of us all [our sin, our injustice, our wrongdoing] To fall on Him [instead of us]. He was oppressed and He was afflicted, Yet He did not open His mouth [to complain or defend Himself]; Like a lamb that is led to the slaughter,*

And like a sheep that is silent before her shearers, So He did not open His mouth.

After oppression and judgment He was taken away; And as for His generation [His contemporaries], who [among them] concerned himself with the fact That He was cut off from the land of the living [by His death] For the transgression of my people, to whom the stroke [of death] was due? His grave was assigned with the wicked, But He was with a rich man in His death, Because He had done no violence, Nor was there any deceit in His mouth.

Yet the Lord was willing To crush Him, causing Him to suffer; If He would give Himself as a guilt offering [an atonement for sin], He shall see His [spiritual] offspring, He shall prolong His days, And the will (good pleasure) of the Lord shall succeed and prosper in His hand.

As a result of the anguish of His soul, He shall see it and be satisfied; By His knowledge [of what He has accomplished] the Righteous One, My Servant, shall justify the many [making them righteous—upright before God, in right standing with Him], For He shall bear [the responsibility for] their sins. Therefore, I will divide and give Him a portion with the great [Kings and rulers], And He shall divide the spoils with the mighty, Because He [willingly] poured out His life to death, And was counted among the transgressors; Yet He Himself bore and took away the sin of many, And interceded [with the Father] for the transgressors."

Isaiah 53:6-12 (AMP)

Like John leaped, definitively to bear witness for Isaiah that right next to him, soon coming after him, was the Lamb of God that he was being born to testify about. The one he was shouting out from the wilderness of his mother's womb and would eventually tell the Pharisees about. And here's the biggest shout. It's like John already knew God's generational success plan before he was formed in his mother's womb.

Organizations can't birth generational success without first raising up forerunners to promote generational successors. Your company's growth plans won't reproduce leadership after its own kind unless you actively cultivate it through a culture of discipleship and mentorship. Your HR succession plans to support their business units will not flourish until you synchronously populate it with teams, talent and treasure that possess shared mentorship interests and are earmarked with similar instincts to increase discipleship.

Mentorship Mastery

Leadership Summary

- **Mentorship is an active call to discipleship duty**. Mentorship must be sustainable. Sustainable enough to produce the desired outcomes over time. Not in blocks of it. Mentorship must be consistent. Consistent enough to shape and mold new behaviors that break old thought patterns.
- **Paul sets the definitive standard for secular and non-secular mentorship.** Paul was a master mentor. Case, and case study closed. He was a master of attracting and equipping others for explosive growth and development. Paul saw mentorship as a process of continuous innovation.
- **Paul saw mentorship as a mutual investment**. In order for this "mentorship thing to work," Paul acknowledged and impressed upon the leaders he invested in that he needed them as much as they needed him. Moreover, Paul may have planted and Apollos watered. But it was God who gave their works the increase.
- **Priscilla is one of the few women mentioned in the New Testament whose influence can't possibly be ignored.** Perhaps, Paul's greatest mastery lies in framing the mentor-mentee relationship with Priscilla and her husband,

"mentorship is mutual investment that breeds shared sacrifice."

- **Paul's greatest legacy is also his most painful lesson.** The lesson he gives us to grow on is not so much in *what he taught* as a mentor, but *who taught him.* Specifically, we can extract much from learning that Paul's thorn is *what mentored and tormented him.*

- **God leaves our thorn intact to make sure we don't come down with a case of "Amazing Grace" amnesia.** He leaves our thorns there to make sure we remember that it is *his infinite grace* that is sufficient, not our finite capabilities.

- **God was more concerned about building Paul's character as a mentor** than his pride. God desires to prevent the type of false pride in mentors that shuns people away.

- **Pain makes it better.** And when pain does come, it's always accompanied by growth. In this way, mentees remind us of who we once were, and where we barely made it out of. But for the grace of God. If we are to be honest as mentors, we must be willing to reveal the story of our thorns to our mentees. We should tell the authentic version that finishes with "God raised me up, brought me out this mess, so I could come back to get you."

- **In his book *The Innovative Church,* Dr. Scott Cormode, of the Fuller Theological Seminary frames this principle of shared stories of hope in the complete context of the Christian tradition.** As Christians, we offer something more specific than "future hope." Christian hope is different from other kids of hope in that our hope is not in some*thing* (like the weather); our hope is in some*one* (our Savior).

- **Paul's relationship with Timothy also leaves us with a wonderful example of Christian mentoring and shared sacrifice.** Both Timothy and Paul had to have the right attitudes for their mentorship relationship to succeed. We also learn from Paul and Timothy the importance of older men providing discipline to younger men. Their relationship growing to the extent Paul referred to Timothy as his "son in the faith."

- **Mentorship carries its own burdens**. After Paul and Barnabas parted ways, Paul chose Silas as a missionary traveling companion, picking up the young disciple Timothy along the way. In the Book of Acts, we learn from Paul, Timothy and Silas that mentorship is a three-way street.

- **The relationship between Elijah and Elisha shows us mentorship and sacrifice travel in both directions.** The mentorship point God bring us to usually begins with one person going the wrong way and the other going in the right direction, but looking the other way. One is ready to follow, but unprepared to lead. The other is prepared to lead, but not quite ready for the follower. One of them willing to give up everything. The other, with nothing else to lose.

- **Mentees are attracted to mentors because they see the results and because they like what they see**. The more they believe in the person, the more willing they become to sacrifice for the results. Individuals within your organization will follow your leaders as far as they believe they can take them.

- **Shared vision and mutual respect go hand in hand.** Mentees will not naturally line up with a leader whose vision they don't respect or narrative they can't relate to. If end results down the road don't appear to lead to an expected end, plan on early exits and detours along the way.

- **Elijah's commitment to Elisha renewed each time and grew manifold into the blessing of a double portion of his spirit**. Elisha discovered this by going after the spirit behind the man, not the mantle itself. God aligns mentorship pairs like Elijah and Elisha quite deliberately in this way.

- **Miracles of mentorship aren't performed overnight**. They are always preceded by sacrifice. No matter what stage or level we are aspiring to or from, do not despise small beginnings. Before Elijah drew crowds, he labored in relative obscurity. God provided him with the time he needed to cultivate his gifts and make his purpose clear. As a leader, you will discover a lot about your organization's effectiveness by looking for the sacrificing going on around you.

- **The story of Elisha cautions us to never take mentorship for granted.** Mentors quickly become paternal and maternal figures who can be taken away, suddenly, in a traumatic instant. In that moment of desperation and detachment, Elijah is impressing upon young Elisha about what is to come through the Messiah. Which is to say, "until you have been my long sufferer, you cannot be my short successor."

- **John is one of the most important figures in the Bible as he carries out God's very own succession plans for Himself.** As a type of Christ, John prepared and paved The Way for the King of Kings and Lord of Lords. John, himself being a type of Christ. Recognizing the supernatural order of things, he consented to baptizing Jesus. John's recognition would open up the windows of heaven for the Spirit of God to descend, providing a spectacular glimpse of the Holy Spirit which was to come.

- **The general opinion of John the Baptist was that he was a prophet of God. Indeed, many thought he was the Messiah.** This, however, was not his interim intent. John knew that once Jesus came on the scene, his work would all but be finished. In that role, he willingly gave up the spotlight to Jesus. Like most "acting CEOs" and interim leaders, John had a clear mandate, vision and focus on what he was being called and asked to do.

- **When it comes to mentorship, there is no greater example of two-way humility in all of humanity than that which has been modeled for us by Jesus and John**. John rightly recognized the Son of God needed no baptism of repentance and like Peter's hesitance to wash the Messiah's feet, felt unworthy of such a mentorship credential as baptizing his personal Savior.

- **In order for succession planning to be successful, we must understand the actions of the runner are of equal importance to those taken by the forerunner.** Jesus is the ultimate company man for the family business and ideal strategic partner. He didn't go running off at the mouth about who he was, and who John wasn't. He didn't feel the need to remove any doubt over who the man next to the man was. How often do we fall short of the Christ mark in our effort to stand taller than others in our titles and standing?

- **Christ is the right type to measure leadership effectiveness by every standard measure because He** *always* **gave credit where credit was due, to the Father.** Jesus also never rebuked John or undermined his authority. Even while John was in prison. Regardless of who the audience is, Christ's first impression is his last impression. Jesus is the type of leader able to speak about his partner and family business with the same level of respect and honor whether they be present or absent from the room.

- **Succession planning in God's Kingdom is witnessed in the profound simplicity of the symbiotic relationship between Mary and Elizabeth's wombs.** You can almost hear Baby John leaping in his mother's womb saying, *"Look! The Lamb of God who takes away the sin of the world!"* Thus, witnessing from umbilical cord to umbilical cord the fact our organizations can't birth generational success without first raising up forerunners to promote generational successors.

BOOK 3

FELLOWSHIP

Chapter 5:
Internal Affairs

"He has told you, O man, what is good; And what does the Lord require of you Except to be just, and to love [and to diligently practice} kindness (compassion), And to walk humbly with your God [setting aside any overblown sense of importance or self-righteousness?

Micah 6:8 (AMP)

Now that we've developed a clear picture of how leadership and discipleship function in the C+Suite, we continue by clearing up our internal dysfunction. Our perspective begins at the top, and starts within. Until we address our internal affairs, everything we've said up to this point is but a garment of praise draped around the spirit of a heavy ask upon our generational succession.

What's the ask?
Ask Micah.
Is that too much to ask?

Apparently so. And considering as though we stockpile hired guns and wax poetic offsite all day in order to white paper mission statements, crystallize our credos, establish brand ethos and implore core values. When in fact, it's been right there in the leather bound book sitting right in front of us, to the left on our coffee table, in black & white. The whole time. Dying to be opened so it can jump off the pages. Not costing a dime of professional services fees.

Is that not priceless?

Apparently not. Seeing as though we search high and low, go from conference to conference and Zoom conference calls to online webinars, seeking out best practices. When in fact, God's Word has been in practice, with his instructions in place, for ages and dispensations of time. There for the taking. And implementation. God's process improvement has been on the move. Long before 1986, Six Sigma and Bill Smith.

The more things stay the same, though, nothing appears to be changing.

A study by Forum Corp. revealed that while 89 percent of managers said they often, or always, apologize for their mistakes at work, only 19 percent of employees said their bosses are willing to say they're sorry.

That's pretty sorry.

During the pinnacle of the pandemic in 2021, the CEO of a mortgage lender who shall remain nameless, but certainly not blameless, terminated 900 of his employees on a virtual conference call, just before the Christmas holiday. Doing so with no shame in his game. As reported by CNN Business, he grinchly said, "your employment here is terminated effective immediately."

That's pretty harsh.

The research conducted by Forum Corp. also found that managers who choose to ignore their workplace missteps are afraid of tarnishing their image. Nearly 80 percent of the bosses surveyed refrain from asking for forgiveness for fear of appearing incompetent, while 22 percent are afraid of looking weak.

That's really sad.

Some of the other traits employees dislike in their bosses include lying, taking credit for others' ideas, blaming employees unfairly, gossiping, not communicating well and not providing enough clarity. All of these behaviors are contributing to employees' lack of trust in their leaders. While both managers and employees report that trust in the workplace is crucial, research shows that this trust has eroded in recent years. Nearly 40 percent of the employees surveyed said they trust managers less today than in past years. Overall, less than 10 percent of workers said they currently trust their leaders "to a great extent."

That's a really bad state of affairs.

"When managers aren't transparent in their actions — and that includes accepting responsibility for errors, being truthful with their employees and acknowledging hard work — that tends to breed mistrust among employees," said Andrew Graham, CEO of Forum Corp.

"The lack of employee engagement is a huge issue among U.S. workers, and our research found that employees who register low levels of trust at work are also the most likely group to report low engagement."

Is this the future state of our internal affairs?

Spotlight On 💡 Bureaucracy

"I like bats much better than bureaucrats. I live in the Managerial Age, in a world of "Admin." The greatest evil is not now done in those sordid "dens of crime" that Dickens loved to paint.

It is not done even in concentration camps and labour camps. In those we see its final result.

But it is conceived and ordered (moved, seconded, carried, and minuted) in clean, carpeted, warmed, and well-lighted offices, by quiet men with white collars and cut fingernails and smooth-shaven cheeks who do not need to raise their voice. Hence, naturally enough, my symbol for Hell is something like the bureaucracy of a police state or the offices of a thoroughly nasty business concern. Milton has told us that "devil with devil damned Firm concord holds."

But how? Certainly not by friendship. A being which can still love is not yet a devil. Here again my symbol seemed to me useful. It enabled me, by earthly parallels, to picture an official society held together entirely by fear and greed. On the surface, manners are normally suave. Rudeness to one's superiors would obviously be suicidal; rudeness to one's equals might put them on their guard before you were ready to spring your mine. For of course "Dog eat dog" is the principle of the whole organization. Everyone wishes everyone else's discrediting, demotion, and ruin; everyone is an expert in the confidential report, the pretended alliance, the stab in the back.

Over all this their good manners, their expressions of grave respect, their "tributes" to one another's invaluable services form a thin crust. Every now and then it gets punctured, and the scalding lava of their hatred spurts out."

C.S. Lewis Fellowship Institute
September 2021
"Bureaucratic Hell"

Power corrupts, and bureaucracy cripples. There's no clear remedy for that. The gravest threat to transforming organizational leadership and corporate culture is the abuse of power through evil, bureaucratic intent. There's no coming back from that. It's true. Trust is the hardest thing to gain and the easiest thing to lose. And it seems our leadership is losing it.

Indeed, C.S. Lewis paints a pretty dark picture of the internal affairs, bureaucracy and evil practices still going on a half-century later within our ongoing business concerns. However, one might also convincingly argue that the thesis of the great apologist, author and theological giant of the last century was merely ahead of its time.

Upon surface glance, it appears to be a rather stark contrast. But, are the blurred lines between hell and bureaucracy really that blurry anymore? At least, considering the marginal extremes.

While the thick layers of bureaucracies we cut through and (ab) normalized stuff we go through in our places of work and worship are presumably nowhere near as dark as the ones Lewis had in mind, there are most certainly "hellish" aspects we have become all too familiar with.

Beyond a shadow of a bureaucratic doubt, there are some shady things we've simply grown accustomed to being able to pinpoint within our corporate locations, business places and sacred spaces. Men of "low degree," and men of "high rank" go hand in hand-shake. This is nothing new, but a natural phenomenon.

> *"Men of low degree are only a breath (emptiness), and men of [high] rank are a lie (delusion). In the balances they go up [because they have no measurable weight or value]; They are together lighter than a breath."*

> *Psalms 62:9 (AMP)*

If you haven't quite discerned it yet, judgment in this chapter starts at the house. But our office buildings, campus and Virtual IIQ doesn't look like a church, or resemble a synagogue. In the biblical sense, if it has four walls containing both believers and non-believers alike within it, then it most certainly qualifies as a house of fellowship *for* the Lord.

We proceed into this discussion as such.

According to Webster's definition, fellowship means to have *companionship*, or to be in (a) *company*. It is the state of being a fellow or *associate*. Fellowship is further defined as the quality or state of being *comradely* (meaningful communication for building trust and fellowship).

As we move further along this chapter and conclusion of the matter, we will see how fellowship has far-reaching potential beyond internal affairs to impact our external affairs. It stands to reason that the aforementioned breach *of* trust in our corporate places and worship spaces is a breach *in* fellowship. Insulated by thick layers of bureaucracy. Without trust, fellowship has punched the clock and left the building.

To be in fellowship is to be connected at the trustworthy source. Indeed, Christ is the common denominator between the dividing wall of hostility in our buildings. Between the C+Suite and reception desk. Between the corner office and the cubicle. Between the owners and the employees. Between the founders and the culture keepers. Between the warehouse plant and factory management.

> *"For he himself is our peace, who has made the two groups one and has destroyed the barrier, the dividing wall of hostility, by setting aside in his flesh the law with its commands and regulations. His purpose was to create in himself one new humanity out of the two, thus making peace, and in one body to reconcile both of them to God through the cross, by which he put to death their hostility."*
>
> *Ephesians 2:14-16 (NIV)*

Between inside sales territory and the workers in the field. Between the managerial level and the executive wing. Between the mail room and the board room. Between the rules and the regulations. Between the fancy titles and "Hello My Name Is" name tags.

He stands in between the gulf between bureaucracy, the breakroom and hallway in between. Between the corner office and the cornerstone. Christ is the common denominator to bridge the divide in employee turnover and the "Great Resignation." How great?

According to *The Washington Post*, **4.3 million** U.S. workers were quitting their jobs in the *previous month*.

What's behind the mass exodus? Basic bureaucratic tendencies.

As reported by *Inc.*, Explorance, a leader in experience management (XM) solutions, commissioned a survey of 2,000 U.S. part-time and full-time employed adults to probe the hidden drivers behind the sudden employee exodus out of the workforce. The survey found that a majority of employees are eager to share feedback with employees and do so in the hopes of driving positive change in the workplace.

No doubt, basic things like, *"sure would be nice to have an annual review this year." Or, "I know we're a private company with per-formance-based metrics and all so not everyone's bonus is earned equally, but shouldn't they at least be distributed equally. I'm still waiting. Meanwhile, it "sure looks like you and your family got yours, boss."*

Bottom line, employers and leaders aren't listening. If leadership begins with listening, it's no wonder employee concerns and constructive feedback are falling upon a vacuum of deaf ears. And employees are finally taking notice. And giving notice. Effectively saying, *"I can ignore myself, by myself. And do myself some good by recognizing I deserve better than to be trapped inside of a bureaucracy."*

Sara Nelson, the American union leader who serves as the international president of the Association of Flight Attendants – CWA, AFL-CIO, put it even more succinctly: "For over 50 years, management has tried to teach workers that they should feel lucky to have a job. For the next 50 years we need to teach management they should feel lucky to have our work."

In that regard, key findings from the Explorance survey also showed that employees want to share feedback, not solely to improve their own fortunes but those of the company as well, which is a hopeful sign of true fellowship. In fact, feedback should be the birthright of fellowship. Surveys, its cornerstone. To that end, 78 percent of the employees surveyed said they're eager to take company surveys, and more than a third (38 percent) say company surveys are the preferred method for sharing feedback.

This, in large part, is what makes a Christ type of leader the common denominator. Think about it for just a moment. Casting religious traditions, denominations and belief systems aside, we can all agree that Christ's effectiveness was based upon His preferred method of leading and teaching – which was to ask thoughtful questions, and solicit open feedback. While there were clearly times he responded by admonishing and correcting false teaching, there never really was a wrong answer to a question he posed.

Jesus was far more interested in creating external change, by changing the internal feedback loop. Even though he already knew the answer, and what was likely to be said, Christ became akin to the CEO in the room that asks more questions for feedback purposes than speaking out for the purposes of being the smartest one in the room to hear Himself speak. His questions were profound yet simple enough for a child to understand. The wisdom and practicality of His responses are spiritual, and relevant to everyday life, regardless of walk of life.

Since we're dealing with matters of internal affairs, fellowship and the crippling effect of bureaucracy, we turn to the Book of Matthew for further witness as Jesus heals the demon-possessed man and solicits the feedback of the Pharisees who subsequently accused Him of being Beelzebub, suggesting He was "the prince of demons."

> *"Jesus knew their thoughts and said to them, "Every kingdom divided against itself will be ruined, and every city or household divided against itself will not stand. If Satan drives out Satan, he is divided against himself. How then can his kingdom stand? And if I drive out demons by Beelzebub, by whom do your people drive them out? So*

*then, they will be your judges. But if it is by the Spirit of
God that I drive out demons, then the kingdom of God has
come upon you."*

Matthew 12:25-28 (NIV)

Here, the Prince of Peace changes the "prince of demons" mental
model of the Pharisees by soliciting their feedback. He could have
just as easily told them straight up, who he was. But that would not
have given them ownership over their own destiny and salvation.
Instead, Christ changed the *external* conditions by challenging the
bureaucratic, demonic forces the Pharisees and others like the man
he had just healed were blindly facing.

He accomplished this by inviting them *inside* the Messianic process. Not leaving them to process things on the outside, like so
many of our bureaucratic entities have a tendency to do. He did so
by changing the preset conditions of their *internal* feedback loop
which were set by self-righteous, religious customs and man's tradition. In essence, Christ provided the Pharisees with a short survey,
and long view of the Kingdom of God.

Taking state of their internal affairs, Christ gave them a much-
needed reality check.

> *"It's not about a salary, it's all about reality
> Teachers teach and do the world good
> Kings just rule and most are never understood
> If you were to rule or govern a certain industry
> All inside this room right now would be in misery
> No one would get along nor sing a song
> 'Cause everyone'd be singing for the king, am I wrong?"*

KRS-ONE "My Philosophy"

What is it about bureaucratic kingdoms we ALL gravitate toward?
What is it about kings and bureaucrats we are ALL drawn to? What
is it about God's rule that we ALL repel from? We go back to the

Book of Samuel for much needed answers. Here, in 1 Samuel 8:7-8 we find that the Israelites have, once again, abandoned their obedience. The rebels are yelling. The renegades are deviating from their faithfulness.

This time, flat out rejecting God's theocratic rule. Instead, behaving like children. Wanting a king for themselves, like everyone else. Just like the other nations around them. As bureaucratic thinking goes, be careful what you wish for. As we pointed out earlier, God granted them their first wish in King Saul. But it didn't take long for the king to crash his own party. Literally, becoming a monument to himself.

Leaving everyone in the room in misery. Including David, who was singing his song for the king. So, was KRS-One's philosophy wrong? No sir. In either case, King Saul's self-centered bureaucracy would leave God no choice but to blow the candlestick out on Israel's own wishes. Was God's judgment wrong. No sir. With the rare exception of brief intervals when Israel was governed by non-corruptible judges or ruled by a righteous king who did right in the eyes of God, spiritual harlotry and idolatry ran rampant in her until God formally divorced her on the grounds of infidelity. Thus, sending Israel and Judah into captivity.

> *"Moreover, the Lord said to me in the days of Josiah the king [of Judah], "Have you seen what that faithless Israel has done—how she went up on every high hill and under every green tree, and there she was a prostitute? I thought, 'After she has done all these things she will return to Me'; but she did not return, and her treacherous (faithless) sister Judah saw it. And I saw [that even though Judah knew] that for all the acts of adultery (idolatry) of faithless Israel, I [the Lord] had sent her away and given her a certificate of divorce, yet her treacherous sister Judah was not afraid; but she went and was a prostitute also [following after idols]. Because of the thoughtlessness of Israel's prostitution [her immorality mattered little to her], she desecrated the land and committed adultery with [idols of] stones and trees. Yet in spite of all this her treacherous sister Judah did not*

return to Me with her whole heart, but rather in [blatant] deception [she merely pretended obedience to King Josiah's reforms]," declares the Lord."

Jeremiah 3:6-10 (AMP)

On Israel's part, it is a complete rejection of her marriage vows; she wants her Benefactor and Husband—God—to have no say in her life, declaring herself free of Him and to be completely and totally a nation of this world and no longer the type of God's Kingdom on earth.

Attitudes Toward Kingship

King. Attitude adjustment. King. Attitude adjustment. King. Attitude adjustment. The overall sentiment towards kingship by the nation of Israel is best characterized by the constant need of one. The need for one (king), would begat the need for another (attitude adjustment). Indeed, our Heavenly Father can be found throughout scripture accommodating the children of Israel with both. Each time, God demonstrating His parenting skills as the children and kings both continued exhibiting their childish ways. Looking closer, we see God taking on familiar roles as parent.

He starts off as the helicopter parent in the Book of Deuteronomy, with Moses instructing his immature brethren in surrogate fashion. *"You shall most certainly set a king over you whom the Lord your God chooses"* (Deuteronomy 17:15). The Israelites, like most minute human beings, proving themselves unable to choose for themselves. Thus, the Lord hovers over them, to make sure they "shall never return that way again."

Parents, can we get a witness? We can all relate. This passage of scripture has the overall feel of a babysitter laying down the law to start "parent's night out" off on solid ground. Lest, we helicopter parents be forced to ground our children again.

Later, in 1 Samuel, we see God taking on the perspective of the accommodating parent, acquiescing to the demands of "give me, give me" and cries of "it's not fair, everyone else has one" coming from His children. As the Lord says to Samuel, *"Listen to the voice of the people in regard to all that they say to you, for they have not rejected you, but they have rejected Me from being King over them"* (1 Samuel 8:7 AMP). Enter Saul, the people's first choice for king, only to exit stage left.

Next, we catch a glimpse of God as the parent who has lost patience with his stubborn children. After instructing Samuel to fill his horn with oil to go anoint David (1 Samuel 16:1), we see God taking matters into His own hands and inviting his unreasonable children into His providential "method behind their madness." Still, showing" "tough love" and providing attitude adjustments along the way and clearing The Way for the Messiah coming through the Key of David.

> *"When your days are over and you rest with your ancestors, I will raise up your offspring to succeed you, your own flesh and blood, and I will establish his kingdom. He is the one who will build a house for my Name, and I will establish the throne of his kingdom forever."*

> *2 Samuel 7:12-13 (NIV)*

Thus, proving to His children once and for all, that Father knows best.

For organizations, it is critical not to gloss over these internal affairs of the Israelites. We submit that a similar push and pull effect can create bureaucratic tension between the immature wants of staff and the dominant needs of management. We must find the middle ground.

It bears repeating. Regardless of your religious tradition or belief system, if you go to the source, you will find that creating a culture of faith and trust is the common denominator. God is the great equalizer. By examining the scriptures, it has become pretty clear that it was part of God's plan for the nation of Israel to have a king or judge. (Genesis 17:6) (Deuteronomy 17:14-20). God has macro intentions, with micro concerns. Having a king was not the real issue.

Indeed, God is a master of organizational behavior. He knows every organization requires effective leadership. As a result, He gave us this handbook called the Holy Bible, outlining how the leader should conduct himself or herself. As we will detail for you in the final chapter, the code of conduct is designed to ensure that the king does not get elevated above the people. It is intended as a framework for leadership to be guided by the attitudes and standards of God.

The "management issue" and employee grievances within our enterprises are the same between God and man, since the beginning of time. It is simply a matter of governance. Specifically, the clash of free will and divine providence.

We can trace this assertion back to Genesis 3 when Adam and Eve rejected God's rule over them. That same spirit of division that slithered its way into the Garden, could be working its way into your culture. Whispering right along. If you have employees quietly, and faithfully, bringing God into their workspace, we would be remiss to think the enemy doesn't want that real estate too. Ultimately, Satan wants to take God out of the work environment just as he deceived our schools into doing so (with tragic consequences), and needs our spirit of rebellion to do it.

The reality check is, if we truly want what God has to offer our enterprises by way of Kingdom principles, we cannot and should not be attempting to retain sovereignty and exclude Him from our internal business affairs. We sure can't have it both ways. And we simply won't receive it this way. At least, not for long.

> *"Come [quickly] now, you rich [who lack true faith and*
> *hoard and misuse your resources], weep and howl over*
> *the miseries [the woes, the judgments] that are coming*

upon you. Your wealth has rotted and is ruined and your [fine] clothes have become moth-eaten. Your gold and silver are corroded, and their corrosion will be a witness against you and will consume your flesh like fire. You have stored up your treasure in the last days [when it will do you no good]. Look! The wages that you have [fraudulently] withheld from the laborers who have mowed your fields are crying out [against you for vengeance]; and the cries of the harvesters have come to the ears of the Lord of Sabaoth. On the earth you have lived luxuriously and abandoned yourselves to soft living and led a life of wanton pleasure [self-indulgence, self-gratification]; you have fattened your hearts in a day of slaughter. You have condemned and have put to death the righteous man; he offers you no resistance."

James 5:1-6 (AMP)

On that cautionary note, as we conclude this matter on bureaucracy, let the people be reminded that God strongly forewarned Israel about the painful future that their wayward desires were creating for themselves. To be clear, their wanting a king was not God's issue.

The problem was theirs. Specifically, the Israelites desired a king who would be like the Gentile kings, not one whom God would appoint from among themselves. In turn, God warned them that their request would open the door for their self-appointed king to steal their hard-earned wealth and diminish the value of their covenant blessings in systematic fashion. In fact, the curse would go far right, and far left beyond what they expected. With that, the king would take their wealth "legally" and then use it for his own political ends to extend his power.

At one extreme end of the spectrum, the bureaucratic entity assumes the right to steal indirectly because it has taxing power to use anything and everything to its own ends. In the end, the bureaucracy becomes master, as opposed to servant of the people. God's leaders are called to serve the people within their organizations, not to serve as masters of the people within their organizations. The moral of the story, be careful which leaders you wish for. Power corrupts. Bureaucracies cripple. And God allows Monarchies to rise and fall. Is He wrong? No sir.

"I took my staff, Favor, and broke it in pieces, breaking the covenant which I had made with all the peoples. So the covenant was broken on that day, and thus the most wretched of the flock who were watching me realized that it was the word of the Lord. I said to them, "If it seems good to you, give me my wages; but if not, do not." So they weighed out thirty pieces of silver as my wages. Then the Lord said to me, "Throw it to the potter [as if to the dogs]—that magnificent sum at which I am valued by them!" So I took the thirty pieces of silver and threw them to the potter in the house of the Lord. Then I broke my second staff, Union, into pieces to break the brotherhood between Judah (the Southern Kingdom) and Israel (the Northern Kingdom)."

Zechariah 11:10-14 (AMP)

Spotlight On 🔮 Valuing The Gifts In The Body Of Christ

(Zac Poonen)

After Christ ascended up to heaven, He gave gifts to the church. These gifts were people. Christ gave the church apostles, prophets, evangelists, shepherds and teachers (Ephesians 4:11). These gifted men had to equip ALL the believers to build up the Body of Christ (Ephesians 4:12). It is important to note this. These gifted men were NOT to build the church by themselves. They were to equip the believers, so that the believers would build up the Body of Christ. Every believer has a part to do in building up the Body of Christ. But such a work is so rarely seen today.

"The purpose of all these ministries is to build up the Body of Christ."

First among the gifted men are the Apostles. These are not the first twelve apostles alone, because it says here that Christ gave them to the church AFTER He ascended into heaven (Ephesians 4:8). In Acts, we read that Paul and Barnabas are also called apostles. And in Revelation 2:2, we read, that at a time when there was only one of the original 12 apostles living (John), the Lord said to the church in Ephesus, "You tested those who claimed to be apostles and found them to be false."

That proves that there were other genuine apostles also at that time. Otherwise there would not have been any need to test anyone who claimed to be an apostle. There are apostles today too. Apostles are not necessarily those who write Scripture. Andrew and many of the original 12 apostles did not write any Scripture.

And there were non-apostles like Mark and Luke who wrote Scripture.

Apostles were men who were sent out by God with a specific task. The word 'apostle' means 'sent one' – a man sent by God to a particular place at a particular time. They establish local churches in a number of places and appoint elders in those places. Then these apostles become elders to those elders, guide them, solve their church problems and lead them to maturity.

Although an apostle may have a home-base in a church, he will not have any responsibility over the members of that local church. His responsibility will be for the elders of the churches.

Next we have the Prophets. These are men who are given the discernment to diagnose the problems in a church. They are like good doctors who can diagnose a patient's sickness, give him the right medicine, or perform the needed surgery, remove the cancer and cure him.

Prophets are not very popular, because they are always exposing the cancer of sin in every church. Many people may not be happy to see the results of their body scan. Even so, many believers are not happy when a prophet tells them about their sinful inner state. But this is the most important ministry in a local church.

For any church to remain in spiritual life, it must have prophets who expose sin in every meeting. Then people will be convicted of their hidden sins and acknowledge that God is present in the meeting and turn to Him (1 Corinthians 14:24, 25).

I am not referring now to the multitude of false prophets in Christendom today who tell people where to go, or whom to marry, or who threaten them with judgement. That is counterfeit prophecy. Directive prophecy is NEVER found in the new covenant. That was the ministry of old covenant prophets, at a time when only the prophets had the Holy Spirit.

But that is not the case today.

Next are the evangelists. These are believers who are given a burden for those who have never heard the gospel and who are given the ability to bring them to the Lord – either through personal evangelism or through evangelistic meetings.

The evangelist is like the hand in the body that takes a slice of bread (type of an unbeliever) and puts it into the mouth. The prophet then is like the teeth that chew that slice and make it small, and also like the stomach that pours acids on it and reduces its size, and finally makes it a part of the body. The gentle ministry of picking up the slice is more appreciated than the acid-pouring ministry. But both are needed if the slice of bread is to become a part of the body. So the evangelist and the prophet have to work together.

Next we have the Shepherds. The Greek words *"poimen"* (noun) and *"poimaino"* (verb) are used 29 times in the New Testament and are always translated as "shepherd," and "to shepherd" respectively in every other place. Here alone it has been translated as "pastor." This has led to a lot of misunderstanding of this ministry in Christendom.

Shepherds are those who look after the sheep, and care for them when they are hungry or wounded. A shepherd's job is to nurture the sheep, tenderly care for the little ones (the lambs), and to ensure that they grow up to maturity.

Every church needs shepherds, not just one pastor. Jesus shepherded only 12 men. So if a church has 120 men, it needs 10 shepherds to look after them. I am not referring to 10 full-time paid workers who have the title of 'pastor.' I am referring to those who have a shepherd's heart to care for those younger to them.

They could be men who are holding secular jobs, but who seek to encourage the younger ones in the church. A 25-year-old man can encourage all the teenagers in his church and thus be a shepherd to them. Many such men can be a great help to the elders in a church. As a church grows in size, it needs more shepherds. Mega-churches are not in God's plan for Christ's Body, but small churches with shepherds who have a father's heart.

Large churches are actually "preaching centres" where people come to be entertained and educated, but not to grow in grace. The leaders of such churches are merely good administrators and preachers/teachers, but not shepherds.

Finally, we have the Teachers. These are the men who can explain the word of God and make it simple and understandable to people. There are not many good teachers in Christendom. But then every church does not need a teacher. One teacher is enough to travel around and teach 20 or 30 churches. And nowadays with CDs, DVDs and the Internet, one teacher can reach hundreds of churches.

In the same way, every church does not need an evangelist, because an evangelist can bring people to Christ and then move on elsewhere. But what every church does need are prophets and shepherds. The purpose of all these ministries is to build up the Body of Christ. An evangelist must not bring souls to Christ and then tell them to go to whichever church they like or to go back to their old dead church.

That's not the type of evangelist spoken of here in Ephesians 4. But unfortunately, today we have evangelists who have their own name attached to their ministry. They conduct meetings and people are saved (hopefully). Then they tell them to go back to their dead churches. In those dead churches, there are no shepherds or teachers to lead them to the truth.

In Ephesians 4, we read of evangelists working together with the apostles, prophets, shepherds and teachers. The evangelist must hand over the converts to good shepherds. This is the type of cooperation we need in the Body of Christ. This is how it was in the early days of the church. Philip was an evangelist, but not an apostle or a shepherd (Acts).

So others in Samaria took over the responsibility from Philip to lead those converts further into the truth of God. Philip did not let them wander around on their own.

Nor, should we allow those within the four walls of our corporate structures wander. Structurally, not ideologically speaking, we should follow the church design and line of thinking Zac Poonen outlines above for our organizations. In other words, who do we have in place within our corporate offices to shepherd our flock of officers, employees, volunteers and temporary staff? How can we expand upon the role and responsibility of the COO to incorporate some Kingdom principles into our operation?

How do we move our corporate body to function like a true body of Christ, valuing our many gifts beyond the ability to bring in new business or rock a spreadsheet? In what ways can we build foundational kingdom structure into our business platforms? Like milk, we would do our bodies good by looking at our org design to replicate *both* our physical and spiritual anatomy.

We ensure our organizational health and overall growth by not treating functions separately, but as parts of the whole. Wholly independent, but totally dependent upon the others. For example, the Sales right hand knows what the Customer Service left hand is doing because it's not attempting to be the Marketing Arm. However, to have an arm without a hand is to have a finger without a pulse. Sounds elementary until you assemble those pieces together.

In order for this to happen, the head of the body must think along those same lines. This is what enables the one to know what the other is doing. As leaders, we must embed cross-functional thought processes into the total vitality of our organizations. How we're located. How we're checking in, and checking up. Bodies stand vertically, but must operate just as effectively (and efficiently) horizontally.

Which brings us to the spiritual anatomy. We talk a "corporate culture" good game. But, how is the heart and soul flowing throughout your business? At its core, how holy is the spirit of your company? We would do well to give a vital check to our internal affairs by further contemplating Brother Poonen's examination of the gifts within the body.

> *"These gifted men were NOT to build the church by themselves. They were to equip the believers, so that the believers would build up the Body of Christ. Every believer has a part to do in building up the Body of Christ. But such a work is so rarely seen today."*

We would be wise to take a moment, or an offsite to ask ourselves: *What* are we building? Are we building companies up to house workers, or are we building up the workers that house the company? Are we equipping people to design functional products and services, or are we equipping our products and services through the functional design of our people? And, in the end, how does it all function, and come together?

If we treat our human capital like an assembly line, barring the defectives, the individual parts should be no greater than the whole. When you add everything, and everyone up, our internal affairs and companies should functionally operate themselves. Culture should be kept by everyone. Accountability should run throughout, in every direction, not just north and south.

Your entire organization should be praying for its leaders. No matter who they are, how well they lead or whether or not you agree with them. The Roman Empire was not known for moral and ethical leadership. Yet, Paul tells Timothy to pray for the king and all who are in places of authority so that the Christians *"may lead a quiet and peaceable life in all godliness and reverence."* Do we pray for our leaders as much as we gossip about them? Perhaps, we should consider praying for them when we are compelled to complain about them at the water cooler.

Paul encourages us in our prayers by reminding us God *"desires all men to be saved and to come to the knowledge of the truth."* So don't stop praying! For God hears our prayers and our pleadings and is at work behind the scenes whether we can see His hidden hand or not. And here is the good news. We have one holy mediator in Christ, between God and mankind's internal affairs. He isn't one of many ways. He is the way, the truth and the life. Christianity is a way of life that is inclusive, and exclusive at the same time. The invitation, and book is an open one.

> *"I urge, then, first of all, that petitions, prayers, intercession and thanksgiving be made for all people – for Kings and all those in authority, that we may live peaceful and quite lives in all godliness and holiness. This is good, and pleases God our Savior, who wants all people to be saved and to come to a knowledge of the truth."*

> *1 Timothy 2:1-4 (NIV)*

In assessing our physical body, or environment, we would also do well to examine our spiritual bodies. Not in terms of what we're *doing* to be a busy body. Rather, in terms of how we're doing at *being* a spiritual body. In other words, is the bodily function of our business under constant distress, and duress? Or, is it being totally productive by combining productivity with functioning periods of rest.

Sounds biological. And pretty hypothetical. But what *exactly* does that look like?

Here's one example. Who is the Chaplain that keeps the team's culture of faith this week? Might not be a bad idea to think about working that in the rotation of your work flow. No pre-qualification necessary, except the believer's honest desire to serve others. One of our primary responsibilities upon entering seminary was to take turns serving as Group Chaplain for our Foundations of Practical Theology class.

While it appeared to be a rudimentary task on balance, no sooner had we moved into the first week of group assignments, then we realized life happens every, single day. Babies were being born into families. Families were losing people close to them. Care fatigue for elderly family members was setting in. The hidden stress of "balancing it all" became readily apparent.

The same holds true for the small group dynamics on your team. Domestic issues, health issues, co-worker issues, management issues, stress and anxiety issues, to name a few. All of which carries traumatic consequences and brings adverse effects upon those we work with, side by side, on a daily basis. Many times, without anyone ever being the wiser.

Inevitably, there are times when what happens between 9-5 can't wait until after 6. Mental Health days are a welcome trend but how about implementing the discretionary, universal "right to rejuvenate" year-round, with pay. Take it when you need it. Even if you don't use it, you won't lose it. Literally, and figuratively.

For sure, most companies now offer real-time digital tools and 24/7 professional resources with employee benefits which is a solid investment in the overall wellness of individuals. They should be applauded for maintaining their iron-clad commitment to this. That said, there's something about having someone *inside* the body that makes it function differently. There's something undeniable about real fellowship and internal group dynamics that helps the corporate body recover from *outside* infections faster, restoring overall health that much more quickly.

> *"Is anyone among you suffering? He must pray. Is anyone joyful? He is to sing praises [to God]. Is anyone among you sick? He must call for the elders (spiritual leaders) of the church and they are to pray over him, anointing him with oil in the name of the Lord; and the prayer of faith will restore the one who is sick, and the Lord will raise him up; and if he has committed sins, he will be forgiven. Therefore, confess your sins to one another [your false steps, your offenses], and pray for one another, that you may be healed and restored. The heartfelt and persistent prayer of a righteous man (believer) is able to accomplish much [when put into action and made effective by God—it is dynamic and can have tremendous power]."*

> *James 5:13-16 (AMP)*

Moving the faith needle of your organization forward by adding a Chaplain to the team roster need not be too formal, though certainly worth its weight in gold to consider adding a properly credentialed one to your future staff plan. Speaking of gold, it's understood my hometown Pittsburgh Steelers are ready for battle on any given Sunday. This is not strictly because of their preparation on the field, or in the film room. It's also because they are going into battle with the abiding presence of the Lord, and wearing the Full Armor of God.

In large part, we have our Team Chaplain and mighty Man of God, Ken Chevalier to thank for the iron sharpening iron in the Steel City. It's also made clear that the entire Steelers organization functions and flourishes in such a way. When asked about his priorities from week-to-week, our Head Coach Mike Tomlin was quick to respond, "the most important thing in my life, is Jesus Christ." Top to bottom. Wayyy up. We're blessed. And we have a body of work, and 6 Super Bowl Rings to prove it!

> *"Planted in the house of the Lord, They will flourish in the courts of our God."*

> Psalms 92:13 (AMP)

We're talking internal affairs.

Statistically speaking, here's another proof point we've discovered, developed and implemented to help mitigate the high turnover rates and number of "Great Migration" data points defecting across organizations. First, we state the facts. According to a recent study by Mind Shares Partners, SAP and Quatrics published in the Harvard Business Review, a whopping *75% of Gen Zers have left their jobs for mental health reasons.*

That's compared to just 20 percent of respondents overall who said they've voluntarily left a job in order to prioritize their mental health. This is emblematic of a "shift in generational awareness," the authors of the report, Kelly Greenwood, Vivek Bapat and Mike Maughan, wrote. For baby boomers, the number was the lowest, with less than 10 percent quitting a job for mental-health purposes. It should come as no surprise that younger generations are paving the way for the de-stigmatization of mental health.

So, why are we surprised we have such high turnover rates? Whereas, employers in previous generations dealt with job hopping, the concern now is jumping ship altogether. Why? With depression diagnoses surging 44 percent among millennials from 2013 to 2016, it's no surprise they are no longer entrusting companies with their care.

As reported in the *Wall St. Journal*, millennials are aptly labeled the "therapy generation." In fact, today's 20-30-somethings are more likely to seek therapy, and with fewer reservations, than young people in previous eras did. This can no longer be ignored. Mental health is taking its toll on the whole corporate body, to the tune of $16.8 billion in losses from employee productivity. The report found that companies are still not doing enough to break down the internal stigma, resulting in a lack of identification in workers who may have a mental health condition.

While millennials were 63% more likely than baby boomers in the study to know the proper procedure for seeking mental health support from outside the company, the question is, who can they turn to *inside* those four walls? Has empathy, in fact, left your building? How can you shepherd it back? We want to help you do just that. Together, let's find, train and raise up Good Shepherds within your organization to tend to your flock, as part of the onboarding process. Together, let's make "shepherding" part and parcel to your recruitment and retention program.

> *"Shepherds are those who look after the sheep, and care for them when they are hungry or wounded. A shepherd's job is to nurture the sheep, tenderly care for the little ones (the lambs), and to ensure that they grow up to maturity."*

There's real wisdom in this type of approach to internal affairs. As the heart of any Good Shepherd knows, *my vocation is my calling, my calling is not my vocation.*

Measuring The Christ Quotient (CQ)

⚜ C+Discernment
"Wisdom For The Ages"
Solomon

> *"Then Solomon said, "You have shown Your servant David my father great lovingkindness, because he walked before You in faithfulness and righteousness and with uprightness of heart toward You; and You have kept for him this great lovingkindness, in that You have given him a son to sit on his throne, as it is today. So now, O Lord my God, You have made*

Your servant king in place of David my father; and as for me, I am but a little boy [in wisdom and experience]; I do not know how to go out or come in [that is, how to conduct business as a king]. Your servant is among Your people whom You have chosen, a great people who are too many to be numbered or counted. So give Your servant an understanding mind and a hearing heart [with which] to judge Your people, so that I may discern between good and evil. For who is able to judge and rule this great people of Yours?"

1 Kings 3:6-9 (AMP)

What eternal wisdom is there to be found in the building (and tearing down) of building structures that we can learn from King Solomon and apply to our internal, corporate affairs? We could certainly wax poetic about King Solomon's "vast as the sand on the seashore" proverbial wisdom for the ages, for days. However, the world does not lack for another volume in this regard. Instead, we magnify our examination on the internal affairs within the temple of your enterprise from the perspective of Solomon's discernment (1 Kings 4:29).

Wisdom and discernment also have a symbiotic relationship.

God gives us one, so that we may exercise the other.

"Now it pleased the Lord that Solomon had asked this thing. God said to him, "Because you have asked this and have not asked for yourself a long life nor for wealth, nor for the lives of your enemies, but have asked for yourself understanding to recognize justice, behold, I have done as you asked. I have given you a wise and discerning heart (mind), so that no one before you was your equal, nor shall anyone equal to you arise after you. I have also given you what you have not asked, both wealth and honor, so that there will not be anyone equal to you among the kings, for all your days."

1 Kings 3:10-13 (AMP)

When Solomon went before the Lord, he wasn't facing a knowledge deficit. Surely, he already knew what a king looked like on the outside. Clearly, he saw how a king acted up close (for better, and for worse) by watching his father David roll with God through the kingdom. Solomon is getting down to the nitty gritty of Israel's internal business affairs. He is discerning the fact that this is not the same company his father was in charge of a generation ago.

These are not the same type of individuals he was set to lead. Their mindset is different. How they communicate is different. The way they roll is different. Their work ethic is different. What they value is different. Who they value is different. In fact, Lord, the way they get down altogether is altogether different. Yet, we're ALL one in the same. In the same body.

Solomon is walking in on his first day, and telling God he is lacking in the internal wisdom on how to "come and go" *between* the people. C'mon somebody! You're not just shepherding "any old" move team to that new city to plant a church. Take a look around. You didn't just close that Series-A funding with a bunch of nobodies running around that loft space. Now, take another look around. It's ok. Say it to yourself: "We've been so busy building this thing, where did all of these people come from. Who is that over there. And, by the way, who sent you? Please tell us what to do with them Lord?"

Solomon is seeking God's wisdom in the area of our Heavenly Father's internal affairs. Note, in our opening scripture, he admits that he is but a boy when it comes to conducting God's grown man business. This is coming from a man who composed three thousand proverbs and more than a thousand songs. Each, would have been certified platinum. Especially, considering people came from all the nations to hear his wisdom. Ask him about trees, he could flow right off the top and speak from the cedar to the hyssop.

That said, Solomon's wisdom didn't come from knowing everything there was and is to know about animals, and birds, and reptiles, and fish. The wisdom of his Christ Quotient is not determined by the knowledge and breadth of understanding he naturally acquired, but is measured by the discernment he spiritually possessed. He intuitively knew to go to God for the leadership answers he needed. He wasn't too proud to beg for wisdom about those God called His own. From Day 1, Solomon's CQ was higher than most and his wisdom surpassed the rest because he was able to discern that he wasn't appointed to lead his nation. He was anointed to lead God's people.

For that reason, he was also anointed to build God's temple. 480 years after the Exodus. The temple that would house the ark of the covenant God made with the Israelites when they came out of the land of Egypt. This was no ordinary new building campaign, HQ move or campus expansion. Without question, as real estate and mixed-use developments go, this was the modern equivalent of God's definitive master plan.

> *"Then Solomon said, The Lord has said that He would dwell in the thick darkness [of the cloud]. I have certainly built you a lofty house, A place for You to dwell in forever."*

> *1 Kings 8:12-13 (AMP)*

Solomon is now handling God's generational affairs.
Solomon is finishing the project his father David would only start in his heart.
We're talking about government buildings.
We're talking about a palatial palace for the Queen.
We're talking about the size of a city.
And we're talking just one part of a larger building program.
We're talking about the elders and the priests bringing up the ark of the Lord,
And the Tent of Meeting, from the City of David to its new place of residence.
We're talking about the two tablets of stone which Moses put there at Horeb (Sinai).
We're talking about the inner sanctuary and Holy of Holies.
We're talking about God being in the center of it all.

And this helps us discern why Solomon was pre-occupied with his own comings and goings.
Solomon is now making good on the promise his Heavenly Father made with his forefathers.

> *"Now the LORD has fulfilled His word which He spoke; I have risen in the place of my father David and have taken my seat on the throne of Israel, just as the LORD promised, and have built the house (temple) for the Name of the LORD, the God of Israel. There I have made a place [in the Holy of Holies] for the ark, in which is the covenant (solemn agreement) of the LORD, which He made with our fathers when He brought them out of the land of Egypt."*

> *1 Kings 8:20-21 (AMP)*

As the late, Pastor Arnold Murray of Shepherd's Chapel might say, when "good time Charlie" starts to roll, we tend to stop holding up our end of the bargain with our Heavenly Father? Why is it, we only remember the good side of God's promises, while fighting tooth and nail to neglect the flip-side of it? We, ourselves would be wise to learn from Solomon's most foolish oversight in managing God's internal affairs. God makes good on ALL of His promises.

(Front-Side of the Promise)

> *"Now it happened when Solomon had finished building the house (temple) of the Lord and the king's house (palace), and all else which he was pleased to do, that the Lord appeared to Solomon a second time, just as He had appeared to him at Gibeon. The Lord told him, "I have heard your prayer and supplication which you have made before Me; I have consecrated this house which you have built by putting My Name and My Presence there forever. My eyes and My heart shall be there perpetually. As for you, if you walk (live your life) before Me, as David your father walked, in integrity of heart and in uprightness, acting in accordance with everything that I have commanded you, and will keep*

*My statutes and My precepts, then I will establish the throne
of your kingdom over Israel forever, just as I promised
your father David, saying, 'You shall not be without a man
(descendant) on the throne of Israel."*

(Flip-Side of the Promise)

*"But if you or your sons turn away from following Me, and do
not keep My commandments and My statutes which I have
set before you, but go and serve other gods and worship
them, then I will cut off Israel from the land which I have
given them, and I will cast out of My sight the house which
I have consecrated for My Name and Presence. Then Israel
will become a proverb (a saying) and a byword (object of
ridicule) among all the peoples. This house (temple) will
become a heap of ruins; everyone who passes by will be
appalled and sneer and say, 'Why has the Lord done such
a thing to this land and to this house?'"*

1 Kings 9:1-8 (AMP)

God's promise begins with an...*If.*

And ends with a...*But if.*
"But if..." is exactly happened to Solomon.
Later in this same chapter of 1 Kings, after executing his 20-year
plan and vision, we see Solomon's reign running into the "Mo'
Money, Mo' Problems" that come with wealth and splendor that
we're all too historically familiar with by now. Regardless, Solomon
was hell bent on repeating the same mistakes. With mixed results.
Solomon built a program on exploitation, pretentiousness and abso-
lute power.
Solomon composed tax districts, centralized power, and replaced
the tribal system.
Solomon imposed forced labor, comprised of conquered people
and his own people.
Solomon associated with many forbidden women, including
Pharaoh's daughter.

Solomon turned away from God, and starting worshipping other gods (and fertility goddesses).

Solomon engaged in evil things, questionable dealings and alliances in the sight of the LORD.

Solomon built a high place for worshipping detestable idols.

Solomon was dripping.

And draped by a gold overlay on his shield.

> *"King Solomon made two hundred large shields of beaten (hammered) gold; six hundred shekels of gold went into each shield. He made three hundred smaller shields of beaten gold; three minas of gold went into each shield. The king put them in the House of the Forest of Lebanon [the king's armory]. Also the king made a great throne of ivory and overlaid it with the finest gold."*

Solomon was slipping.

And heading down a slippery, ivory throne slope.

> *"The throne had six steps, and a round top was attached to the throne from the back. On either side of the seat were armrests, and two lions stood beside the armrests. Twelve lions stood there, one on either end of each of the six steps; there was nothing like it made for any other kingdom. All King Solomon's drinking vessels were of gold, and all vessels of the House of the Forest of Lebanon were of pure gold. None were of silver; it was not considered valuable in the days of Solomon. For the king had at sea the [large cargo] ships of Tarshis with the ships of Hiram. Once every three years, the ships of Tarshish came bringing gold, silver, ivory, monkeys, and peacocks. So King Solomon exceeded all the Kings of the earth in wealth and in wisdom."*

> *1 Kings 10:16-23 (AMP)*

Solomon was tripping.

And about to learn a painful lesson about God's promises.

Revisiting the symbiotic relationship between wisdom and discernment which Solomon exhibited on his very first day on the job, we now rightfully divide the word to see just how far Solomon's discernment completely split from God's wisdom, landing him in the precarious position between God's promises of "but if" and "or else."

> *"Further, he shall not acquire many [war] horses for himself, nor make the people return to Egypt in order to acquire horses [to expand his military power], since the LORD said to you, 'You shall never return that way again.' He shall not acquire multiple wives for himself, or else his heart will turn away [from God]; nor [for the same reason] shall he acquire great amounts of silver and gold."*

> *Deuteronomy 17:16-17 (AMP)*

With the evidence mounting and abounding, we turn to 1 Kings 10 and 11 to see how Solomon's discernment measures up against his actions with the above passage of scripture in Deuteronomy 17 alone.

On "not multiplying horses…"

> *"Now Solomon collected chariots and horsemen; he had 1,400 chariots and 12,000 horsemen, which he stationed in the chariot cities and with the king in Jerusalem."*

> *1 Kings 10:26 (AMP)*

And just where did Solomon send his people in order to acquire those horses (where God specifically said not to)?

> *"Solomon's horses were imported from Egypt and from Kue, and the king's merchants acquired them from Kue for a price. A chariot could be imported from Egypt for six hundred shekels of silver, and a horse for a hundred and fifty; and in the same way they exported them, by the king's*

merchants, to all the Kings of the Hittites and to the Kings of Aram (Syria)."

1 Kings 10:28-29 (AMP)

On "not acquiring multiple wives…"

"Now Solomon [defiantly] loved many foreign women along with the daughter of Pharaoh: Moabite, Ammonite, Edomite, Sidonian, and Hittite women, from the very nations of whom the LORD said to the Israelites, "You shall not associate with them, nor shall they associate with you, for the result will be that they will turn your hearts to follow their gods." Yet Solomon clung to these in love. He had seven hundred wives, princesses, and three hundred concubines, and his wives turned his heart away [from God]. For when Solomon was old, his wives turned his heart away after other gods; and his heart was not completely devoted to the LORD his God, as was the heart of his father David."

1 Kings 11:1-4 (AMP)

On "not multiplying silver or gold…"

"Now the weight of the gold that came to Solomon in one [particular] year was six hundred and sixty-six talents of gold, besides the taxes of the traders and from the wares of the merchants, and [the tribute money] from all the Kings of the Arabs (Bedouins) and the governors of the country."

1 Kings 10:14-17 (AMP)

Remember, God's promise to Solomon was built on a rock solid "if."

"If you walk in My ways, keeping My statutes and My commandments, as your father David did, then I will lengthen your days."

1 Kings 3:14 (AMP)

If Solomon only had the wisdom to discern the most valuable thing to God was something he didn't even have to ask him for, God's promise would never have collapsed from within.

> *"So the Lord became angry with Solomon because his heart was turned away from the Lord, the God of Israel, who had appeared to him twice, and had commanded him concerning this thing, that he should not follow other gods; but he did not observe (remember, obey) what the Lord had commanded. Therefore, the Lord said to Solomon, "Because you have done this and have not kept My covenant and My statutes, which I have commanded you, I will certainly tear the kingdom away from you and give it to your servant. However, I will not do it in your lifetime, for the sake of your father David, but I will tear it out of the hand of your son (Rehoboam). However, I will not tear away all the kingdom; I will give one tribe (Judah) to your son for the sake of My servant David and for the sake of Jerusalem which I have chosen."*

> *1 Kings 11:9-13 (AMP)*

If Solomon only had the discernment to know God sees the end from the beginning so when He says *"but if,"* it's because He *already* knew it was coming.

If Solomon only had the discernment to understand how God keeps both sides of His promises and judgment, when it came time for his son Rehoboam's turn at the promise, Solomon never would have blown it for him.

If Solomon only had the discernment to perceive what God values most is so simple a child could see it, just as he did as a little boy as his father was coming and going.

> *"Then Solomon said, "You have shown Your servant David my father great lovingkindness, because he walked before You in faithfulness and righteousness and with uprightness*

of heart toward You; and You have kept for him this great lovingkindness, in that You have given him a son to sit on his throne, as it is today."

1 Kings 3:6 (AMP)

If Solomon only had a double portion of wisdom to ascertain that a man after God's own wisdom must first and foremost be like his father David was, a man after God's own heart, for the sake of future generations. Which is to say, out of the material abundance and carnality of Solomon's heart, his issues would speak for themselves. In the final analysis, swinging the pendulum of this king's discernment and wisdom to worldly ways, far away from God's Kingdom.

If Solomon only had the discernment to learn his most valuable lesson, without having to pay such a hefty price. Which is to say, all of the money, women, horses, chariots and precious metals in the world may increase your *net wealth*, but it will never equal your *net wisdom*. Goodness and honor speaks for itself.

"The [intrinsically] good man produces what is good and honorable and moral out of the good treasure [stored] in his heart; and the [intrinsically] evil man produces what is wicked and depraved out of the evil [in his heart]; for his mouth speaks from the overflow of his heart."

Luke 6:45 (AMP)

Christ ↑ Type

Melchizedek

"For this Melchizedek, king of Salem, priest of the Most High God, met Abraham as he returned from the slaughter of the Kings and blessed him, and Abraham gave him a tenth of all [the spoil]. He is, first of all, by the translation

of his name, king of righteousness, and then he is also king of Salem, which means king of peace. Without [any record of] father or mother, nor ancestral line, without [any record of] beginning of days (birth) nor ending of life (death), but having been made like the Son of God, he remains a priest without interruption and without successor."

Hebrews 7:1-3 (AMP)

In Psalm 110, a messianic psalm written by David (Matthew 22:43), Melchizedek is presented as a type of Christ. This theme is repeated in the book of Hebrews, where both Melchizedek and Christ are considered kings of righteousness and peace. By citing Melchizedek and his unique priesthood as a type, the writer shows that Christ's new priesthood is superior to the old Levitical order and the priesthood of Aaron (Hebrews 7:1–10).

Some propose that Melchizedek was actually a pre-incarnate appearance of Jesus Christ, or a Christophany. This is a possible theory, given that Abraham had received such a visit before. Consider Genesis 17 where Abraham saw and spoke with the Lord (*El Shaddai*) in the form of a man.

Hebrews 6:20 says, "[Jesus] has become a high priest forever, in the order of Melchizedek." This term *order* would ordinarily indicate a succession of priests holding the office. None are ever mentioned, however, in the long interval from Melchizedek to Christ, an anomaly that can be solved by assuming that Melchizedek and Christ are really the same person. Thus the "order" is eternally vested in Him and Him alone.

Hebrews 7:3 says that Melchizedek was "without father or mother, without genealogy, without beginning of days or end of life, resembling the Son of God, he remains a priest forever." The question is whether the author of Hebrews means this *actually* or *figuratively*. If the description in Hebrews is literal, then it is indeed difficult to see how it could be properly applied to anyone but the Lord Jesus Christ.

No mere earthly king "remains a priest forever," and no mere human is "without father or mother." If Genesis 14 describes a theophany, then God the Son came to give Abraham His blessing (Genesis 14:17–19), appearing as the King of Righteousness (Revelation 19:11,16), the King of Peace (Isaiah 9:6), and the Mediator between God and Man (1 Timothy 2:5).

If the description of Melchizedek is figurative, then the details of having no genealogy, no beginning or ending, and a ceaseless ministry are simply statements accentuating the mysterious nature of the person who met Abraham. In this case, the silence in the Genesis account concerning these details is purposeful and better serves to link Melchizedek with Christ.

Are Melchizedek and Jesus the same person? A case can be made either way. At the very least, Melchizedek is a type of Christ, prefiguring the Lord's ministry. But it is also possible that Abraham, after his weary battle, met and gave honor to the Lord Jesus Himself.

"Now if perfection [a perfect fellowship between God and the worshiper] had been attained through the Levitical priesthood (for under it the people were given the Law) what further need was there for another and different kind of priest to arise, one in the manner of Melchizedek, rather than one appointed to the order of Aaron? For when there is a change in the priesthood, there is of necessity a change of the law [concerning the priesthood] as well. For the One of whom these things are said belonged [not to the priestly line of Levi but] to another tribe, from which no one has officiated or served at the altar.

For it is evident that our Lord descended from [the tribe of] Judah, and Moses mentioned nothing about priests in connection with that tribe. And this becomes even more evident if another priest arises in the likeness of Melchizedek, who has become a priest, not on the basis of a physical and legal requirement in the Law [concerning his ancestry as a descendant of Levi], but on the basis of the power of an indestructible and endless life.

For it is attested [by God] of Him, "You (Christ) are a Priest forever According to the order of Melchizedek." For, on the one hand, a former commandment is cancelled because of its weakness and uselessness [because of its inability to justify the sinner before God] (for the Law never made anything perfect); while on the other hand a better hope is introduced through which we now continually draw near to God.

And indeed it was not without the taking of an oath [that Christ was made priest] (for those Levites who formerly became priests [received their office] without [its being confirmed by the taking of] an oath, but this One [was designated] with an oath through the One who said to Him, "The Lord has sworn And will not change His mind or regret it, 'You (Christ) are a Priest forever '"). And so [because of the oath's greater strength and force] Jesus has become the certain guarantee of a better covenant [a more excellent and more advantageous agreement; one that will never be replaced or annulled].

The [former successive line of] priests, on the one hand, existed in greater numbers because they were each prevented by death from continuing [perpetually in office]; but, on the other hand, Jesus holds His priesthood permanently and without change, because He lives on forever. Therefore, He is able also to save forever (completely, perfectly, for eternity) those who come to God through Him, since He always lives to intercede and intervene on their behalf [with God].

It was fitting for us to have such a High Priest [perfectly adapted to our needs], holy, blameless, unstained [by sin], separated from sinners and exalted higher than the heavens; who has no day by day need, like those high priests, to offer sacrifices, first of all for his own [personal] sins and then for those of the people, because He [met all the requirements and] did this once for all when He offered up Himself [as a willing sacrifice]. For the Law appoints men as high priests who are weak [frail, sinful, dying men], but the word of the oath [of God], which came after [the institution of] the Law, permanently appoints [as priest] a Son who has been made perfect forever."

Hebrews 7:11-28 (AMP)

Internal Affairs

Leadership Summary

• **Clearing dysfunction in the C+Suite begins at the top, and starts within.** Until we properly address our internal house cleaning, everything else is but a garment of praise draped around the spirit of a heavy ask upon our leadership and generational success. God is the common denominator and great equalizer in creating a culture of trust and faith.

• **We search high and low, go from conference to conference and zoom to webinars, seeking out internal best practices.** In fact, God's Word for process improvement has always been on the move. Long before 1986, Six Sigma and Bill Smith.

• **The more things stay the same, nothing changes.** A study by Forum Corp. revealed that while 89 percent of managers said they often, or always, apologize for their mistakes at work, only 19 percent of employees said their bosses are willing to say they're sorry. Nearly 40 percent of the employees surveyed said they trust managers less today than in past years. That's a sad state of internal affairs.

• **The inability for managers to be transparent in their actions and be truthful with their employees breeds mistrust.** Lack of employee engagement is a huge issue among U.S. workers. Employees who register low levels of trust at work are the most likely group to report low engagement. This, is the present state of our current internal affairs.

• **Power corrupts and "bureaucratic hell" cripples**. There's no clear remedy for it. The gravest threat to transforming organizational leadership and corporate culture is the abuse of power. Trust is the hardest thing to gain and the easiest thing to lose. It seems our leadership is losing it. Beyond the shadow of a bureaucratic doubt, there are dark and shady things we can pinpoint behind closed office doors in our business locations, meeting places and sacred spaces.

• **According to the Webster's definition, "Fellowship" is to be *in company*.** While our office buildings, campus or HQ may not look like a church, or resemble a synagogue, if it has four walls containing both believers and non-believers alike, it qualifies as a house of *fellowship* for the Lord (in the biblical sense). To be in fellowship is to be connected to a trustworthy source.

• **Basic bureaucratic tendencies are behind the "Great Resignation" and mass exodus from the workforce.** Employees are anxious to provide feedback. Bottom line, leadership begins with listening and employers are showing lackluster performance. And the results speak for themselves. Upwards of 4.3 million U.S. workers are quitting their jobs *by the month*.

• **Religious traditions, doctrines and denominations aside, Christ should be the cornerstone for leadership and common denominator for our internal affairs.** By asking questions and soliciting feedback Jesus gives us a powerful example of leadership beginning with listening. As a teacher, Christ was more interested in creating external change by changing the internal feedback loop.

• **There is something about bureaucratic kingdoms and monarchies we gravitate to, while repelling God's theocratic rule.** Behaving like disobedient children, the Israelites wanted a king for themselves, "like everybody else." God granted them their wish, in King Saul, knowing what they wished for would eventually be the thing He would take away. Eventually, resulting in God blowing out their candlesticks and divorcing Israel because of her harlotry and idolatry.

• **The overall attitude toward kingship is one of attitude adjustment.** The need for one (king), would begat the need for the other (attitude adjustment). Over time, our Heavenly Father assumes different roles to administer attitude adjustments. We see him going from "helicopter parent" in the Book of Deuteronomy (with Moses acting as surrogate), to accommodating parent and the one who has lost patience. Finally, after he has chosen David to be king over Israel, clearing the way for the Messiah, he shows them the role of Father knows best.

• **God is a master of organizational behavior.** He provides us with a manual for how leaders should conduct themselves, intended to serve as a framework for leaders to be guided by the attitudes and character of God. Management issues and grievances in our enterprises is a derivative of the same issue and spirit of division between God and man, since the beginning of time. The clash in the Garden between God's divine providence and man's rebellious, free will.

• **Mankind wants to retain authority over governance of his affairs.** However, if we truly want what God has to offer our enterprises by way of Kingdom principles and favor, we commit the original sin when we attempt to wrestle away his sovereign rule by excluding Him from our business environments and internal affairs.

• **The children of Israel remind us to be careful which leaders we wish for.** We must take an active role in our internal affairs by making sure we aren't advocating for, or supporting leaders who seize the opportunity to promote their selfish interests at the expense of the company's hard-earned human capital.

• **We ensure our organizational health and overall company growth by treating functions of the corporate body holistically, not separately.** Like milk, we do our corporate bodies good by having our org design replicate physical and spiritual anatomy. The left and right hand both know what the other is doing when the head of the body is thinking along those lines. As leaders, we must embed cross-functional thought processes into the total vitality of our organizations.

• **We talk a good "corporate culture game" but need to examine ourselves, and the vital signs of the heart and soul that are flowing throughout our enterprise.** We would be wise to ask ourselves *"what"* we are building. We would do well to examine our physical environment from the perspective of the spiritual body *within* it. We do this, not in terms of what we're *doing* to be a "busy body," but rather how we're doing at *being* a spiritual body.

• **One example for making sure we are spiritually and anatomically correct is to incorporate a "Chaplain" into your team's dynamic.** Without need of making it too formal (though to formalize such a position does have exponential fellowship benefits), this role may prove invaluable in helping make spiritual sense out of the day-to-day issues confronting our co-workers that come trudging along with adverse effects for the workplace.

• **Invariably, there are times when what happens between 9-5 can't wait until after 6.** While companies have answered the bell by offering internal benefits and external resources to support overall health and wellness, there's nothing like investing in someone on the *inside* whose primary function is the vital functioning of the corporate body. This, particularly holds true for helping shepherd Millennial workers who are no longer wholesale entrusting employers to their care (*a whopping 75% of Gen Zers have left their jobs for mental health reasons*).

• **We are wise to measure our Christ Quotient (CQ) by the discernment shown by Solomon, in both the building up and destroying of our buildings and corporate structures.** Wisdom and discernment have a symbiotic relationship. God gives us one, so we may exercise the other. Solomon didn't go to God on his first day in the office as king with a knowledge deficit. After all, he knew how a king functioned watching his father growing up. Instead, he showed discernment by recognizing he lacked internal wisdom on the "comings and goings" between those he was to lead. He was seeking wisdom on how to manage God's internal affairs.

• **If Solomon only had the discernment to recognize what God values most in a leader is a man after God's own heart.** In the end, if Solomon had the discernment to learn his most valuable, timeless lesson. All of the money, women, horses, chariots and precious metals in the world may increase your net wealth, but it will never equal your net wisdom.

• **Are Melchizedek and Jesus the same person? A case can be made either way**. At the very least, Melchizedek is a type of Christ, prefiguring the Lord's ministry. But it is also possible that Abraham, after his weary battle, met and gave honor to the Lord Jesus Himself.

Chapter 6:
External Relations

"You are the light of the world. A city set on a hill cannot be hidden. Nor do people light a lamp and put it under a basket, but on a stand, and it gives light to all in the house. In the same way, let your light shine before others, so that they may see your good works and give glory to your Father who is in heaven."

Matthew 5:14-16 (ESV)

Having spiritually meddled in our internal affairs, we now expose ourselves to the fuller examination of fellowship by setting our sights and casting light upon our works outside of the corporate body. We're talking eternal relations. Community relations, and community affairs. We're talking about the mission critical, mission alignment of our philanthropic, non-profit and corporate responsibility endeavors to meet the unmet needs of those around us.

For all the right reasons, in all fiscal seasons.

Not just in tax season, for write-off purposes.

Spotlight On 💡 Gratitude

"...in order that in the coming ages he might show the incomparable riches of his grace, expressed in his kindness to us in Christ Jesus. For it is by grace you have been saved, through faith – and this is not from yourselves, it is the gift

of God – not by works, so that no one can boast. For we are God's handiwork, created in Christ Jesus to do good works, which God prepared in advance for us to do."

Ephesians 2:7-9 (AMP)

As Dr. Scott Cormode frames for us in *"The Innovative Church,"* gratitude and generosity are *"two sides of the same practice."* In effect, *"gratitude is about choosing **what** to remember – and about choosing **whom** to remember."* If you think about it, this is what makes the Salvation Army so successful. For whom their iconic red bell tolls, it strikes us with a reminder to be grateful during the Holiday Season because we are *choosing* to remember those less fortunate.

For the right reason.

As he continues, *"the Christian practice of gratitude is different from secular gratitude in that it is choosing to remember what God has done. It is choosing to remember the abundance God provides rather than the scarcity that can seem apparent."* Dr. Cormode illuminates our thinking further around placing our generosity into external relations practice for several key reasons:

1.) **Gratitude is not complete until it becomes generosity** – gratitude is about choosing to remember the gift of God's grace. To choose gratitude is to choose my identity. Gratitude is not complete until it becomes generosity. If I lack gratitude, I lack generosity. My purpose then becomes about my own, selfish interests.

2.) **Generosity is no more and no less than grace in action** – sincere gratitude flows into generosity. Generosity is not just about money. It is a generous spirit – a willingness to give others the same benefit of the same doubt we received.

3.) **We practice generosity because we have received grace** – we give because God gave and because God continues to give. We cannot turn God's gift of grace into a transaction – as if God were a dealmaker and we stand to get the better of Him. And we cannot pretend that we owe God nothing. When I am so overwhelmed by the gifts and grace I've received, it's easy to let others have a little of my good fortune.

4.) **We owe God gratitude** – the kind of gratitude that makes us want to be generous in return, in equal and proper proportion to how generous God has been to us.

5.) **We don't want things to be fair, we want grace** – if we're really given what we deserve, that thinking sets a dangerous precedent. If God were being fair, we'd no longer be here, much less in the position we're in.

Jesus did not always think things should be "fair." Indeed, as Matthew 20 is our witness, he thought the *"last should be first."* If you're not familiar with that passage of scripture, no doubt you are quite familiar with the saying it prompted which was co-opted by the American Federation of Labor movement.

"A fair day's wage for a fair day's work."

Indeed, this tidy declaration doing a yeoman's job capturing the spirit behind the labor movement, trade unions and other worker's groups push to increase pay and adopt reasonable hours of labor. Like beauty, though, fairness is in the eye of the beholder. One man's beautiful, conservative arrangement is yet another woman's ugly reality of unequal pay. Such harsh realities get progressively worse when the workforce capitalizes off of unsuspecting women of ALL colors to profit one's advantage. Leaving pay scales woefully unbalanced.

March 24 is "Equal Pay Day," a symbolic date representing the number of additional days that women, on average, must work to earn what men, on average, earned the year before. Unfortunately, for the majority of women of color, this date falls much later in the year. According to Bureau of Labor Statistics data, in 2020, women's annual earnings were 82.3% of men's. The gap is even wider for women of color (65% for Black and Latina women).

Let's give fair assessment by going inside the Equal Pay Day numbers.

To earn what white, non-Hispanic men earned in 2020, Asian American and Pacific Islander women had to work until March 9th. For women of color, Equal Pay Day falls even later in the year. For Black women, not until August 3rd. For Native American women it finally arrives on September 8th. Lastly, for Latinas, the scales of Equal Pay Day are even more unevenly balanced, with their Equal Pay Day landing 9 months into the year on Oct. 21st.

Clearly, women are giving more than their fair share of a full day's work for less than a fair day's wages in return. In the end, for workers galore, it all adds up to being just enough to make ends meet. That's less than a fair exchange.

One man totally agreed with this premise. In 1881, Friedrick Engels critiqued and tweaked the *"fair day's wage"* slogan in the inaugural issue of *The Labour Standard*. Engels argued that workers were exchanging the full power of their labor for a day in return, for just enough subsistence necessary to maintain them for a day. As he wrote: *"The workman gives as much, the Capitalist gives as little, as the nature of the bargain will admit."*

He also opined that capitalists can force a better bargain as they can live off of their capital. Whereas, workers without reserves are forced to accept work at a less advantageous rate. Engels went on to call for the old motto to be terminated in favor of another, more radical version: *"Possession of the Means of Work, Raw Material, Factories, Machinery, by the working people themselves."* His critique would ultimately inform the preamble of the Industrial Workers of the World, founded in Chicago in 1905, which called for the total "abolition of the wage system."

While clear progress has been achieved since the Equal Pay Act of 1963, momentum slowed after the global pandemic. What can we do achieve pay equity? Chief Economist Janelle Jones with The U.S. Department of Labor concedes there's "clearly a lot of work to be done," but also suggests "it is possible to level the playing field for equal pay by increasing transparency around wages across the board, disrupting occupational segregation, expanding access to paid leave and child and elder care, and creating more good union jobs."

Parable of the Vineyard Owner

"For the kingdom of heaven is like the owner of an estate who went out in the morning at dawn to hire workmen for his vineyard. When he had agreed with the laborers for a denarius for the day, he sent them into his vineyard. And he went out about the third hour (9:00 a.m.) and saw others standing idle in the market place; and he said to them, 'You also go into the vineyard, and I will pay you whatever is right (an appropriate wage).' And they went.

He went out about the sixth hour (noon) and the ninth hour (3:00 p.m.), and did the same thing. And about the eleventh hour (5:00 p.m.) he went out and found others standing around, and he said to them, 'Why have you been standing here idle all day?' They answered him, 'Because no one hired us.' He told them, 'You go into the vineyard also.' "When evening came, the owner of the vineyard said to his manager, 'Call the workers and pay them their wages, beginning with the last [to be hired] and ending with the first [to be hired].'

Those who had been hired at the eleventh hour (5:00 p.m.) came and received a denarius each [a day's wage]. Now when the first [to be hired] came, they thought they would get more; but each of them also received a denarius. When they received it, they protested and grumbled at the owner of the estate, saying, 'These men who came last worked [only] one hour, and yet you have made them equal [in wages] to us who have carried [most of] the burden and [worked in] the scorching heat of the day.' But the owner of the estate replied to one of them, 'Friend, I am doing you no injustice. Did you not agree with me for a denarius?

Take what belongs to you and go, but I choose to give to this last man [hired] the same as I give to you. Am I not lawfully permitted to do what I choose with what is mine? Or is your eye envious because I am generous?' So those who are last [in this world] shall be first [in the world to come], and those who are first, last."

Matthew 20:1-16 (AMP)

As you will recall from our last chapter, Christ models transformational leadership through listening. He demonstrates best teaching practices by speaking in parables and soliciting feedback. By framing the vineyard owner's question to the workers in the context of the *"last being first, and the first being last,"* Christ changes our mental model around gratitude, entitlement, victimization, fairness and generosity. All in one fell swoop.

In the process, He implies new meaning and extols fresh virtue into our definition of what gratitude is. And what fairness looks like. And, more importantly, Jesus is reshaping our misconstrued mentality around generosity. In other words, let's be real. Do we truly want God to give us what we really deserve?

How generous of Him not to!

"since all have sinned and continually fall short of the glory of God, and are being justified [declared free of the guilt of sin, made acceptable to God, and granted eternal life] as a gift by His [precious, underserved] grace, through the redemption [the payment for our sin] which is [provided] in Christ Jesus."

Romans 3:23-24 (AMP)

In the Book of Romans, Paul is reminding "the holier than thou" within us to be grateful for the gift that keeps on giving. This is more than enough to keep our bell ringing with generosity all year long. Paul also cautions us while we're constantly calculating what's owed to us. Indeed, he quiets our noisy spirit of ungratefulness to silent mode.

While we're busy complaining about how God is somehow shorting us into our reaching out and giving to others with short arms (and alms) during this drought of a season, he challenges us to start another tally. Let's begin by adding up the past due wages from our past sins. And multiply that by the wounds of our transgressions. When we check the ledger, we find our account doesn't balance and is long overdue. Who has every right to file that grievance claim, now? How generous of Him to reconcile the books, and blot it all out!

> *"For the wages of sin is death, but the free gift of God [that is, His remarkable, overwhelming gift of grace to believers] is eternal life in Christ Jesus our Lord."*

> *Romans 6:23 (AMP)*

God blots everything out except our responsibility to assume the same external posture toward generosity and gratitude. Here, we come to understand what it truly means to be blessed. More than a statement t-shirt, "truly blessed" is more about being in a *condition* than it is to be in a *position*. Being blessed is a condition of putting ourselves in the position of being *in* God's unconditional will. Thereby, supernaturally placing us in a natural position to be blessed.

In other words, we're not blessed because our life is in *"this position,"* we're blessed as a result of our lives being *"in His condition."* Once we juxtapose our thinking, we unearth the true riches of the kingdom, and principles behind seed time and harvest time. Truth is, the only way we will be a blessing to others is if we are truly honest enough with ourselves and others to let them know the blessing we possess in our *current position* is the direct result of our *previous condition*. For far too long, we have come to equate "being blessed" as a position in direct proportion to the amount of "stuff" we have to show and prove for it.

Far too often, we wait until we feel like we are *finally* in a position of being blessed in order to be a blessing to others. *"La, la, la, la, wait 'til I get my money right."* This self-fulfilling prophecy becomes but a generosity myth. Internal profits are down, so our external giving is on the low. Our fortunes are closing, so our coffers can't open up. We're losing our shirt and cutting our losses this quarter, so we're going to treat our quarterly employee bonuses like a pair of jeans and squeeze them in our little front pocket.

Once we put ourselves in a position of gratitude and begin operating within God's will, following His precepts and commands to love on others and take care of others, the blessing will follow and take care of itself. His blessings will pour out and rain down on us. God is a way maker and a rainmaker. How much rain? How about this, for good measure?

> *"Give, and it will be given to you. They will pour into your lap a good measure – pressed down, shaken together, and running over [with no space left for more]. For with the standard of measurement you use [when you do good to others], it will be measured to you in return."*

> *Luke 6:38 (AMP)*

Spotlight On 💡 Giving

> *"Bring all the tithes (the tenth) into the storehouse, so that there may be food in My house, and test Me now in this," says the LORD of hosts, "if I will not open for you the windows of heaven and pour out for you [so great] a blessing until there is no more room to receive it."*

> *Malachi 3:10 (AMP)*

We're talking external relations. Internal proceeds going toward outside giving. In ancient times, special storehouses were established in the temple to receive the tithes of the harvest. If the people were not faithful, the priests could not continue to serve and perform their duties.

By all measures, corporations and business concerns today are doing a good job storing up top heavy, fat bonuses and concerning themselves with paying house dividends. Right off the top. In extreme cases, until there is not much more room to receive it.

Nothing wrong with the good times rolling but since we're all in this together, now more than ever, we should pause for a minute to think about those for whom they've stopped altogether. In all fairness, the true measure of company growth in our annual report these days should be taken by the amount and percentage of our treasury reserved for sustaining the community around us.

Inquiring shareholder minds seated around the private dining room table should want to know how much resource allocation is being deployed externally to keep the local service industry gainfully employed, and able to continue performing their duties – as we perform ours tonight?

This is not to paint a grim picture.

Rather, we seek to encourage with a pen stroke and accentuate the positive, wholesale strides made in the midst of the global pandemic. With more travails certainly ahead. Surely, there was nothing more gratifying than watching the applied, collective effort unfold across the spectrum to support small businesses, minority-owned retailers and women founders of mom and pop shops alike. Some, whose very existence, literally, hung by inventory threads on the balance sheet.

If the pandemic taught us anything, it is not to be deceived. God is not mocked. He will not allow Himself to be ridiculed, nor treated with contempt nor allow His precepts to be scornfully set aside];

"for whatever a man sows, this and this only is what he will reap (Galatians 6:7)." If the disruption from the pandemic reinforces anything for us about Kingdom principles, it would be that the outpouring (or not) speaks for itself.

Reaping & Sowing

"Now [remember] this: he who sows sparingly will also reap sparingly, and he who sows generously [that blessings may come to others] will also reap generously [and be blessed]. Let each one give [thoughtfully and with purpose] just as he has decided in his heart, not grudgingly or under compulsion, for God loves a cheerful giver [and delights in the one whose heart is in his gift]. And God is able to make all grace [every favor and earthly blessing] come in abundance to you, so that you may always [under all circumstances, regardless of the need] have complete sufficiency in everything [being completely self-sufficient in Him], and have an abundance for every good work and act of charity.

As it is written and forever remains written, "He [the benevolent and generous person] scattered abroad, he gave to the poor, His righteousness endures forever!"

Now He who provides seed for the sower and bread for food will provide and multiply your seed for sowing [that is, your resources] and increase the harvest of your righteousness [which shows itself in active goodness, kindness, and love]. You will be enriched in every way so that you may be generous, and this [generosity, administered] through us is producing thanksgiving to God [from those who benefit]. For the ministry of this service (offering) is not only supplying the needs of the saints (God's people), but is also overflowing through many expressions of thanksgiving to God.

Because of this act of ministry, they will glorify God for your obedience to the gospel of Christ which you confess, as well as for your generous participation [in this gift] for them and for all [the other believers in need], and they also long for you while they pray on your behalf, because of the surpassing measure of God's grace [His undeserved favor, mercy, and blessing which is revealed] in you. Now thanks be to God for His indescribable gift [which is precious beyond words]!"

2 Corinthians 9:6-15(AMP)

Not only have we juxtaposed what it means to be blessed, we have convoluted the good intent behind God's laws and precepts regarding our giving and lending to the poor. God never intended lending or debt to be leveraged as a predatory vehicle. He didn't design borrowing to become a Fintech platform through which those in positions to lend and facilitate lending could, technically, take advantage of the poor. For a small, success fee. Without kicking some back.

Personal loans are the fastest-growing debt category, increasing about 12% year-over-year since 2015. That's due in part to the rise of Fintech and peer-to-peer lending companies, which make accessing these loans cheaper and easier than ever. In other words, *"the problem we solve is..."* helping consumers fall deeper into personal debt much faster. Not to pick on Fintech either, as these are real individual choices and real problems that warrant real solutions.

Besides, somebody's going to do it.

God is simply saying wait a minute. The neighborhood supports, so put some money in it. God is saying, check my biblical records. The purpose for borrowing was intended as an instrument for the poor among you to ensure they would always have a place of some solid, if not equal, footing in society. This, being a contingency requirement of God's blessing.

And so it was for the nation of Israel.

It may be Old Testament, but there is something new our country could learn from revisiting God's precepts. It seems, though, we are more inclined and doomed to repeating history as opposed to learning from it. For our educational purposes here, we make a return visit to the old schoolmaster, the Book of Deuteronomy.

God is warning the Israelites not to throw caution to the wind.

He is reminding them that their blessing is not the result of their financial position or standing. He is placing further stipulations on future proceeds, contingent upon them recognizing they are to be a blessing to others, which is the condition upon which their blessings will continue to flow. As previously stated, we act upon our gratitude with generosity and give benefit of the doubt because we honor God as the source of our generational good fortune.

In the following passage of scripture, God is humanizing the condition of the less fortunate by instructing the most fortunate among the Israelites to see the "priceless" worth of His children, regardless of their net worth or net present value. In fact, God wanted them to put their money where his mouth was. Seed time and harvest time speaking.

He was speaking out, on behalf of those on the fringes of their society. God was *not* talking about lending handouts. He was addressing the need for creditors to give reprieve for debts. Specifically, He was putting His foot down on the foot stool every seven years as a seasonal "*grace period*" to help pull everyone up by the sandal straps.

The Sabbatical Year

"At the end of every seven years you shall grant a release (remission, pardon) from debt.

This is the regulation for the release: every creditor shall forgive what he has loaned to his neighbor; he shall not require repayment from his neighbor and his brother, because the Lord's release has been proclaimed. You may require repayment from a foreigner, but whatever of yours is with your brother [Israelite] your hand shall release. However, there will be no poor among you, since the Lord will most certainly bless you in the land which the Lord your God is giving you as an inheritance to possess, if only you will listen to and obey the voice of the Lord your God, to observe carefully all these commandments which I am commanding you today.

When the Lord your God blesses you as He has promised you, then you will lend to many nations, but you will not borrow; and you will rule over many nations, but they will not rule over you. "If there is a poor man among you, one of your fellow Israelites, in any of your cities in the land that the Lord your God is giving you, you shall not be heartless, nor close-fisted with your poor brother; but you shall freely open your hand to him, and shall generously lend to him whatever he needs.

Beware that there is no wicked thought in your heart, saying, 'The seventh year, the year of release (remission, pardon), is approaching,' and your eye is hostile (unsympathetic) toward your poor brother, and you give him nothing [since he would not have to repay you]; for he may cry out to the Lord against you, and it will become a sin for you. You shall freely and generously give to him, and your heart shall not be resentful when you give to him, because for this [generous] thing the Lord your God will bless you in all your work and in all your undertakings. For the poor will never cease to be in the land; therefore I command you, saying, 'You shall freely open your hand to your brother, to your needy, and to your poor in your land."

Deuteronomy 15:1-11(AMP)

Yes. For all God's Kingdom intents and purposes, this is the divine origin of what a grace period was *intended* to look like. Nothing like it looks today. Grace periods today are given in windows of

30-60 days, not 365. Grace periods today are never fully satisfied until the debt and interest are both satisfied. Debts are never retired. They pass down generationally. Nothing could compare, or stand in more clear contrast, to the way God was reconciling debt for Israel than the Sabbatical year. Generationally, and generously speaking.

The fine print of this Law binds us to framing the cure to poverty and how we view the poor among us in terms of the symbolic (and symbiotic) relationship between indebtedness, gratitude and God's generosity. Indeed, gratitude is not complete until it travels the distance between one's indebtedness and someone else's need for generosity.

In this case, every seven-year period.

In placing a time out on collections and canceling debts held by their brethren, the Israelites are reminded *"there need be no poor people among you, for in the land the Lord your God is giving you to possess as your inheritance, he will richly bless you."* God is reminding the Israelites of their indebtedness to Him as the generous source of their prosperity.

Therefore, they should be moved to forgive any outstanding debts so the abundance of His generosity flows to the entire nation and extends to the poor. Finally, God is saying generosity is not just about the money, but a willingness to give (and forgive) in the same generous spirit in which God has so freely given, even when it was undeserved.

Stands to wonder and reason what profound impact implementing such a sabbatical period would have on the imposing numbers of poor folks facing the homelessness crisis facing our nation. Based on statistics from *Endhomelessness.org*, in January 2020, there were 580,466 people experiencing homelessness in America.

A devastating 30 percent of the homeless population comprised families with children. If ever there were a just, patriotic cause for such a sabbatical, it would find sufficient probable cause in the more than 6% of our country's veterans that are homeless. More than clearing the accounting books, God is urging us to carry one another's burdens and clearing the spirit from sin, as Moses warns against harboring "the wicked thought" and not "showing ill will." (Deuteronomy 15:9).

Bottom line, sincere gratitude flows quite naturally from a mindset of generosity.

> *"Carry one another's burdens and in this way you will fulfill the requirements of the law of Christ [that is, the law of Christian love]. For if anyone thinks he is something [special] when [in fact] he is nothing [special except in his own eyes], he deceives himself. But each one must carefully scrutinize how own work [examining his actions, attitudes, and behavior], and then he can have the personal satisfaction and inner joy of doing something commendable without comparing himself to another."*
>
> *Galatians 6:2-4 (AMP)*

This scripture speaks volumes on the topic of indebtedness, gratitude and generosity in contemporary society. Unfortunately, such precepts have all but lost empathetic relevance today. Rarely do we see these three triangulated in our modern society as evidenced by increasing levels of debt, poverty and homelessness.

As such, it is beyond reproach and quite polarizing to even suggest such an approach (much less enacting it into policy or law) without it being labeled, politicized or characterized by one group or another. Irrespective of which side of the aisle we're on, or wavering in the middle, we are all stuck in the same boat when it comes to economic debt and economic uncertainty.

According to CNBC, the average American has $90,460 in debt. These numbers have a ripple effect inside of our enterprises and organizations in terms of low productivity, turnover, human resources and aforementioned mental health.

Average debt balances by age group:

- Gen Z (ages 18 to 23): $9,593
- Millennials (ages 24 to 39): $78,396
- Gen X (ages 40 to 55): $135,841
- Baby boomers (ages 56 to 74): $96,984
- Silent Generation (ages 75 and above): $40,925

The reverberating impact of "making ends meet" while "keeping up with the Kardashians" has particular resonance among younger professionals entering the workforce. Millennials have seen the largest debt increase in the last five years. For example, in 2015, the average Millennial had about $49,722 in debt.

By 2019, they carried an average of $78,396 in total debt – an increase of 58%. Gen Z has the lowest overall debt balance on average, but they struggle the most to make payments. About 12.24% of Gen Z's credit card accounts were 30 days or more past due in 2019.

Throughout scripture, from Moses in the Book of Deuteronomy to the Apostle Paul in the great Book of Galatians, God is providing our conscious with its own grace period by constantly taking measure of our giving culture vs taking culture. Not as a constant measure to see who gets to be "one up," but as a measure of spiritual integrity.

Measuring The Christ Quotient (CQ)

♛ C+Ethics
"Eli & Sons"

> *"A poor yet wise youth is better than an old and foolish king who no longer knows how to receive instruction and counsel (friendly reproof, warning)— for the poor youth has [used his wisdom and] come out of prison to become king, even though he was born poor in his kingdom. I have seen all the living under the sun join with the second youth (the king's*

*acknowledged successor) who replaces him. There is no
end to all the people; to all who were before them. Yet those
who come later will not be happy with him. Surely this also
is vanity (emptiness) and chasing after the wind."*

Ecclesiastes 4:13-16 (AMP)

When it comes to biblical leadership authority, the story of Eli con-
stitutes a convincing case study for measuring the integrity of our
leaders by the ethical framework around the standards of giving
and taking.

*"If the person said to him, "Let the fat be burned first, and
then take whatever you want," the servant would answer,
"No, hand it over now; if you don't, I'll take it by force. This
sin of the young men was very great in the LORD's sight,
for they were treating the LORD's offering with contempt."*

1 Samuel 2:16-17 (NIV)

The wicked, internal affairs of these young men marring the
excellence of Eli's external affairs, having given so much to
his fellow man as a revered judge over Israel. Eli's inability to
manage the integrity of his family leading to his downfall after
having the distinction of holding the high office as a member of
the priesthood.

Scripture informs us, with sufficient reproof and correction, if we
do not faithfully and ethically handle the internal affairs of our own
house, we lack the credibility to lead outside of it. As was the case
with King Solomon, and taking ethical stock of our leadership ranks
today, we glean as many key learnings from their personality and
character shortcomings as we do their highest expression. In this
regard, we now apply the ethical framework to Eli.

Eli in the Bible was a Jewish priest living in the days of the judges and
serving God at the tabernacle in Shiloh, a city near the hill country of
Ephraim (1 Samuel 1:1, 3). Eli is best remembered for his blessing

on Samuel's mother and for his part in Samuel's first prophecy. Eli had two wicked sons named Hophni and Phineas; they also served in the tabernacle but did not know the Lord (1 Samuel 2:12). They violated the Law by keeping and eating meat from the sacrifices that was not allocated to them. They also had sex with the women who served at the doorway to the tent of meeting (1 Samuel 2:22).

The bad behavior of Eli's sons was widely known (1 Samuel 2:24), and the report came back to Eli. When he found out about these things, he rebuked his sons but failed to make them stop, allowing them to continue to profane the tabernacle (1 Samuel 2:25). Apparently, there was some lack of zeal on Eli's part; some part of Eli's heart was with his sons and not with the Lord. We know this because God sent a prophet to Eli to deliver a dire message concerning Eli's household: "I will cut short your strength and the strength of your priestly house, so that no one in it will reach old age...What happens to your two sons, Hophni and Phinehas, will be a sign to you—they will both die on the same day" (1 Samuel 2:31, 34).

This was a terrible curse, because the Levites depended on the priesthood for their living (1 Samuel 2:36). Eli's family line would be supplanted by another, more faithful priest: "I will raise up for myself a faithful priest, who will do according to what is in my heart and mind. I will firmly establish his priestly house, and they will minister before my anointed one always" (1 Samuel 2:35). The priest God raised up was a boy named Samuel, who was dedicated to the tabernacle by his mother, Hannah, a formerly barren woman who had prayed for a child.

Hannah spoke her prayer in Eli's presence, and he had blessed her: "Go in peace, and may the God of Israel grant you what you have asked of him" (1 Samuel 1:17). God answered Hannah's prayer, and she had a son. After Samuel was weaned, she gave him to the Lord's service (1 Samuel 1:24–28). Hannah's birthing of this future prophet demonstrates the ethical power of persistence and faith. During a time when infertility earned women both ridicule and scorn, dished out in equal amount, Hannah took the high road when she became the subject of mockery by her husband's other wife.

Yes, his *other* wife. Instead of acting out like the unreal housewives we see on television today, shunning ethics in favor of unscripted debauchery, she took her sorrow, her longings and her losses to God. In the face of infidelity and infertility, she refused to believe her situation would remain barren. Instead of cursing her rival, she blessed God. Instead of resorting to low blows to put the "other woman" in her place, she took her rightful place on her knees and prayed earnestly.

In a real sense, she was wise enough to know even Iyanla Vanzant turned to God to fix her life. In turn, when the time came for her to honor her word and give her son Samuel to God, she kept the framework of God's ethical house in order. There's power in a praying woman.

This is not mere euphemism.

The power of a praying woman gives birth and rise to God's generational effect. Prayer not only changed the course of Hannah's life, but would impact the entire nation of Israel. As we undoubtedly now know, God used her son Samuel in the key role as the prophet that would unlock the Key of David. The young Samuel lived in the tabernacle, under the tutelage and care of Eli. Each year, Hannah brought Samuel a robe for him to wear in the house of the Lord (1 Samuel 2:19).

Eli again blessed Hannah and her husband, asking God to give Hannah children to replace the one she had dedicated to the Lord (1 Samuel 2:20). Hannah eventually gave birth to three more sons and two daughters (verse 21). No doubt, Eli's ethical influence played an instrumental role in Samuel's most difficult, and direct response to prophetic inside information he had received from the Lord concerning Eli and his family's external affairs. When Samuel was a little older and Eli's eyes were so weak that he could barely see, the Lord Himself spoke to Samuel.

In the middle of the night, the Lord "came and stood" in Samuel's room (1 Samuel 3:10) and told the young boy to deliver the message to Eli that it was almost time for the prophesied judgment to fall upon his family (verses 11–14). Samuel spent a long and sleepless night, no doubt gripped by the thought and overwhelming fear of being the bearer of the bad news God instructed him to deliver to Eli.

> *"The Lord said to Samuel, "Behold, I am about to do a thing in Israel at which both ears of everyone who hears it will ring. On that day I will carry out against Eli everything that I have spoken concerning his house (family), from beginning to end. Now I have told him that I am about to judge his house forever for the sinful behavior which he knew [was happening], because his sons were bringing a curse on themselves [dishonoring and blaspheming God] and he did not rebuke them. Therefore, I have sworn to the house of Eli that the sinful behavior of Eli's house (family) shall not be atoned for by sacrifice or offering forever." So Samuel lay down until morning. Then he opened the doors of the Lord's house. But Samuel was afraid to tell the vision to Eli. But Eli called Samuel and said, "Samuel, my son." And he answered, "Here I am."*
>
> *Then Eli said, "What is it that He said to you? Please do not hide it from me. May God do the same to you, and more also, if you hide from me anything of all that He said to you." So Samuel told him everything, hiding nothing from him. And Eli said, "It is the Lord; may He do what seems good to Him."*
>
> *1 Samuel 3:11-18 (AMP)*

Knowing that he could handle it, Eli convinced Samuel it was far more dangerous to withhold the truth than to reveal what God had shown him. So Samuel laid out the whole truth. Eli humbly accepted God's decree. And because of this obedience, God raised the young man up and Samuel was confirmed as a prophet of the Lord in Shiloh (1 Samuel 3:19–21). In this prophetic moment of truth, God revealing that there are always multiple sides to every ethical framework.

Eli and Samuel's adherence to truth and Kingdom ethics confirming for us that the man or woman who is fit to lead God's people is the one who has learned to hear His voice, heed His words, and speak His truth, no matter the earthly consequences. No matter the career repercussions. Who among us is willing to follow a leader with this kind of give and take? Unlike Eli, Samuel exuded integrity and honestly within each area of his life. People trusted him and knew he had their best interests in mind. They considered Samuel utterly trustworthy and depended upon him to intercede on their behalf with God. The people listened when Samuel spoke because he was a powerful communicator.

Unlike Eli, Samuel's words lined up with his actions. That represents the highest standard definition of character and integrity. And the more his character grew in integrity, the more God's trust in his messenger increased, ensuring his words would never fall short, or fail him.

> *"The LORD was with Samuel as he grew up, and he let none of Samuel's words fall to the ground. And all Israel from Dan to Beersheba recognized that Samuel was attested as a prophet of the LORD. The LORD continued to appear at Shiloh, and there he revealed himself to Samuel through his word."*

> *1 Samuel 3:19-21 (NIV)*

We're still talking external affairs. Words matter. Actions matter most. Anything else falls outside the ethical framework of transformative, Christ-centric leadership. Faulty actions lead to faulty communication and disconnects. This is the self-fulfilling prophecy of poor marketplace management. Peter Drucker, the father of American management, asserts that 60 percent of our management problems stem from faulty communications.

Fortunately, for those of us who aspire to higher levels of ethical leadership, the success formula is full proof. Its pure ingredients of honor, character, integrity and positive influence are mainstays.

Unfortunately for Eli, he and his family would be left out of God's ethical mix. A short time after receiving the fateful news from Samuel, the Philistines came against Israel to attack them. Eli's sons, Hophni and Phineas, went to battle, and they brought with them the Ark of the Covenant thinking it would guarantee protection against their enemies.

However, God was not with them. Eli's two sons were killed, along with about 30,000 foot soldiers of Israel. In addition, the Ark was captured by the Philistines. When Eli heard the bad news, he fell off of his seat, and his neck was broken "for he was old and heavy" (1 Samuel 4:3, 10, 17–18). Meanwhile, Eli's pregnant daughter-in-law, Phinehas's wife, went into labor; she died during delivery, but not before she named her son "Ichabod, saying, 'The Glory has departed from Israel'" (verse 21).

Eli's grandson, born on a day of death and defeat, was given a name meaning "No Glory." Eli had been a priest in Israel and a judge for forty years. Perhaps, fittingly, the name of his grandson on the bookend of his life also informing our final takeaway on Eli's story and conclusive measurement of the ethical framework. Indeed, in the end, by failing to rebuke his sons for their unethical behavior and blaspheming God, Eli proved himself worthy of the label *"No Guts, No Glory."*

Christ ↑ Type

Abraham

> *"Now pause and consider how great this man was to whom Abraham, the patriarch, gave a tenth of the spoils. It is true that those descendants of Levi who are charged with the priestly office are commanded in the Law to collect tithes from the people—which means, from their kinsmen— though these have descended from Abraham.*

But this person [Melchizedek] who is not from their Levitical ancestry received tithes from Abraham and blessed him who possessed the promises [of God]. Yet it is beyond all dispute that the lesser person is always blessed by the greater one."

Hebrews 7:4-7 (AMP)

As the saying goes, we only keep what we have, by giving it away.

This is true in the parenthetical sense of the word tithing. And, if it was true of Abraham and the tithing in his house, surely it should be good enough for ours. In his case, Abraham was giving glory to the Father's house by honoring the son's vacant office.

The lesser being blessed by the greater one to come. That's the good work of faith working in Abraham. This is what it means to operate in good faith. Counted up as righteousness. There are numerous points we can tally in favor of the argument for Abraham being a type of Christ. We start the conversation out with the stirring similarities between them symbolic of sacrifice.

Like Christ, Abraham knew what it meant for a son of promise to be a living sacrifice.

"God said, "Take now your son, your son [of promise], whom you love, Isaac, and go to the region of Moriah, and offer him there as a burnt offering on one of the mountains of which I shall tell you. So Abraham got up early in the morning, saddled his donkey, and took two of his young men with him and his son Isaac; and he split the wood for the burn offering, and then he got up and went to the place of which God had told him."

Genesis 22:3 (AMP)

Out of complete obedience and love for God, Abraham was willing to give up his world by serving up his son Isaac to the Lord as a burnt offering. Unbeknownst to the young lad. Unbeknownst to

Abraham, there was more to the story he was sparing and foretelling his son that God would be providing a young lamb for sacrifice.

> *"And Isaac said to Abraham, "My father!" And he said, "Here I am, my son." Isaac said, "Look, the fire and the wood, but where is the lamb for the burnt offering?" Abraham said, "My son, God will provide for Himself a lamb for the burnt offering." So the two walked on together."*

> *Genesis 22:7-8 (AMP)*

In complete obedience to the Father, Christ offered himself as a sacrifice for God's highest expression of love, as his only begotten son, because God so loved the world. In the process, fulfilling the law and doing away with such animal sacrifices.

> *"Therefore, when Christ enters into the world, He says, "Sacrifice and offering You have not desired, But [instead] You have prepared a body for Me [to offer]; In burnt offerings and sacrifices for sin You have taken no delight. Then I said, 'Behold, I have come To do Your will, O God— [To fulfill] what is written of Me in the scroll of the book.'" After saying [in the citation] above, "You have neither desired, nor have You taken delight in sacrifices and offerings and whole burnt offerings and sacrifices for sin" (which are offered according to the Law) then He said, "Behold, I have come to do Your will." [And so] He does away with the first [covenant as a means of atoning for sin based on animal sacrifices] so that He may inaugurate and establish the second [covenant by means of obedience]. And in accordance with this will [of God] we [who believe in the message of salvation] have been sanctified [that is, set apart as holy for God and His purposes] through the offering of the body of Jesus Christ (the Messiah, the Anointed) once for all."*

> *Hebrews 5-10 (AMP)*

Like Christ, Abraham was a sojourner.

By faith, Abraham left his people and tribe to answer God's calling and obeyed by going to the place he and his family was to receive as an inheritance. Abraham was an heir to the promise, along with his son Isaac and his offspring Jacob, just as we are joint heirs to the promise and reconciled as "first fruits" adopted back into God's patriarchal family through Christ.

By the spirit of prophecy, it was also said about Christ, *"I have become a stranger to my brothers, and an alien to my mother's children"* (Psalms 69:8). Christ leads us in sojourning (passing through) our perished earth to his heavenly Jerusalem. Through the good faith of his surety, we entered into a new relationship and covenant with God.

> *"...remember that at that time you were separated from Christ [excluded from any relationship with Him], alienated from the commonwealth of Israel, and strangers to the covenants of promise [with no share in the sacred Messianic promise and without knowledge of God's agreements], having no hope [in His promise] and [living] in the world without God."*

> *Ephesians 2:12 (AMP)*

Like Christ, Abraham was cut from the same rock.

> *"Listen to Me, you who pursue righteousness (right standing with God), Who seek and inquire of the LORD: Look to the rock from which you were cut And the excavation of the quarry from which you were dug. Look to Abraham your father And to Sarah who gave birth to you in pain; For I called him when he was but one, Then I blessed him and made him many."*

> *Isaiah 51:1-2 (AMP)*

God made Abraham a rock of righteousness, from which believers among all of the nations (Jews and Gentiles) would be cast. Abraham, himself being a gentile, first, before becoming the father of the Jews. Christ, himself, becoming the cornerstone of the new covenant, for Jews and Gentiles alike.

> *"But Jesus looked at them and said, "What then is [the meaning of] this that is written: 'THE [very] STONE WHICH THE BUILDERS REJECTED, THIS BECAME THE CHIEF CORNERSTONE'?*

> *Luke 20:17 (AMP)*

> *"Do not tremble nor be afraid [of the violent upheavals to come]; Have I not long ago proclaimed it to you and declared it? And you are My witnesses. Is there a God besides Me? There is no other Rock; I know of none."*

> *Isaiah 44:8 (AMP)*

Like Christ, Abraham was a chosen forerunner for God's covenant with the Gentiles.

> *"What shall we say then? That Gentiles, who did not pursue righteousness [who did not seek salvation and a right relationship with God, nevertheless] obtained righteousness, that is, the righteousness which is produced by faith; whereas Israel, [though always] pursuing the law of righteousness, did not succeed in fulfilling the law. And why not? Because it was not by faith [that they pursued it], but as though it were by works [relying on the merit of their works instead of their faith]. They stumbled over the stumbling Stone [Jesus Christ]. As it is written and forever remains written, "Behold I am laying in Zion a Stone of stumbling and a Rock of offense; And he who believes in Him [whoever adheres to, trusts in, and relies on Him] will not be disappointed [in his expectations]."*

> *Romans 9:30-33 (AMP)*

While the major religions (Judaism, Christianity and Islam) point to Abraham as the great patriarch of their faith, they miss the subtle mark and broader point of God's divine plan for the ages inherent in the promise He gave to Abraham as the "Father of Nations."

Specifically, in Genesis 12:2, God promises to make Abram "a great nation," in the singular sense. In the next verse, however, God expands the Abrahamic covenant to include "all the families (nations) of the earth." In the plural sense of the word. Translation: Gentiles. We catch a further glimpse of what God had in mind (and its far-ranging implications for the Jews and Gentiles) later in the Book of Genesis outside of Abram's tent.

> *"And the Lord brought Abram outside [his tent into the night] and said, "Look now toward the heavens and count the stars - if you are able to count them." Then He said to him, "So [numerous] shall your descendants be."*
>
> *Genesis 15:5(AMP)*

Furthermore, God's covenant with Abram was made *prior* to establishing the Covenant of circumcision of the foreskin in Genesis 17. Point being, Abraham *himself* was first a Gentile. God would use him, like Christ, but not solely for the raising up of one nation or religion. Just as Abraham's faith was counted as righteousness, so it would be for the Gentiles. With that, we turn to the Book of Romans for further witness from Paul.

> *"Is this? blessing only for the circumcised, or also for the uncircumcised. For we say, "FAITH WAS CREDITED TO ABRAHAM AS RIGHTEOUSNESS." How then was it credited [to him]? Was it after he had been circumcised, or before? Not after, but while [he was] uncircumcised. He received the sign of circumcision, a seal or confirmation of the righteousness which he had by faith while [he was still] uncircumcised - this was so that he would be the [spiritual] father of all who believe without being circumcised - so that righteousness would be credited to them, and [that he*

would be] the [spiritual] father of those circumcised who are not only circumcised, but who also walk in the steps of the faith of our father Abraham which he had before he was circumcised. For the promise to Abraham or to his descendants that he would be heir of the world was not through [observing the requirements of] the Law, but through the righteousness of faith."

Romans 4:9-13 (AMP)

Like Abraham, Christ was ahead of his time.

"Are You greater than our father Abraham, who died? The prophets died too! Whom do You make Yourself out to be?" Jesus answered, "If I glorify Myself, My glory is [worth] nothing. It is My Father who glorifies Me, of whom you say, 'He is our God.' Yet you do not know Him, but I know Him fully. If I said I did not know Him, I would be a liar like you. But I do know Him and keep His word. Your father Abraham [greatly] rejoiced to see My day (My incarnation). He saw it and was delighted." Then the Jews said to Him, "You are not even fifty years old, and You [claim to] have seen Abraham?" Jesus replied, "I assure you and most solemnly say to you, before Abraham was born, I Am. So they picked up stones to throw at Him, but Jesus concealed Himself and left the temple."

John 8:53-59 (AMP)

Here, the builders are once again rejecting the cornerstone by casting stones at the rock of Abraham, and going against their own good faith. How fitting.

External Relations

Leadership Summary

• **Gratitude and Generosity are "two sides of the same practice."** In effect, "gratitude is about choosing *what* to remember – and about choosing *whom* to remember." This is what makes the Salvation Army successful. Their iconic red bell signaling a gratitude reminder for us during the Holiday Season to remember those less fortunate.

• **We put our generosity into external relations practice for several key reasons:**

√ **Gratitude is not complete until it becomes generosity** – gratitude is about choosing to remember the gift of God's grace. Choosing gratitude is choosing my identity. If I lack gratitude, I lack generosity and my purpose then becomes all about my selfish interests.

√ **Generosity is no more and no less than grace in action** – sincere gratitude flows into generosity. Generosity is not just about money. It is a generous spirit and willingness to give others the benefit of the doubt.

√ **We practice generosity because we have received grace** – we give because God gave and because God continues to give. We cannot turn God's gift into a transaction. And we cannot pretend that we owe God nothing. When we are overwhelmed by the gifts and grace we've received, it's easier to let others have a little of our good fortune.

√ **We owe God gratitude** – the kind of gratitude that makes us want to be generous in return, in equal and proper proportion to how generous God has been to us.

√   **We don't want things to be fair, we want grace** – if we're really given what we deserve, that thinking sets a dangerous precedent. If God were being fair, we'd no longer be here, much less in the position we're in.

• **Jesus did not think things should always be "fair."** His teaching of the parable of the vineyard owner in Matthew 20 changes our mental model around gratitude, fairness and generosity. Christ implies new meaning and extols fresh virtue into our definition of what gratitude is. And what fairness looks like. Most importantly, He reshapes our warped mentality around generosity.

• **IF we are to be truly honest with ourselves, we don't want God to give us what we truly deserve.** While we're busy calculating what's owed to us, and how God is somehow shorting us into reaching out and giving to others with short arms (and alms), Paul cautions us to add up our wages from past sins and transgressions. In doing our fuzzy math, we find our past due account balance is long overdue. How generous of God to reconcile the books by blotting them all out.

• **God blots everything out except our responsibility to assume the posture of generosity and gratitude.** More than a t-shirt, "truly blessed" is more about being in a *condition* than being in a *position*. In other words, we're not blessed because we're in "*this position*," we're blessed as a result of being in "*His condition*."

• **Far too often, we wait until we feel like we are *finally* in a position of being blessed in order to be a blessing to other**s. This self-fulfilling prophecy becomes but a generosity myth. Internal profits are down, so our external giving is on the low. Our fortunes are closing, so our coffers can't open up.

• **Once we put ourselves in a position of gratitude and operating within God's will, following His precepts and commands to love on others and take care of others, the blessings supernaturally follow**. God will bless kingdom enterprises "*exceedingly,* *abundantly above what we ask or think, according to the power that works in us. (Ephesians 3:20-21 NKJV).*

• **Like beauty, fairness is in the eye of the beholder**. One man's beautiful arrangement is another woman's ugly reality of unequal pay, leaving the pay scales unbalanced. According to Bureau of Labor Statistics data, in 2020, women's annual earnings were 82.3% of men's. The gap is even wider for women of color (65% for Black and Latina women). Clearly, women are giving more than their fair share of a full day's work for less than a fair day's wages in return.

• **Equal Pay Day symbolically represents the number of additional days that women, on, average, must work to earn what men earned on average the year before**. To earn what white, non-Hispanic men earned in 2020, Asian American and Pacific Islander women had to work until March 9th. Black women, August 3rd. Native American women, September 8th. For Latinas, the scales of Equal Pay Day are even more unevenly balanced, with their Equal Pay Day landing 9 months into the year on Oct. 21st.

• **In ancient times, special storehouses were established in the temple to receive the tithes of the harvest.** If the people were not faithful, the priests could not continue to serve and perform their duties. Corporations and business concerns today are doing a good job storing up top heavy, fat bonuses and concerning themselves with paying house dividends. In all fairness, the true measure of company growth in our annual report these days should be applied against what percentage and amount from our treasury is reserved for sustaining the community around us.

• **In the midst of the global pandemic, there was nothing more gratifying than watching the collective effort unfold to support small businesses, minority-owned retailers and women founders of mom and pop shops alike.** Some, whose very existence, literally, hung by inventory threads on the balance sheet. If the pandemic teaches us anything, it is not to be deceived, *"for whatever a man sows, this and this only is what he will reap (Galatians 6:7)."* If the pandemic informs anything for us about Kingdom principles, it is the outpouring (or not) that speaks for itself.

• **Not only have we juxtaposed what it means to be blessed, we have convoluted the intent behind God's laws and precepts regarding our giving and lending to the poor**. God never intended lending or debt to be leveraged as a predatory vehicle through which those in positions to lend and facilitate lending and borrowing could, technically, take advantage of the poor.

• **It may be Old Testament, but there is something new our country could learn from revisiting God's precepts**. God is warning the Israelites in the Book of Deuteronomy not to throw their giving caution to the wind. He is reminding them that their blessing is not a result of their financial position or standing. God is humanizing the condition of the less fortunate by instructing the most fortunate among the Israelites to see the "priceless" worth of ALL of his children. God was *not* talking about handouts. He was addressing the need for reprieve. He was putting His foot down every seven years as a seasonal *"grace period"* to pull everyone back up.

· **Debts are never retired.** They pass down generationally. Nothing is more symbolic of the debt of forgiveness God was reconciling for Israel through its generations than His imposing the law of a "sabbatical year," whereby the nation would forgive all debts owed by their brethren. The fine print of the scripture in Deuteronomy 17 teaches us to frame the place of indebtedness and poverty in society in terms of the symbiotic relationship between indebtedness, gratitude and God's generosity. Indeed, gratitude is not complete until it travels the distance between one's indebtedness and someone else's need for generosity.

• **God is saying generosity is not just about money, but a willingness of spirit to give (and forgive) in the same generous spirit which God has so freely given to us, even when undeserved**. Stands to wonder what profound impact implementing such a sabbatical period would have on the imposing numbers of people facing the homelessness crisis in our nation. If ever there were a just, patriotic cause for such a sabbatical, we find probable cause in the more than 6% of our country's veterans who are homeless.

• **Irrespective of which side of the aisle we're on, or wavering in the middle, we are all in the same boat when it comes to economic debt and economic uncertainty.** According to CNBC, the average American has $90,460 in debt. The reverberating impact of "making ends meet" while "keeping up with the Kardashians" has particular resonance among younger professionals entering the workforce. In 2015, the average Millennial had about $49,722 in debt.

• **Throughout scripture, from Moses in the Book of Deuteronomy to the Apostle Paul in the great Book of Galatians, God provides our conscious with its own grace period by constantly taking measure of our culture of giving vs taking.** Not as a constant measure to see who gets to be "one up," but as a measure of spiritual integrity.

• **The story of Eli and his sons gives us an "all too familiar" case study on measuring the integrity of our leaders within the ethical framework of giving and taking.** The wicked, unethical internal affairs of his two sons marred the ethical excellence of Eli's external affairs as a revered judge in Israel. Eli's inability to manage the integrity of his family led to his downfall as a leader. As scripture informs us, if we do not faithfully handle the internal affairs of our own household enterprise, we lack the credibility to lead outside of it.

• **As the saying goes, we only keep what we have by giving it away.** This is true in the parenthetical sense of the word tithing. And, if it was true of Abraham and the tithing in his house, then it should be good enough for ours. In his case, Abraham was giving glory to the Father's house by honoring the son's vacant office. The lesser being blessed by the greater one to come. That's the good work of faith working in Abraham. This is what it means to operate in good faith. Counted as righteousness.

• **There are numerous points we can tally in favor of the argument for Abraham being a type of Christ.** The conversation starts with the stirring similarities between them which are symbolic of sacrifice. Like Christ, Abraham knew what it meant for a son of promise to be a living sacrifice. Like Christ, Abraham was a sojourner, traveling with an heir of inheritance. Like Christ, Abraham was cut from the same rock and cornerstone the builders rejected. Like Christ, Abraham was a chosen forerunner for God's covenant with the Gentiles. Like Christ, Abraham was ahead of his time.

BOOK 4

PARTNERSHIP

Chapter 7:
Strategic Alliances

"I have seen that every [effort in] labor and every skill in work comes from man's rivalry with his neighbor. This too is vanity (futility, false pride) and chasing after the wind. The fool folds his hands [together] and consumes his own flesh [destroying himself by idleness and apathy]. One hand full of rest and patience is better than two fists full of labor and chasing after the wind. Then I looked again at vanity under the sun [in one of its peculiar forms]. There was a certain man—without a dependent, having neither a child nor a brother, yet there was no end to all his labor. Indeed, his eyes were not satisfied with riches and he never asked, "For whom do I labor and deprive myself of pleasure?" This too is vanity (a wisp of smoke, self-conceit); yes, it is a painful effort and an unhappy task. Two are better than one because they have a more satisfying return for their labor; for if either of them falls, the one will lift up his companion. But woe to him who is alone when he falls and does not have another to lift him up."

Ecclesiastes 4:4-10 (AMP)

Spotlight On 💡 Cooperation

The best way to compete, is to not compete.

The best form of competition requires cooperation. This is not simply rooted in natural economic theory, but has fertile application in the supernatural laws governing the marketplace. Our creator designed all things in the universe to function as a cooperative in the midst of *what appears to be* fierce competition. From our perspective, competition can be healthy.

From God's perspective, competition is healthiest when it is filtered through cooperation.

In fact, such a view of "competition as partnership" is quite vital to the operation of His strategic alliance network effects. More on that later. Our premise: if competition is inherently good for God's world, we must believe it is practically good for the corporate world.

On the pure basis of Economics 101, competition forces companies to lower prices and segment the market to prevent one company from monopolizing the entire market. Competition also forces companies to make more quality products in order to foster loyalty and build consumer trust. Fundamentally, competition in the marketplace is healthy as long as unhealthy strategies are not deployed, such as the stealing of trade secrets or lying about a competitor's product.

Unfortunately, it is more common in today's business environment to eliminate the competition than it is to cooperate with it. This is where we go left, and drift away from God's intent.

> *"Do nothing from selfishness or empty conceit [through factional motives, or strife], but with [an attitude of] humility [being neither arrogant nor self-righteous], regard others as more important than yourselves. Do not merely look out for your own personal interests, but also for the interests of others."*
>
> *Philippians 2:3-4 (AMP)*

By eliminating competition, we reduce necessary cooperation and extinguish our natural instincts to thrive collectively. Think about that in the context of the rainforest. National Geographic states the facts. Rainforests are Earth's oldest living ecosystems, some having survived in their present form for at least *70 million years!*

They are incredibly diverse and complex, and home to more than half of the world's plant and animal species – even though they cover just 6% of the Earth's surface. The Amazon rainforest is the world's largest tropical rainforest. It is home to around 40,000 plant species, nearly 1,300 bird species, 3,000 types of fish, 427 species of mammals and 2.5 million different insects. Red-bellied piranhas and pink river dolphins both swim its waters.

The rainforest finds a way to get along with such vast, treacherous dichotomy. When you think about a rainforest, you think, see, hear and *feel* harmony. Like a symphony orchestra. While there will always be competitive, cataclysmic clashes going on underneath, no matter where you are standing inside of the rainforest, you can look around or close your eyes and name that cooperative tune.

> *"When the flowing waters enter the sea, its water becomes fresh. Wherever the river flows, every living thing that moves will thrive. There will be great schools of fish, because when these waters enter the sea, it will be fresh. Wherever the river flows, everything will live."*
>
> Ezekiel 47:8-9 (AMP)

Despite the competition to survive, the rainforest thrives *as a result* of it, *not in spite* of it. According to the International Society for Behavioral Ecology, various studies have found that in tropical forests the different primate species often not only tolerate each other but also form mixed-species groups. Such strategic alliances form, presumably to cooperate in anti-predatory defense against leopards, crowned eagles and chimpanzees.

Mixed-species associations are common throughout Africa both East and West and only very few species are known to avoid them. Plants and animals throughout the rainforest work together in subtle, surprising ways. In an environmental process known as *mutualism*, two organisms work together in such a way that each benefits, or is helped in some way by the cooperation.

Often times, in the most minute fashion. For example, ants and termites rely on each other and work as a team to build mounds where the group will live, or hunt together to find food. In other words, these tiny insects know not to sweat the small stuff. They innately understand that by not competing over their shared resources, they are competing together *for it* and not against each other to the detriment *of it*.

Mutualism maintains the delicate balance of the rainforest. Without it, certain plants and animals would have a difficult time of surviving. Much less thriving. The structure of the rainforest has a lot to do with this. Most rainforests are structured in four layers: emergent, canopy, understory, and forest floor. Each layer has unique characteristics based on differing levels of water, sunlight, and air circulation. While each layer is distinct, they exist in an interdependent system: processes and species in one layer influence those in another.

Structure is God's external network *effect.*
Reciprocity is God's intended *affect.*

By competing "without competing" in our environments, we cooperate with natural laws of give and we take. In balanced proportion. When the leaves fall to the ground, forming windfall piles in your yard, it may be a nuisance and look unattractive to you, but is a sight for mother earth's soil eyes. Most "leaf litter" has potential to add nutrients and rich soil to your lawn's care.

During the Fall season, the leaves of deciduous trees turn an array of vibrant hues and colors of red, yellow and orange. As they swirl to the ground, they are honoring nature's Law of Return: plants use up nutrients during the growing season, and give them back when the season is over. By raking up the leaves in "Lawn of the Month" competition with our shared environment, we deplete this natural, shared resource until we require the use of fertilizers or compost to make our lawns green or grow our gardens more robustly.

Our independent actions also have a reciprocal impact upon the deeper structure involved beneath the surface, such as the "decomposer food web." Invertebrates, including earthworms, beetle larvae, millipedes, mites, slugs and snails that live in the soil, shred plant materials into smaller and smaller pieces, increasing the surface area on which soil bacteria and fungi can prey. Mulching the leaf litter and taking it up with your mower too prematurely may very well take up land's natural fertility along with it.

In natural areas, like rainforests, nature and mutualism take care of all this reciprocal work.

We also hold these truths to be self-evident in our business environment. We call this phenomenon "*marketplace mutualism*." This is a positive indicator that emerged more fully from the pandemic. By most accounts, key sectors within the retail environment were (and still are) threatened with extinction. The pandemic spelled a death knell for some, more than others.

In natural response, the retail environment reimagined and restructured itself as an interdependent ecosystem and sector. Grubhub's thriving became just as important to the fortunes of the local pizza shop which has its own delivery drivers and mechanisms in place.

Why? Because like the ants and termites, they were both building a mole hill of consumer confidence. Indeed, they were getting busy, doubling down their cooperative efforts to boost spending back up in support of their "shared" local business economy.

They were competing together *for it* and not against each other to the detriment *of it.* They were competing less, for more "share of wallet." Although there were clashes still going on underneath, they were able to survive and show signs of thriving by shifting their focus from vertical domination to horizontal cooperation.

Thereby, maintaining the health of the overall takeout ecosystem.

In this age of digital competition and platforms, our marketplace efforts and valuations are hinging upon our application's capturing of verticals and ownership of ecosystems. However, the problems we're solving are becoming more of a benefit than a burden to the ecosystem by hyper-competitively keeping data, engagement and user experiences locked up within verticals.

Such activity has contributed to an unhealthy atmosphere of privacy breaches, including cyber-attacks and cyber ransoms. Notwithstanding the proprietary rationale of defensibility, who among us is thinking about structuring cross-platform mobile applications and alliances that enhance the overall ecosystem in horizontal fashion, both online and offline.

Google was clearly thinking about the overall benefits that market-place mutualism provides in the face of the pandemic's life threat-ening impact on the small business environment, both online and offline. The search engine giant optimized leadership in this regard with their structured, micro-level support for the black business ecosystem as a vehicle for search optimization, while optimizing the corresponding benefits for the macro economy.

Specifically, Google added new ways to help users find and support Black-owned businesses. US merchants with a verified Google Business Profile were able to add a Black-owned business attribute to their profile so customers could identify them as being Black-owned when they located that business through Google Search and Maps. Google also extended the attribute to the site's shopping tab, so people could more easily find and buy from Black-owned businesses.

The feature will remain available to all US-based shops and vis-ible to shoppers in the coming months, the company reported in a recent blog post. Searches on Google for "Black owned businesses" jumped 600% over a 12 month-period, according to the company.

Reports also found that 41% of Black-owned businesses had been closed due to COVID-19.

Google then partnered with Opportunity Finance Network to provide more than $30 million in micro loans and grants to support these businesses, as part of the tech giant's $50 million commitment through the Grow with Google Small Business Fund. As part of Google's monetary commitment to support underrepresented entrepreneurs, the company has integrated the Black-owned business attribute into the digital skills training programs offered to Black business owners through Grow with Google Digital Coaches.

Digital Coaches offer free mentorship, networking and workshop opportunities to Black and Latino businesses across the US. Google recently expanded its Grow with Google Digital Coaches program to 20 cities across the US, reaching an additional 50,000 Black-owned businesses. Google's digital coaches have trained more than 58,000 Black and Latino small business owners to date, according to the post.

This is interdependent thriving of the community body at its best, informed by God's Kingdom structured principles. Google was not alone. The many membered body of essential and non-essential business public and private parts, along with vital secular and non-secular organs, all came together limb by limb to compensate for weaknesses in one area by adding strength to the other. Altogether, proving it is the individual parts that make the whole body greater.

> *"For the [human] body does not consist of one part, but of many [limbs and organs]. If the foot says, "Because I am not a hand, I am not a part of the body," is it not on the contrary still a part of the body? If the ear says, "Because I am not an eye, I am not a part of the body," is it not on the contrary still a part of the body? If the whole body were an eye, where would the hearing be? If the whole [body] were an ear, where would the sense of smell be? But now*

[as things really are], God has placed and arranged the parts in the body, each one of them, just as He willed and saw fit [with the best balance of function].

If they all were a single organ, where would [the rest of] the body be? But now [as things really are] there are many parts [different limbs and organs], but a single body. The eye cannot say to the hand, "I have no need of you," nor again the head to the feet, "I have no need of you." But quite the contrary, the parts of the body that seem to be weaker are [absolutely] necessary; and as for those parts of the body which we consider less honorable, these we treat with greater honor; and our less presentable parts are treated with greater modesty, while our more presentable parts do not require it.

But God has combined the [whole] body, giving greater honor to that part which lacks it, so that there would be no division or discord in the body [that is, lack of adaptation of the parts to each other], but that the parts may have the same concern for one another. And if one member suffers, all the parts share the suffering; if one member is honored, all rejoice with it."

1 Corinthians 12:14-26 (AMP)

We declare and decree this to be a marketplace move of the Holy Spirit. And we fully anticipate seeing more of it. Human organisms are functioning in the profitable ways in which we were designed. By cooperating. By co-laboring. By practicing natural laws of reciprocity. By approaching carnal business affairs with supernatural connectivity. By recognizing that the oil of anointing flowing from the crown of Aaron's head, down his beard and to the soles of his feet, is analogous to our corporate body being connected at the source.

"How good and pleasant it is when God's people live together in unity. It is like precious oil poured on the head, running down on the beard, running down on Aaron's beard, down on the collar of his robe. It is as if the dew of Hermon were falling on Mount Zion. For there the LORD bestows his blessing, even life forevermore."

Psalms 133:1-3 (NIV)

We are finally beginning to observe universal signs of the realization that who we are connected to matters for our joint survival. We are finally starting to bear witness to the fact that our strategic alliances we form on earth possess power in the heavenly realm. Enough to command favor and result in windows of opportunity opening up and pouring out blessings, simply by virtue of our associations. *This* is the seasonal opportunity we find ourselves in. *This,* is the pleasant aroma of honor and spirit of the strategic alliance (and covenant) God promised and entered into with man back in Genesis 8.

"The LORD smelled the pleasing aroma [a soothing, satisfying scent] and the LORD said to Himself, "I will never again curse the ground because of man, for the intent (strong inclination, desire) of man's heart is wicked from his youth; and I will never again destroy every living thing, as I have done. While the earth remains, Seedtime and harvest, Cold and heat, Winter and summer, And day and night, Shall not cease."

Genesis 8:21-22 (AMP)

Measuring The Christ Quotient (CQ)

👑 *C+Collaboration*
"How Saul and Samuel Partnered Together to Lead God's People"
Source: Maxwell Leadership Bible

> *"Then Samuel took the flask of oil and poured it on Saul's head, kissed him, and said, "Has the LORD not anointed you as ruler over His inheritance (Israel)?"*

> *1 Samuel 10:1 (AMP)*

This passage of scripture paints a marvelous picture of how pastors and business leaders can partner together in strategic alliance to fulfill God-given vision. The Book of 1 Samuel shows how God sovereignly uses both Samuel the priest (ministry leader) and Saul the king (marketplace leader). Because he feels secure, Samuel is able to fulfill his role as spiritual leader to big and strong Saul. He finds security in his divine call and in the One who called him, not in people.

While Saul could be an intimidating, daunting leader (1 Samuel 9:2), Samuel does not envy Saul's role, nor can he be diverted from his work in Saul's life. Note the following observations regarding the partnership of these two in fulfilling God's plan.

1. *Samuel could speak into Saul's life because he felt secure in his calling (9:17-19).*

   While God told Samuel to anoint Saul as king, the prophet never considered the son of Kish to be a celebrity. Saul became king over Samuel – but Samuel never placed his security or emotional health in a mere man. With poise and confidence, he said to Saul, "I am the prophet." He then instructed Saul concerning the spiritual matters he would face as king.

2. Samuel affirmed Saul's complimentary role and honored him for it (9:21-23).

   Although Samuel had been the visible leader in Israel, he intentionally gave away his status by publicly honoring Saul. He reserved special food for him and a special place at the table, so no one would question whom they were to follow.

3. Samuel took initiative and anointed Saul for the role he was to fulfill (10:1).

   Samuel didn't feel competition or envy over this new king; he knew that both would serve as leaders among God's people as complementary partners. As Coach Bill McCartney once said to some Promise Keeper speakers, "We are not here to compete with each other, but to complete each other."

4. *Samuel helped Saul to receive a new heart for serving people* (10:6-9).

   At this point Samuel had every reason to feel awkward or displaced; now Saul was doing the very thing Samuel had been gifted to do. But Samuel didn't resist helping Saul to develop into the spiritual leader God called him to be.

5. *Samuel encouraged Saul to use his spiritual gifts* (10:10-13).

   Samuel faithfully brought God's word to Saul. He prepared Saul to receive his spiritual gifts by explaining what would happen and when to look for it.

6. *Samuel did not feel intimidated by or envious of Saul's conquests* (13:8-13).

   Samuel allowed neither Saul's position as king nor his success as conqueror to move him. While Samuel affirmed the king, he also understood his role in Israel and in the king's life. Samuel confronted Saul's disobedience and clarified their roles.

7. *Samuel spoke words of direction to Saul* (15:1-3).

Even after confronting Saul's disobedience, Samuel was able to provide direction for the king and affirm his work on the battlefield. He didn't shrink from playing his role in Saul's life and again clarified Saul's place in the grand scheme of things. He furnished Saul with great confidence and support as he led the armies of Israel.

8. *Samuel prayed and hurt for Saul when the king failed* (15:10,11).

Samuel grieved when God rejected the disobedient Saul. He knew that God intended great things for Saul – and the king's failure broke Samuel's heart. As Saul's spiritual leader, Samuel hurt for the king.

9. *Samuel could confront Saul when he sinned and provide him perspective* (15:22-23).

Samuel felt called to continually provide the big-picture perspective to Saul and remind him of his roots, of God's call and mission. He offered an eternal perspective to the king and refused to let him try to do God's will in his own way.

10. *Samuel possessed the spiritual credibility to call for repentance and worship from Saul* (15:24-31).

Samuel ministered to Saul with a beautiful combination of grace and truth. He spoke the truth in love, never out of spite or superiority. When he returned with Saul, he did it not out of intimidation, but to leave Saul with as much dignity as possible.

What Every Pastor Should Know About These Partnerships

The Scripture illustrates the partnership role that ministry leaders and marketplace leaders can enjoy, if only they will work cooperatively.

1. Samuel illustrates the role of the pastor (the ministry leader). Saul illustrates the role of the entrepreneur (the marketplace leader).

2. The issue ministry leaders (pastors) must settle: personal security. The issue marketplace leaders (laymen) must settle: personal submission.

3. The pastor often envies the entrepreneur's success (the money). The entrepreneur often envies the pastor's significance (the mission).

4. Pastors must develop a vision big enough to attract entrepreneurs. Entrepreneurs must develop a generous spirit to enable pastors to fulfill it.

5. Pastors must include business leaders in decisions so they can own the ministry. Entrepreneurs must include pastors in both their checkbook and calendar.

6. Pastors must give the church's ministry to Entrepreneurs/marketplace leaders. Entrepreneurs must give their spiritual gifts to the church's ministry.

7. Pastors fail in this partnership because they feel intimidated. Entrepreneurs fall in this partnership because they feel independent.

8. Pastors can offer one thing that entrepreneurs want most: fulfillment. Entrepreneurs can offer one thing that pastors need most: resources.

The leadership key to successful partnerships and strategic alliances lies within the same spirit of reciprocity and give and take we've been presenting here. The success path in our strategic alliances is forged in the willingness to put others first, in order to get ahead. Through the strategic alliance of Saul and Samuel, and subsequently David and Jonathan, we bear witness to the redeeming value of cooperation upon transformative leadership.

Reciprocity...

- Helps others see the contribution of every man or woman's gift in the partnership.
- Reminds everyone in the alliance that God is the source of every good gift, and each anointing that flows into the partnership, by virtue of association.
- Promotes goodwill in other potential allies.
- Enables future alliances and networks.
- Develops a natural atmosphere of added-value, mutual benefit and good faith.

Scripture also informs us that reciprocity works against man's natural inclinations and often produces strange alliances of cooperating bedfellows. Indeed, the story of the three kings in the book of 2 Kings reveals how God uses man's natural inclination for victory by annihilation over the competition to ensure His divine purpose ultimately prevails.

> *"So the king of Israel went with the king of Judah and the king of Edom. They made a circuit of seven days' journey, but there was no water for the army or for the cattle that followed them. Then the king of Israel said, "We are doomed, for the Lord has called these three Kings to be handed over to Moab." But Jehoshaphat said, "Is there no prophet of the Lord here from whom we may inquire of the Lord?" One of the servants of the king of Israel answered, "Elisha the son of Shaphat is here, who used to pour water over Elijah's hands." Jehoshaphat said, "The word of the Lord is with him." "So the king of Israel and Jehoshaphat and the king of Edom went down to Elisha. Now Elisha said to the king of Israel, "What business do you have with me? Go to the prophets of your [wicked] father [Ahab] and to the prophets of your [pagan] mother [Jezebel]." But the king of Israel said to him, "No, for the Lord has called these*

three Kings together to be handed over to Moab." Elisha said, "As the Lord of hosts (armies) lives, before whom I stand, were it not that I have regard for Jehoshaphat king of Judah, I would not look at you nor see you [king of Israel]."

God forges a strategic alliance between these competing king factions of Israel, Judah and Edom to go up against and destroy the Moabites in order for His competitive ambitions and sole purpose for the Israelites to prevail.

"Now all the Moabites heard that the [three] Kings had come up to fight against them, and all who were able to put on armor, as well as those who were older, were summoned and stood [together in battle formation] at the border. When they got up early the next morning, the sun shone on the water, and the Moabites saw the water across from them as red as blood. And they said, "This is blood! Clearly the Kings have fought together, and have killed one another. Now then, Moab, to the spoil [and the plunder of the dead soldiers]!"

2 Kings 3:6-23 (AMP)

Connectivity...

- Commands a blessing from God. We must be careful how we treat our alliances and associations as the oil of anointing flows based on connectivity. If you breach the natural connectivity (e.g. breaking laws of reciprocity), you disrupt the supernatural flow.
- Implies reciprocity in return for what we pour back into others. In Paul's last letter, he was dying from a lack of reciprocity. Paul planted, Apollos watered and God gave the increase. But nobody Paul was sowing into reproduced after his own kind when it came time for Paul to receive it back. Without reciprocity, you lose connectivity at the source. When you selfishly take more than you give, you risk self-sabotaging the partnership.

- Requires we share the common language of anointing and are able to translate it into the blessing. Our leadership and strategic alliances must not only be bi-lingual in nature, but must speak the multi-lingual language of supernatural favor in order for it to move on our behalf. God was even able to command the frogs to go into Egypt (Exodus 8:1-8).
- Demands we recognize the need for help. Because God designed us to be connected, and the network effects of His blessings come through our alliances, partnerships and associations, we must recognize that *"our ask"* as leaders and entrepreneurs is not a sign of trouble, but a sign God wants to help us by giving us double for our trouble.
- Places us in the fellowship of suffering together, with one another, in the fixed position of the cross. Torn between our selfish interests and the greater good of the relationship.

Spotlight On ♥ The Fellowship of Suffering

(Andrew Murray)

"It is my cross, that makes my crown."

Taking up the cross was always spoken of by Christ as the test of discipleship. On three different occasions (Matthew 10:38; Matthew 16:24; Luke 15:27) we find the words repeated, "If any man will come after me, let him take up his cross and follow me." While the Lord was still on His way to the cross, this expression - taking up the cross - was the most appropriate to indicate that conformity to Him to which the disciple is called.

But now that He has been crucified, the Holy Spirit gives another expression, in which our entire conformity to Christ is still more powerfully set forth, - the believing Disciple is Himself crucified with Christ. The cross is the chief mark of the Christian as of Christ; the crucified Christ and crucified Christian belong to each other.

ONE OF THE CHIEF ELEMENTS OF LIKENESS TO CHRIST CONSISTS IN BEING CRUCIFIED WITH HIM. WHOEVER WISHES TO BE LIKE HIM MUST SEEK TO UNDERSTAND THE SECRET OF FELLOWSHIP WITH HIS CROSS.

At first sight the Christian who seeks conformity to Jesus is afraid of the truth; he shrinks from the painful suffering and death with which the thought of the cross is connected.

As his spiritual discernment becomes clearer, however, this word becomes all his hope and joy, and he glories in the cross, because it makes him a partner in a death and victory that has already been accomplished, and in which the deliverance from the powers of the flesh and of the world has been secured to him. To understand this, we must notice carefully the language of Scripture.

"I am crucified with Christ," Paul says; "nevertheless I live; yet not I, but Christ liveth in me." Through our faith in Christ we become partakers of Christ's life. That life is a life that has passed through the death of the cross, and in which the power of that death is always working.

When I receive that life, I receive at the same time the full power of the death on the cross working in me and its never ceasing energy. "I have been crucified with Christ; yet I live; and yet no longer I, but Christ liveth in me;" the life I now live is not my own life, but the life of the Crucified One, is the life of the cross. The being crucified is a thing past and done: "Knowing this, that our old man was crucified with Him;"

"They that are Christ's have crucified the flesh;" "I glory in the cross of our Lord Jesus Christ, by whom the world hath been crucified unto me, and I unto the world." These texts all speak of something that has been done in Christ, and into which I am admitted by Faith. It is of great consequence to understand this, and to give bold utterance to the truth; I have been crucified with Christ; I have crucified the flesh. I thus learn how perfectly I share in the finished work of Christ.

If I am crucified and dead with Him, then I am a partner in His life and victory. I learn to understand the position I must take to allow the power of that cross and that death to manifest itself in mortifying or making dead the old man and the flesh, in destroying the body of sin. For there is still a great work for me to do. But that work is not to crucify myself:

I have been crucified; the old man was crucified, so the scripture speaks. But what I have to do is always to regard and treat it as crucified, and not to suffer it to come down from the cross. I must maintain my crucifixion position; I must keep the flesh in the place of crucifixion. To realize the force of this I must notice an important distinction. I have been crucified and am dead; the old Adam was crucified, but is not yet dead.

When I gave myself to my crucified Savior, sin and flesh and all, he took me wholly; I with my evil Nature was taken up with Him and his crucifixion. But here a separation took place. In fellowship with Him I was freed from the life of the flesh; I myself died with him; in the in most center of my being I received new life: Christ lives in ME.

But the flesh, in which I yet am, the old man that was crucified with Him, remained condemned to an accursed death, but is not yet dead. And now it is my calling, in fellowship with and in the strength of my Lord, to see that the old nature be kept nailed to the cross, until the time comes that it is entirely destroyed. All its desires and affections cry out, "Come down from the cross, save thyself and us."

It is my duty to glory in the cross, and with my whole heart to maintain the dominion of the cross, and to set my seal to the sentence that has been pronounced, to make dead every uprising of sin, as already crucified, and so not to suffer it to have dominion.

Christ ↑ Type

Peter

"Now when Jesus went into the region of Caesarea Philippi, He asked His disciples, "Who do people say that the Son of Man is?" And they answered, "Some say John the Baptist; others, Elijah; and still others, Jeremiah, or [just] one of the prophets." He said to them, "But who do you say that I am?" Simon Peter replied, "You are the Christ (the Messiah, the Anointed), the Son of the living God." Then Jesus answered him, "Blessed [happy, spiritually secure, favored by God] are you, Simon son of Jonah, because flesh and blood (mortal man) did not reveal this to you, but My Father who is in heaven.

And I say to you that you are Peter, and on this rock I will build My church; and the gates of Hades (death) will not overpower it [by preventing the resurrection of the Christ]. I will give you the keys (authority) of the kingdom of heaven; and whatever you bind [forbid, declare to be improper and unlawful] on earth will have [already] been bound in heaven, and whatever you loose [permit, declare lawful] on earth will have [already] been loosed in heaven." Then He gave the disciples strict orders to tell no one that He was the Christ (the Messiah, the Anointed)."

Matthew 16:13-20 (AMP)

Takes one (rock), to know One (Rock). And to be on One strategic alliance accord. Here in Philippi, we gather that it was not only John that recognized Christ was in the world unrecognized. Peter goes on record for being second, and the only one among the disciples to answer Christ correctly by seeing the "I Am" in the Son of Man.

Here, in this fertile plain through which much trade and many travelers passed through on their way to Rome. Here, in this city that was named after the father of Alexander the Great and would become the capital of the Greek empire. Here, where the gospel writer Luke is believed to have studied medicine. Indeed, it would be here on this spot and upon this rock where the church at Philippi would be planted and built by the Apostle Paul on his second missionary journey around AD 50 or 51.

Indeed, becoming the first Christian church in Europe. From the very time it was established, the church at Philippi was healthy, strong, and generous. It would become a model church that only experienced minor problems of disunity. Though the gates of hell surely tried, they could not overpower it.

God is not a man that he should lie.

> *"God is not man, so he does not lie. He is not human, so he does not change his mind. Has he ever spoken and failed to act? Has he ever promised and not carried it through?"*

> *Numbers 23:19 (NLV)*

Ask yourself.
Do you recognize *who* your partner is?
And what their capabilities *really* are…
When you're out there trying to build something together?

It's critical for the success of your operation to know that you're strategically aligned with the right one. If you registered no response to the question posed in the scripture above, the question becomes do you know Him? Or, perhaps you choose to recognize Him (or deny Him) at your convenience. Like Peter.

> *"Jesus said to them, "**You will all fall away** [and be ashamed and be afraid to be associated with Me as disciples], **because it is written, 'I WILL STRIKE THE SHEPHERD, AND THE SHEEP WILL BE SCATTERED.' But after I have been raised** [from the dead], **I will go ahead of you to Galilee."** But Peter said to Him, "Even if they all*

*fall away [and desert You, ashamed and afraid of being associated with You], yet I will not [do so]! Jesus said to him, "**I assure you and most solemnly say to you, this very night, before a rooster crows twice, you will deny** [that you even know] **Me three times**." But Peter kept saying insistently, "If I have to die with You, I will not deny You!" And they all were saying the same thing as well."*

Mark 14:27-31 (AMP)

Ask yourself.
Does your partner recognize who *you* are?
And what your capabilities *really* are?
When you're no longer cozied up in the upper room together...
And you're now facing His opposition, seeking to kill the entire operation.

"They led Jesus away to the high priest, and all the chief priests and the elders and the scribes (Sanhedrin, Jewish High Court) gathered together. Peter had followed Him at a distance, right into the courtyard of the high priest; and he was sitting with the officers [guards and servants] and warming himself at the fire."

Mark 14:53-54 (AMP)

Now ask yourself again.
Do you remember how adamant you were about forming that strategic alliance?
Pledging to never deny your partnership, no matter the circumstance.
And when the time came to make a decision on recognizing the partnership or your selfish interests, what did you *actually* do?

"While Peter was down below in the courtyard, one of the servant-girls of the high priest came, and when she saw Peter warming himself, she looked intently at him and said, "You were with Jesus the Nazarene, too." But he denied it, saying, "I neither know nor understand what you are

talking about." Then he went out [of the courtyard] to the porch, [and a rooster crowed.] The servant-girl saw him, and began once more to tell the bystanders, "This [man] is one of them." But again he denied it. After a little while, the bystanders again said to Peter, "You are in fact one of them, for [it is clear from your accent, that] you are a Galilean, too." But he began to invoke a curse [on himself] and to swear [an oath], "I do not know this man you are talking about!" Immediately a rooster crowed the second time. And Peter remembered what Jesus said to him: "Before a rooster crows twice, you will deny Me three times." And thinking of this, he began weeping [in anguish].

Mark 14:66 72 (AMP)

Strategic partnerships and alliances abound in the secular and non-secular space. Sometimes, between them. And this is good. The operative, implied term in alliance is alignment. With an emphasis on strategic. Once you are no longer lined up strategically against the desired outcomes of the partnership, it dies. It never fails, one partner eventually denies the other. Question is, which type of partner are you, or will you be? Will you become the one who conveniently denies, or like the One type that never lies?

Going back a short distance in time to Mark 14:27, we bear second witness to the fact that the Son of Man was the only One who would tell no lie. While he accurately foretold Peter that he would betray his own "ride or die" oath and deny their alliance and association thrice before the rooster crowed twice, He also foretold the truth about meeting the disciples in Galilee *after all of that.*

After "all of that" meaning after the accusing, after the denying, after the dying on the cross and after the resurrection. After the Sabbath was over, Mary Magdalene, Mary the mother of James, and Salome bought spices that they could use to anoint Jesus' dead body. But when they looked up, they saw that the rock had been rolled away and inside the tomb, they saw a young man in a white robe *seated on the right side.*

Did anyone just catch that? The young man inside the tomb, in the white robe, was seated on the right side. Our Father is so good.

Clearly, they were startled. That's when the young man started in on the power of their alliance by telling them "*not to be alarmed, Jesus of Nazareth was crucified and had been raised.*" But that's not the shout. The shout is, Christ was no longer there in the space where they laid Him because He had some place to be. He *still* had 12 disciples to meet, including Peter. Yes, after all of that, He was still counting Peter amongst their strategic discipleship alliance.

> "*Go tell his disciples, especially Peter, that he is going ahead of you into Galilee. You will see him there, just as he told you.*"

> *Mark 16:7 (CEB)*

And before all was said and done, it was Peter the rock who would deliver the inaugural message to the church on the Day of Pentecost. The day that the new covenant, and our new strategic alliance with the Holy Spirit was born.

> "*And Peter said to them, "Repent [change your old way of thinking, turn from your sinful ways, accept and follow Jesus as the Messiah] and be baptized, each of you, in the name of Jesus Christ because of the forgiveness of your sins; and you will receive the gift of the Holy Spirit.*"

> *Acts 2:38 (AMP)*

All of that to say, this.
Don't take ours, take the Word for it.
It's important to recognize who your partner is.
Just ask Peter.

Strategic Alliances

Leadership Summary

• **The best way to compete is to not compete**. The best form of competition is derived from cooperation. This is rooted in economic theory and natural law but has fertile application as Kingdom principle for the marketplace. Our creator designed us to function as a cooperative, even in the midst of what *appears* to be competition.

• **By eliminating competition, we reduce necessary cooperation and extinguish our natural instincts to thrive collectively**. Despite the competition to survive, the rainforest thrives *as a result of it, not in spite of it.* According to the International Society for Behavioral Ecology, various studies have found that the different primate species in tropical forests often not only tolerate each other but also form mixed-species groups as an anti-predatory response.

• **The physical structure of the rainforest has a lot to do with this level of cooperation**. Most rainforests are structured in four layers: emergent, canopy, understory, and forest floor. Each layer has unique characteristics based on differing levels of water, sunlight, and air circulation. While each layer is distinct, they exist in an interdependent system: processes and species in one layer influence those in another. These are God's network effects.

• **In an environmental process known as *mutualism*, two organisms work together in such a way that each benefits, or is helped in some way by the cooperation**. These ecological truths are also self-evident in our business environment. We call this *"marketplace mutualism."* In the pandemic, Grubhub and DoorDash thriving became as important to the fortunes of the local pizza shop with its own takeout mechanisms in place. Like the rainforest ants and termites, they rebuilt a mole hill of consumer confidence together and doubled down on their cooperative efforts to boost spending back up in support of their "shared" local business environment.

• **The natural law of *Reciprocity* is critical toward the survival of our alliances.** It helps others see the contribution of every man or woman's gift in the partnership and reminds everyone in the alliance that God is the source of every good gift. It also promotes goodwill in other potential allies, enables future alliances and networks and develops a natural atmosphere of added-value, mutual benefit and good faith. We must be careful of how we treat our alliances and associations as the oil of anointing flows based on connectivity. When we breach the natural connectivity (e.g. breaking laws of reciprocity), we disrupt the supernatural flow.

• **The natural law of *Connectivity* commands a blessing from God.** Connectivity implies reciprocity, as a blessing in return for what we pour out into others. In Paul's last letter (2 Timothy 1:1-14), he was dying from a lack of reciprocity. Paul planted, Apollos watered and God gave the increase but nobody Paul sowed into reproduced after his own kind when it came time to reciprocate. Because of Paul's respect for God's natural law of reciprocity, He promised Paul earthly reparations through a heavenly reward. Without reciprocity, we lose connectivity at the source. Selfishly taking more than you give, self-sabotages the partnership.

• **God naturally demands we recognize the need for help.** Because He designed us to be connected and the network effects of His blessings come through our alliances, partnerships and associations, "*our ask*" as leaders is not a sign of trouble, but a sign God wants to give us double for our trouble. He also places us in the fellowship of suffering together, in the fixed position of the cross, torn between selfish interests and the greater good of the relationship.

• **We declare and decree a marketplace move of the Holy Spirit.** Human organisms are functioning in the profitable ways we were designed to by cooperating, co-laboring and practicing natural laws of reciprocity. We are observing universal signs of the realization that who we are connected to matters for joint survival. We bear witness to the fact that our strategic alliances possess enough power in the heavenly realm to command favor and windows of opportunity opening up with blessings being poured out, by virtue of our associations.

• **Scripture provides a marvelous picture of how pastors and business leaders can partner together to fulfill a God-given vision**. 1 Samuel shows how God uses both Samuel the priest (ministry leader) and Saul the king (marketplace leader) in cooperative fashion. Thereby, illustrating the partnership role that ministry leaders and marketplace leaders can enjoy, if only they work together. Pastors must give the *church's ministry* to entrepreneurs and marketplace leaders. Entrepreneurs must give their *spiritual gifts* to the church's ministry.

• **The leadership key to successful partnerships and strategic alliances lies in the spirit of reciprocity and give and take**. The success path in our strategic alliances is forged in the willingness to put others first, in order to get ahead. Through the strategic alliance of Saul and Samuel, and subsequently David and Jonathan, we bear witness to its redeeming value on transformative leadership.

• **Scripture also informs us that reciprocity works against man's natural inclination to compete and often produces strange alliances of cooperating bedfellows**. Indeed, the story of the three kings shows us how God uses man's natural inclination to annihilate one another through competition to ensure His purpose ultimately prevails.

• **One of the chief elements of likeness to Christ consists in being crucified with him.** Whoever wishes to be like Him must seek to understand the secret of fellowship with His cross. Now that He has been crucified, the Holy Spirit gives another expression in which our entire conformity to Christ is still more powerfully set forth - the believing Disciple is Himself crucified with Christ. The cross is the chief mark of the Christian as of Christ; the crucified Christ and crucified Christian belong to each other.

• **If I am crucified with Christ, then I am a partner in His life and victory**. I learn to understand the position I must take to allow the power of that cross and that death to manifest itself in making dead the old man and the flesh, in destroying the body of sin. For there is still a great work for me to do. This is the work of the cross.

284

• **What my alliance with Christ is calling me to do in the working of the cross is to always regard and treat it as crucified, and not to suffer it to come down from the cross**. I must maintain my crucifixion position; I must keep the flesh in the place of crucifixion. When I gave myself to my crucified Savior, sin and flesh and all, he took me wholly. But here a separation took place. In fellowship with Him I was freed from the life of the flesh; I myself died with him; in the in most center of my being I received new life: Christ lives in ME.

• **It takes one (rock), to know One (Rock).** And to be on One strategic alliance accord. In Philippi, we gather it was not only John who recognized Christ was in the world unrecognized. Peter goes on record as being the second. Indeed, he was the only one among the 12 disciples to answer Christ correctly by seeing the "I Am" in the Son of Man.

• **It's critical for the success of your operation to know if you're strategically aligned with the right one**. The question becomes "do you know *Him*?' Or, perhaps, do you choose to recognize Him (or deny Him) at your convenience. Like Peter. Ask yourself. Do you recognize who your partner *really* is? And what their capabilities *really* are? Does your partner recognize you and what your capabilities *really* are when you're no longer cozied up in the upper room together, and facing opposition threatening to kill the entire operation?

• **In Mark 14, we bear second witness to the fact that the Son of Man was the *only* One telling no lie.** While Jesus foretold Peter he would deny their association thrice before the rooster crowed twice, He also foretold the truth about meeting the disciples in Galilee *after all of that*. Especially, Peter. He still counted Peter as one among their discipleship alliance. And before all was said and done, it was Peter the rock who delivered the inaugural message to the church on the Day of Pentecost. The day our strategic alliance with the Holy Spirit was born.

Chapter 8:
Code of Conduct

"Remember your leaders [for it was they] who brought you the word of God; and consider the result of their conduct [the outcome of their godly lives], and imitate their faith [their conviction that God exists and is the Creator and Ruler of all things, the Provider of eternal salvation through Christ, and imitate their reliance on God with absolute trust and confidence in His power, wisdom, and goodness]. Jesus Christ is [eternally changeless, always] the same yesterday and today and forever."

Hebrews 13:7-8 (AMP)

How then are we to conduct ourselves, now operating in such alliance with the Holy Spirit in the marketplace? Now that our organizations have been armed with this transformational information, what are next steps? How do we make this revelation knowledge and supreme intelligence actionable for leadership in the C+Suite and throughout our office structure?

It's true. Actions speak louder than words. But it's the quiet, unassuming ones on both counts that *mean* the most. Sincerely, nothing changes externally until we change our internal code of conduct. These facts can no longer be denied. While we have developed a treasure trove of resources, delivery mechanisms and scalable platform to support this book, in order to take your organization from "*A to G*," it only works if *you* work it. It has to become part of your DNA.

Which brings us to the G-code.

Spotlight On 💡 The G-code

Quite simply, the G-code is identifying the presence of God within the structural composite of our marketplace activity and enterprise solutions. Not at all scientific, but certainly microscopic. We must view our businesses through the lens of us being living, breathing organisms with the ability to mutate God's kingdom principles in the form of our business operations.

This is not religion, but reality.
This is not fanaticism, but practicality.

We shouldn't go on thinking business as usual will simply go on in perpetuity. Things should not be getting *back to normal*, nor should we be entertaining such folly with our precious opportunity costs. Rather, we must go back to faith's basics. We should have the courage to *change the course*, not just change course in the direction of a poor substitute, and go along with it. Corporate America is in need of revival.

Lord knows, we need it.
Bo knows we need to evangelize a new Nike crusade.
Call it "*Just Do The Right Thing.*"
Because *El-Roi*, the "God who sees me," is looking.

This is the G-code.

I do the right thing, and the next right thing that follows, not just to please my manager but to be just, and pleasing to God. I *do right* by my staff because I want to *be right* with God. I make the right business decisions and personnel moves because *my maker* is *in me*. Because I'm a believer. And I truly believe He sees all. Everything I do. And you, too. And even though I can't see Him, it doesn't change how I treat you or decide whether or not cheat you. Imagine that.

And if that's not enough to move you, the following will definitely make a believer out of you.

"The Empty Chair Effect"

There is a fascinating illustration of this notion of God's relational influence to our conduct and human nature, as the "invisible seeing all," in the acclaimed National Geographic documentary series *"Story of God"* with Morgan Freeman. In this particular episode, psychologist Jesse Bering schools a group of unsuspecting, early childhood learners in New Zealand (ages of 5 to 9) on the cognitive science of religion and innate nature of the G-code. He does so with an experiment you might characterize as "the empty chair effect."

The hypothesis, simple but profound. Bering and his PhD students Jared Piazza and Gordon Ingram sought to validate their sound premise: When no other actual person is around, and we're tempted to do something we know we shouldn't, the illusion of a supernatural watcher should meaningfully influence our behavioral decision-making.

In essence, the children are gathered in their classroom and given a fun, competitive yet difficult challenge to perform. They are given a clear set of instructions to follow. They are to toss a Velcro ball backwards over their shoulders from a fairly considerable distance *behind a marked line* on the floor with hopes of landing a bullseye on a mounted dartboard against the wall.

Per normal rules, each section of the dartboard has corresponding point levels. As the game goes, the students are informed that whomever scores the most points wins a prize at the end. The students then leave the room. One by one, the students come back into the classroom and go through the task quite unsuccessfully while their teacher remains absent from the room.

Absent, but monitoring their actions via closed-circuit television in his adjacent office.

Naturally, what follows is adolescent human behavior. Of course, not a single child is able to manage tossing a ball over their shoulder to reach the dartboard, much less land on it. After a couple of failed attempts, the students come to the realization they can just as easily get the ball to land on the dartboard by sneaking across the forbidden line on the floor and walking right up to place it there themselves. Sure enough, the children begin cheating in order to achieve the task. No doubt, fueled by the immediate gratification of a potential reward.

Armed with knowledge, and now aware of their forbidden nature to cheat, they have disregarded their absentee teacher and changed the rules of the game. Knowing this, and right from wrong, one student even walks up to open the classroom door ever so slightly to take a peek and see if anyone (assuming his teaching authority) was on the outside of the room, looking in.

We could conclude this matter here having made our point on code of conduct rather elementary. But the story and lesson both get better. For the next round, the teacher gives them the same task, rules and instructions but tells the kids they now have a "special guest" observing the game. This special guest, "Princess Alice" is a loving, supernatural entity with the magical power to make herself invisible. Thus, occupying an otherwise empty chair at the head of the classroom. The chair, strategically positioned right next to the dartboard.

Before leaving the room this time, Bering tells the students their special guest will keep them company, observing and encouraging everything they do while performing the task. You don't need supernatural powers to guess what happens next. Amazingly, one by one, the students approached the task and looked *to* the empty chair as if the special guest were *really there.*

Without fail, despite failing at the challenge, the majority of the students opted to play by the rules instead of cheating. One particularly charming young girl actually went to the chair and had an affectionate exchange with Princess Alice. As you might imagine, the results of the study were conclusive. When assigned to play the game under "no supervision," the children were more likely to cheat.

In fact, more than half were so brazen in their transgressions that they walked right up to the wall and manually placed the ball on the target (usually just shy of the bulls-eye to cleverly simulate some relative degree of marginal error), thereby breaking all of the rules at once.

Bering points out one last important caveat. This rather astonishing Princess Alice effect panned out to be more significant statistically for those children who said they *believed she was real*. The more skeptical children, by contrast, were just as likely to cheat in the presence of the invisible Princess Alice in the empty chair than those in the "no supervision" condition.

Yet even those who adamantly denied that Princess Alice was real during their initial introduction to her, when left alone in the room, seemed to display some curious signs of ambivalence about her. For example, for those kids in "her presence" that did cheat, the majority only did so after "disconfirming" her non-existence by running their hand across the chair. Is this all child's play? Or, is it more indicative of man's pure unwillingness to depart from his own childish behavior and put away childish things.

> *"When I was a child, I talked like a child, I thought like a child, I reasoned like a child; when I became a man, I did away with childish things. For now [in this time of imperfection] we see in a mirror dimly [a blurred reflection, a riddle, an enigma], but then [when the time of perfection comes we will see reality] face to face. Now I know in part [just in fragments], but then I will know fully, just as I have been fully known [by God]."*
>
> *1 Corinthians 13:11-12 (AMP)*

Lord knows who we are. Here's another illustration. Remember playing *"Pin The Tail On The Donkey"* at birthday parties growing up? Before Jungle Gyms and trampoline stadiums. Just the neighborhood kids, our cousins and 'them playing at someone's house.

Our parents came up with fun stuff like that for us to do. Of course, being blindfolded made the game the classic one that it is. When it came time for you to turn around and play, how many times did you cheat? A lot.

Lord knows, it's *in us*.
Knowing the Lord brings it out *of us*.

> *"Good and evil exist, within us all. And we must make the choice for good. Each one of us has to purge evil from within us. Every day, by doing good...doing the right thing. Purging the world of evil is not the work of messiahs, kings, prophets. It's the work of each one of us."*

> *-Morgan Freeman, "Story of God"*

This is the true meaning of the G-code. We are genetically predisposed to many things. A predisposition doesn't always cause a trait to develop, but instead it tends to *contribute* to its development. There are many other contributing factors, not the least of which is our environment. Therefore, we may be predisposed to something and never actually have it develop.

Like the good,
And evil within us.
Like our Faith.

Faith is an *innate*, learned behavior. Learned behaviors develop from observing our surrounding or through direct experience. Scientifically speaking, learned behavior can be learned through associating one stimulus with another (classical conditioning), in the early stages of life by imitating parents (imprinting), or by not responding to a stimulus after repetition (habituation).

In other words, as we saw with the children in Bering's study, the action toward cheating or not cheating came through directly observing the "empty chair" in their immediate surroundings and by associating *that* stimulus with *another*. The other stimulus being the imprint of faith placed upon them (or not) from their outside environments or experience.

More than likely, the kids who actually believed that the make-believe, special guest Princess Alice was there with them, were not merely using their imagination. If that were so, the overwhelming consensus of children that age would not need much convincing to play a game of make believe with Alice inside of their classroom.

The difference is, her *presence* was tied to a moral choice.

When presented with a choice, the reality of human nature has proven that imagination and morality can both quickly go out the window. This is where faith comes in. Through imitating and repeating the behavior associated with faith learned in their homes, presumably from their parents, the children who "believed she was real" have learned *how* to believe God is real.

On the flipside, those children bent on "disconfirming" her existence presumably adopted such behavior in similar fashion. Either way, the beauty of children lies in reminding us what comes naturally. They instruct us back toward our innate innocence. Doing the right thing feels more natural to them. Even in doing wrong, it's clear when their actions are prompted by some external stimulus (e.g. peer pressure) going against the purity of their own internal make-up.

> *"Start children off on the way they should go,*
> *and even when they are old they will not turn from it."*

> *Proverbs 22:6 (NIV)*

We may further conclude that faith, at its best, is an "*early intervention*" style of learned behavior that starts from the outside looking within. And going from "*faith to faith and glory to glory*," the learning outcomes never end. This is not by accident. Our fallen nature all boils down to choice and God's reconciling everything back to Himself by our own free will. It is what it is.

As covered in our opening chapter, God designed it to be this way. His desire has always and forever more will be for us to *choose Him,* or not. And to know right from wrong, or not. To grow up, and put away childish things, or not. That's how we got here, like it or not. He didn't rig the test for us to become Gnostic. We did. Our desire for the knowledge of good and evil got our signals and wireframe within our complex cell structures crossed. Life is pretty simple. It's building blocks are not. That's where things grew complicated for us.

> *"It is not a simple life to be a single cell, although I have no right to say so, having been a single cell so long ago myself that I have no memory at all of that stage of my life."*
>
> *- Lewis Thomas (1913 – 1993)*
> *author, biologist, physician*

The Human Body is comprised of *trillions* of cells, which are the building blocks of life. In fact, we all began as a single cell structure. The *"self,"* is a collection of living cells. We could very well be called the *"cellf."* Every cell has a job and a function. They move, think, see, laugh and talk. When they come together, they make us.

When you think you're hungry, it's your cells that are growling. When you wake up with the urge for a Morning Joe or tobacco, it's your cells making a fixed decision *for* you. Same goes for all of our addictions, afflictions, temptations, triggers and so on. This is what it means to be a slave, (*in*slaved) or prisoner to sin. Right or wrong, this is right where the enemy wants to ensnare us. We, literally, become confined and *locked up in the fleshly desires of our cells.*

Sometimes voluntarily, sometimes involuntarily. Our confinement, always solitary.

To master one's *self,* is to master "our*cellves.*"
This is when we become free.
This is what it means to be a Bond Servant.
This is what it costs to be redeemed.

This is the price He paid.
This unlocking from the captivity of our cells is the Key of David.
This is not hyperbolic.
As His word is our witness:

"Set me free from my prison,
That I may praise your name.
Then the righteous will gather about me
Because of your goodness to me."

Psalm 142:7 (NIV)

"Who executes justice for the oppressed,
Who gives food to the hungry.
The LORD sets free the prisoners."

Psalm 146:7 (AMP)

"The Spirit of the LORD GOD is upon me,
Because the LORD has anointed and commissioned me
To bring good news to the humble and afflicted;
He has sent me to bind up [the wounds of] the brokenhearted,
To proclaim release [from confinement and condemnation]
To the [physical and spiritual] captives
And freedom to prisoners;"

Isaiah 61: 1 (AMP)

To become regenerated is to put your cells back in check.
To discover Him, is to find our way of escape.

"No temptation has overtaken you except what is common to
mankind. And God is faithful; he will not let you be tempted
beyond what you can bear. But when you are tempted, he
will also provide a way out so that you can endure it."

1 Corinthians 10:13 (NIV)

Satan may be tempting you, but it's your cells that are carrying out the orders. Literally. Satan is trying to possess you, by possessing your cells. He's after the red and white in your blood cells because He is after the *light* in your blood cells. If we believe nothing else, that *alone* should be liberating enough to set *all* of us captives free.

Yet, we *choose* to stay bound by sin.
Why then?
When it comes to our business conduct.
We still behave like juvenile delinquents.

Fundamentally, the 5-year-old spiritual child inside you must believe God is there, seated next to you in your cubicle chair, before filling out that bogus expense report. When tempted to turn the sales meeting time away from our significant others into a smorgasbord full of sin, there must be something inside of us that believes *"greater is he that is in me than he that is in the world."*

This, is *"the older serving the younger."*
This, is *"the putting on the new man."*
This, is *"the reverse engineering of the G-code."*

Imagine that. Now, imagine this working for your organization. Picture reserving an empty chair, in every room, for every meeting and every discussion that takes place within your offices. And making it plainly understood that God is *always* seated in the empty chair. And is to be respected as such. Not as a one-off game of tongue and cheek but as a fact of life for doing business there.

If we want our start-up cultures, corporate environments, cross-functional teams and upstart ministries to thrive, we must bring these words to life within the context and code by which we conduct ourselves. Which is to say, we must encode the basics of faith back into our operational DNA. We must fundamentally honor our agreements, respect our associations, value our people and keep our word as if God is seated right next to us signing off on our every move.

We must understand that honor means everything to our Father. We must be willing to place God's office at the very top of our building directory. If God is truly our silent partner and seed investor, we must factor Him, our faith, our character and our integrity into the valuation equation. Seriously. We must give new rise to the meaning and definition of what it means to go by the book. And be good with that.

We must no longer view our faith and belief system in God as somehow being offensive, separate from, or a threat *to* the work-place while the enemy continues to make sure his agents are armed and dangerous *in* it. We must begin to have the courage to abandon the lewd desire to have "the best of both worlds," while leaving God's Kingdom out of it.

We must rebuke the spirit of division dividing our enterprises and view our various expressions of faith as being one in the same, in God's eyes. We must stop breaking all of the rules, and stop playing games with His. We must discipline ourselves by showing respect for His ultimate authority in all circumstances, including those situations when we *think* nobody is watching. If not, we're just playing Adam and Eve.

We must resolve the conflict of interest between our two natures.

> *"We know that the law is spiritual; but I am unspiritual, sold as a slave to sin. I do not understand what I do. For what I want to do I do not do, but what I hate I do. And if I do what I do not want to do, I agree that the law is good. As it is, it is no longer I myself who do it, but it is sin living in me. For I know that good itself does not dwell in me, that is, in my sinful nature. For I have the desire to do what is good, but I cannot carry it out. For I do not do the good I want to do, but the evil I do not want to do—this I keep on doing. Now if I do what I do not want to do, it is no longer I who do it, but it is sin living in me that does it.*

So I find this law at work: Although I want to do good, evil is right there with me. For in my inner being I delight in God's law; but I see another law at work in me, waging war against the law of my mind and making me a prisoner of the law of sin at work within me. What a wretched man I am! Who will rescue me from this body that is subject to death? Thanks be to God, who delivers me through Jesus Christ our Lord! So then, I myself in my mind am a slave to God's law, but in my sinful nature a slave to the law of sin."

Romans 7:14-25 (NIV)

Spotlight On 💡 Discipline

"Do you not know that in a race all the runners run [their very best to win], but only one receives the prize? Run [your race] in such a way that you may seize the prize and make it yours! Now every athlete who [goes into training and] competes in the games is disciplined and exercises self-control in all things. They do it to win a crown that withers, but we [do it to receive] an imperishable [crown that cannot wither]. Therefore I do not run without a definite goal; I do not flail around like one beating the air [just shadow boxing]. But [like a boxer] I strictly discipline my body and make it my slave, so that, after I have preached [the gospel] to others, I myself will not somehow be disqualified [as unfit for service]."

1 Corinthians 9:24-27 (AMP)

It is in the maturing of our discipline, and putting away of those childish things that we do in the flesh, that makes us fit for reasonable service in partnership with the Holy Spirit. This is not a natural phenomenon but the byproduct of how God supernaturally disciplines us. When the fighter is ready, the trainer appears.

Sometimes, whether we know it or not, asked for it or not. Ready or not, we've all experienced the rod of correction and discipline coming from our Heavenly Father. Perhaps, in rebellion though, we stopped short of the realization that it was His chasing and chastening that followed. Not the other way around.

One makes us run *from* Him.
The other makes us run *to* Him.
But what exactly is God chastening us *to* and chasing us *for*?

Because our ways are not the Father's, we naturally consider discipline as the correction of a wrong. This has been our primary orientation as children and parents. However, in the above passage of scripture, Paul is urging and encouraging the church of Corinth to walk their faith life out with the same discipline of an athlete. Not by constantly beating yourself up. Edifying yourself, your church or your organization requires a different kind of discipline.

One beats you down, the other builds you up. Before muscles can build their memory, and get ripped, they must first remember what it feels like to be torn. Both matters of discipline produce hardship and require the full training commitment of obedience and perseverance.

Like a sparring prize fighter, it calls for us to focus on our techniques and see past the pain to the outcome of the process. We have Jesus as our undisputed example.

> *"When he had received the drink, Jesus said, "**It is finished.**" With that, he bowed his head and gave up his spirit."*
>
> *John 19:30 (NIV)*

"Surrender To Win"

Christ fought the good fight to the finish on the cross. He received His rank, earned His title and took His rightful place at the right hand of God the Father. In like fashion, we too need to endure the battles, tests and bouts with temptations in this life by looking to our heavenly reward and our rightful position as more than con-querors. Like Christ, we hold the belt of truth up high and do so by (voluntarily) surrendering the fight with the flesh.

That's surrender, spelled with a victory, not ending in defeat.

If we were preaching this message right now, we'd say "I wish I had someone in here who's been in a fight. Somebody who's been sparring with the enemy their whole life. Round by round. Blow by bloody blow. And that's *when* Christ came in and stopped the fight!"

> *"For our struggle is not against flesh and blood [contending only with physical opponents], but against the rulers, against the powers, against the world forces of this [present] darkness, against the spiritual **forces** of wickedness in the heavenly (supernatural) **places**.*
>
> *Therefore, put on the complete armor of God, so that you will be able to [successfully] resist **and** stand your ground in the evil day [of danger], and having done everything [that the crisis demands], to stand firm [in your place, fully prepared, immovable, victorious]."*
>
> *Ephesians 6:12-13 (AMP)*

Ladies and Gentlemen, we are training for a heavenly prize in eternal life. As such, this life on earth is meant to be hard. This life is not our zenith. It's the undercard. Let's get ready to rumble in this wilderness full of evil entrapments, sure death and pain. Let's welcome our fair share of it. Knowing God is with us and will never forsake us. And *"if He be for us, who can be against us."* Really. God is behind the scenes working all things out for our good, including evil, so that "we may be partakers of His holiness."

The discipline we walk with today will yield *"the peaceable fruit of righteousness to those who have been trained by it"* tomorrow. Regardless of what each one of us is currently going through on the job, or being out of a job. Whether our leadership and character is undergoing fiery trial, or under pressure, let's look to our head trainer who put our fight plan together in the first place.

Like good boxers, let's trust our cornerstone and instructions He has given us in the final round.

Like a good trainer, God recognizes our weaknesses as well as our fight or flight tendencies. Ultimately, it is by our faith and trust in Him, not by our good works alone, that we are declared righteous and worthy to be victorious. When in doubt, we remember those nervous moments we were on the ropes, dancing around the ring of doubt and fear. Falling victim to our bad habits. It was His voice that urged us to get back to fighting squarely in the middle of the ring.

It is then we recollect back to our senses that our success and body of work is not solely based on our skills and abilities. In this way, it is good to be reminded that our obedience alone is what God is looking for out of his prize fighters. He is responsible for the tale of the tape and outcome of that obedience. In the middle of the fight, there are times where His instructions may not look anything like a strategy for success to us.

It is then we recall that His ways are not our ways. His reach is far higher and much longer than ours. We may throw a lot of punches but he lands way more. In this way, we take comfort in the fact that it is in obedience to the bruising of our reproof and taking the cuts from our activity errors in faith that we are commended, and made fit for the fight.

> *"All Scripture is God-breathed [given by divine inspiration] and is profitable for instruction, for conviction [of sin], for correction [of error and restoration to obedience], for training in righteousness [learning to live in conformity to God's will, both publicly and privately—behaving honorably with personal integrity and moral courage]; so that the man of God may be complete and proficient, outfitted and thoroughly equipped for every good work."*

> *2 Timothy 3:16-17 (AMP)*

"Coarse Correction"

It is inevitable. There are times we must submit ourselves in obedience to correction. No matter what level of the game we're on, we are subject to a higher authority. By submitting ourselves to God's correction and subjecting our leadership to Him as a matter of conduct, we level the playing field. In turn, subjecting ourselves to those we are leading. Unfortunately, we are so hung up, and get so caught up on submission. This is quite detrimental to our code of conduct.

Let's clear the error. Submission *is not a passive adjective*. Submission *is an active noun*.

The active component in the definition of submission is in the *"sub"* portion. It is performed in the act of *"coming under"* someone else's mission. His or hers. Mine or theirs. Anybody else but yours. Come on, somebody! We can feel ourselves starting to preach.

> *"Have confidence in your leaders and submit to their authority, because they keep watch over you as those who must give an account. Do this so that their work will be a joy, not a burden, for that would be of no benefit to you. Pray for us. We are sure that we have a clear conscience and desire to live honorably in every way."*
>
> *Hebrews 13:17-18 (NIV)*

How do you react to coarse correction? Probably defensively. Preaching to the choir now. No one among us enjoys being rebuked or admonished. Certainly, not corporately. However, the Bible urges us to *"bear with the word of exhortation."* In other words, correction is intended to earnestly advise, not ridicule. The intent is to course correct toward faithful action. This is what makes great coaches, and allows supervisors to supernaturally transform themselves.

If we take time to think on them, and the rod of correction they applied to motivate us, very often their words of rebuke actually stirred up conviction in us, bringing us through our false pride to true repentance. To repent, is to change course - not to feel sorry, or ashamed, or embarrassed but to be convicted about going in the right direction when all signs were pointing opposite. If we never get to the place of repentance and instead remain defensive beyond the point of no return, our conduct never changes and we miss the opportunity to grow further in the Spirit.

It's the little things that add up to a culture of feedback and thriving team dynamic. It's these minor adjustments to our attitude, hearts and minds that make us better co-workers, better managers, better partners, better collaborators. It's the major corrections we make to the activity errors in our personal life that do the work of transforming us more and more into the professional image of Christ.

When we are easily offended and defensive after presentations, shift blame or justify our false sense of entitlement, we grieve the strategic alliance we formed with the Holy Spirit in the previous chapter to do His job sanctifying us. This is not to suggest every rebuke is correct, or of God. In any business environment, there are invariably times the load of guilt, obligation or accountability someone heaves upon us is clearly theirs, and not ours to carry.

When our conscience is clear and our conduct is clearly in alliance with the Holy Spirit, instead of reacting sensitively, we are sensitive enough to discern the difference. This is how we measure the yield between His discipline and the working of our obedience.

As the above passage of scripture in this chapter of the Book of Romans continues in subsequent verse, this is how God *"equips you with every good thing to carry out His will and strengthen you [making you complete and perfect as you ought to be], accomplishing in us that which is pleasing in His sight."*

Or, as Philippians 1:6 conducts and instructs us, *"He who has begun a good work in you will complete it until the day of Jesus Christ."*

And in Philippians 2:13, Paul adds further witness and encourages us that *"it is God who works in you both to will and to do for His good pleasure."* This is what it means to subject ourselves in the workplace by giving Him full and total access to do His work and carry out His mission in our marketplace.

This means coming under conviction for deceptive business practices and repentance for discrimination and harassment. Past and present. This means the individual laying down of bad habits that no longer serve us and are not useful for His Kingdom. It means the casting down of thoughts and imaginations that are detrimental to us or those we work with. This means relinquishing our need to right, just as we hold fast to another's inalienable right to be wrong.

While we're leaning in on everything else, we should also lean into this discipline we are undergoing, in order that our partnerships might be strengthened, our enterprises made fit and ready for the journey He has laid out for us. If we reject His discipline, we will end up fighting among ourselves instead of allowing God to heal us. If we resist His discipline, we will miss the opportunity for our Heavenly Father to raise us above our childish standards.

> *"And have you completely forgotten this word of encouragement that addresses you as a father addresses his son? It says, "My son, do not make light of the Lord's discipline, and do not lose heart when he rebukes you, because the Lord disciplines the one he loves, and he chastens everyone he accepts as his son." Endure hardship as discipline; God is treating you as his children. For what children are not disciplined by their father? If you are not disciplined—and everyone undergoes discipline—then you are not legitimate, not true sons and daughters at all. Moreover, we have all had human fathers who disciplined us and we respected them for it. How much more should we submit to the Father of spirits and live! They disciplined us for a little while as they thought best; but God disciplines us for our good, in order that we may share in his holiness.*

No discipline seems pleasant at the time, but painful. Later on, however, it produces a harvest of righteousness and peace for those who have been trained by it."

Hebrews 12:5-11 (NIV)

Pursuing peace with all people we work with or partner with means training ourselves and our teams in the discipline of forgiveness and asking others to forgive us. Otherwise, bitterness, resentments and lack of forgiveness can run *wide and deep* through our work environments like the roots of the mulberry tree. Christ used this tree and its complex root system to instruct His disciples with a cautionary tale and parable that illustrates the importance of forgiveness.

"So watch yourselves. If your brother or sister sins against you, rebuke them; and if they repent, forgive them. Even if they sin against you seven times in a day and seven times come back to you saying 'I repent,' you must forgive them. The apostles said to the Lord, Increase our faith!"

He replied, if you have faith as small as a mustard seed, you can say to this mulberry tree, 'Be uprooted and planted in the sea,' and it will obey you."

Luke 17:3-6 (NIV)

For instance, the bitterness over being passed over for that promotion takes up root in one of your shift supervisors and branches out, connecting to shared resentments among other workers in the warehouse. Once this "root system" gets embedded in the hearts and knotted in the minds of your team, it is virtually impossible to uproot it without repentance and increasing your faith.

"Work at living in peace with everyone, and work at living a holy life, for those who are not holy will not see the Lord. Look after each other so that none of you fails to receive the

grace of God. Watch out that no poisonous root of bitterness grows up to trouble you, corrupting many."

Hebrews 12:14-15 (NLT)

Spotlight On 💡 Empathy

"O my son, give me your heart."

Proverbs 23:26 (NLT)

Empathy. We need it. Empathy has long been perceived to be a critical, emotional quotient for leaders. And, rightfully so. However, the reality of the new leadership paradigm we now find ourselves in has evolved empathy to new heights as a top priority for leadership *effectiveness*. Indeed, empathy has flipped its perceptual map positioning on its axis, rearranging from soft skill to proprietary know how. Shifting from producing an intangible character trait, to manufacturing tangible business results.

As reported in *Forbes* by career contributor Tracy Brower, demonstrating empathy has always been considered as a positive attribute for managers but new research demonstrates its profound, wide-ranging importance on everything from innovation to retention. No doubt, as she argues, great leadership demands a fine assortment of skills to create the conditions for engagement, happiness and performance. However, empathy now tops the list of what leaders must get right, and not merely figure out how not to be on the wrong side of.

Bower suggests the reason empathy is so necessary is because people are experiencing "multiple kinds of stress at work" as the world turns and our work-life balance has been turned upside down. For example, research at the University of Illinois found when employees receive rude emails at work, they tend to experience negativity and spillover into their personal lives and particularly with their partners. In addition, a study at Carleton University found when people experience incivility at work, they tend to feel less capable in their parenting.

Furthermore, a study published in the *Academy of Management Journal* found when people are on the receiving end of rudeness at work, their performance suffers and they are less likely to help others. And a new study at Georgetown University found workplace incivility is rising and the effects are extensive, including reduced performance and collaboration, deteriorating customer experiences and increased turnover.

"Empathy Contributes to Positive Outcomes"

Brower further asserts that, as we go through tough times, struggle with burnout or find it challenging to find happiness at work, empathy can be a powerful antidote and contribute to positive experiences for individuals and teams. She points to a study of 889 employees by *Catalyst* which found empathy has some significant constructive effects:

- Innovation. When people reported their leaders were empathetic, they were more likely to report they were able to be innovative - 61% of employees compared to only 13% of employees with less empathetic leaders.

- Engagement. 76% of people who experienced empathy from their leaders reported they were engaged compared with only 32% who experienced less empathy.

- Retention. 57% of white women and 62% of women of color said they were unlikely to think of leaving their companies when they felt their life circumstances were respected and valued by their companies. However, when they didn't feel that level of value or respect for their life circumstances, only 14% and 30% of white women and women of color respectively said they were unlikely to consider leaving.

- Inclusivity. 50% of people with empathetic leaders reported their workplace was inclusive, compared with only 17% of those with less empathetic leadership.

- Work-Life. When people felt their leaders were more empathetic, 86% reported being able to navigate the demands of their work and life - successfully juggling their personal, family and work obligations. This is compared with 60% of those who perceived less empathy.

Cooperation is also a factor. According to a study published in *Evolutionary Biology*, when empathy was introduced into decision making, it increased cooperation and even caused people to be more empathetic. Empathy fostered more empathy. The study by Qualtrics found when leaders were perceived as more empathetic, people reported greater levels of mental health.

"Wired for Empathy"

In addition, empathy seems to be inborn. In a study by Lund University, children as young as two demonstrated an appreciation that others hold different perspectives than their own.

Research at the University of Virginia found when people saw their friends experiencing threats, they experienced activity in the same part of their brain which was affected when they were personally threatened. People felt for their friends and teammates as deeply as they felt for themselves. All of this makes empathy an important part of our human condition—at work and in our personal lives.

"Leading with Empathy"

Brower emphasizes that leaders can demonstrate empathy in two ways. First, they can consider someone else's thoughts through cognitive empathy ("If I were in his/her position, what would I be thinking right now?"). Leaders can also focus on a person's feelings using emotional empathy ("Being in his/her position would make me feel ___").

But leaders will be most successful not just when they personally consider others, but when they express their concerns and inquire about challenges directly, and then listen to employees' responses. Leaders don't have to be experts in mental health in order to demonstrate they care and are paying attention. It's enough to check in, ask questions and take cues from the employee about how much they want to share.

Leaders can also be educated about the company's supports for mental health so they can provide information about resources to additional help. Great leadership also requires action. One leader likes to say, "You're behaving so loudly, I can hardly hear what you're saying." People will trust leaders and feel a greater sense of engagement and commitment when there is alignment between what the leader says and does.

All that understanding of someone else's situation should turn into compassion and action. Empathy in action is understanding an employee's struggles and offering to help. It is appreciating a person's point of view and engaging in a healthy debate that builds to a better solution. It is considering a team member's perspectives and making a new recommendation that helps achieve greater success. As the popular saying goes, people may not remember what you say, but they will remember how you made them feel.

In the final analysis, empathy contributes to positive relationships and organizational cultures and it also drives results. As she concludes, "empathy may not be a brand new skill, but it has a new level of importance and the fresh research makes it especially clear how empathy is the leadership competency to develop and demonstrate now and in the future of work."

"Need-Based Leadership"

More encouraging empathy trends and new theories have emerged across the industry landscape. One such noteworthy theory indicates *"need-based leadership"* is the shift we need. *Greg Sumpter, Ph.D., brings forth his disruptive theory on pandemic-era leadership in his book of the same title, influenced by Trust-Based Relational Intervention and motivational interviews.*

As Dr. Sumpter highlighted for *SmartBrief,* "need-based leadership can be simply defined as a relationship whereby the leader's responsibility is to meet the needs of those in their care." Citing authors and leadership thought leaders James Kouzes and Barry Posner, he aims at the discovery that essentially all people exhibit leadership behaviors.

It is a matter of drawing these behaviors out, and behaviors are simply a result of beliefs, thoughts and feelings that may come out of deeper needs. Kouzes and Posner have further established that leadership is everyone's business. This developing of everyone's leadership capacity is the role of a need-based leader.

From Dr. Sumpter's perspective, need-based leadership is an intentional, continual move away from a leader-centric approach toward *meeting the needs of future leaders,* or what some texts have called "followers." As he suggests, "this approach is the intentional bringing out of existing leadership behaviors in all employees by setting the appropriate conditions for people to be their best selves and sustaining these behaviors." For example, in the sciences and behavioral health professions, we have seen a movement toward meeting client needs.

Accordingly, meeting needs is the path to creating a healthy workplace culture. Retired United States Navy captain and bestselling author David Marquet has stated, "In healthy cultures, people take responsibility for their behavior and leaders take responsibility for the environment. In unhealthy cultures people blame the environment and leaders blame the people."

Dr. Sumpter believes that, given the ability to have their needs met, people will take ownership of their behavior and will be able to show up as their full, best selves. He concludes: "For too long in organizations, we have tried to balance two things that are almost diametrically opposed: control and relationships. In a focus on meeting workplace needs, leaders will shift this narrow view and create more balance."

> *"My research has convinced me that we all have extraordinary creative, humanitarian, and spiritual possibilities but are often alienated from them because we are so focused on a very narrow slice of who we are. As a result, we aren't fulfilling our full potential."*

> *- Scott Barry Kaufman*

We believe Dr. Sumpter's hypothesis holds significant potential to be proven correct. We also believe it to be a lasting, manual gear shift toward organizations finally fulfilling their full potential and achieving a perpetual state of high-performance homeostasis. We see it as the softening, not the hardening of the leadership heart. And that's the main thing empathy brings.

"The Heart"

(J.C. Ryle)

The heart is the main thing in true religion. I make no excuse for asking the special attention of my readers, while I try to say a few things about the heart. The head is not the principal thing. You may know the whole truth as it is in Jesus, and consent that it is good. You may be clear, correct, and sound in your religious opinions.

But all this time you may be walking in the broad way which leads to destruction. It is your heart which is the main point. "Is your heart right in the sight of God?" Your outward life may be moral, decent, respectable, in the eyes of people. Your minister, and friends, and neighbors, may see nothing very wrong in your general conduct.

There are three things which I propose to do in order to impress the subject of this paper upon your mind.

I.   First, I will show you the immense importance of the heart in religion.

II. Secondly, I will show you the heart which is wrong in the sight of God.

III. Lastly, I will show you the heart which is right in the sight of God.

May God bless the whole subject to the soul of everyone into whose hands this may fall! May the Holy Spirit, without whom all preaching and writing can do nothing, apply this paper to many consciences, and make it an arrow to pierce many hearts!

I.   In the first place, I will show the immense IMPORTANCE of the heart in religion.

How shall I prove this point? From whence shall I fetch my arguments? I must turn to the Word of God. In questions of this kind it matters nothing what the world thinks right or wrong. There is only one sure test of truth. What says the Scripture? What is written in the Bible? What is the mind of the Holy Spirit? If we cannot submit our judgments to this infallible umpire, it is useless to pretend that we have any religion at all.

For one thing, the Bible teaches that the heart is that part of us on which the state of our soul depends. *"Out of it are the issues of life"* (Proverbs 4:23). The reason, the understanding, the conscience, the affections, are all second in importance to the heart. The heart is the man. It is the seat of all spiritual life, and health, and strength, and growth.

It is the hinge and turning-point in the condition of man's soul. If the heart is alive to God and quickened by the Spirit, the man is a living Christian. If the heart is dead and has not the Spirit, the man is dead before God. The heart is the man! Tell me not merely what a man says and professes, and where a man goes on Sunday, and what money he puts in the collecting plate. Tell me rather what his heart is, and I will tell you what he is. *"As a man thinks in his heart, so is he"* (Proverbs 23:7).

For another thing, the Bible teaches that the heart is that part of us at which God especially looks. "Man looks at the outward appearance - but the Lord looks on the heart" (1 Samuel 16:7). "Every way of man is right in his own eyes - but the Lord ponders the heart" (Proverbs 21:2). Man is naturally content with the outward part of religion, with outward morality, outward correctness, outward regular attendance on means of grace.

But the eyes of the Lord look much further. He regards our motives. He "weighs the spirits" (Proverbs 16:2). He says Himself, "I the Lord am the searcher of the heart, the tester of the thoughts" (Jeremiah 17:10). For another thing, the Bible teaches that the heart is the first and foremost thing which God asks man to give him. "My son," He says, "give Me your heart" (Proverbs 23:26).

We may give God a bowed head and a serious face, our bodily presence in His house, and a loud amen. But until we give God our hearts, we give Him nothing of any value. The heart is what the husband desires to have in his wife, the parent in his child, and the master in his servant. And the heart is what God desires to have in professing Christians.

What is the heart in man's body?

It is the principal and most important organ in the whole frame. A man may live many years in spite of fevers, wounds, and loss of limbs. But a man cannot live if you injure his heart. Just so it is with the heart in religion. It is the fountain of life to the soul.

What is the root to the tree?

It is the source of all life, and growth, and fruitfulness. You may cut off the branches, and wound the trunk, and the tree may yet survive. But if you hurt the root, the tree will die. Just so it is with the heart in religion. It is the root of life to the soul.

What is the mainspring to the watch?

> It is the cause of all its movements, and the secret of all its usefulness. The case may be costly and beautiful. The face and figures may be skillfully made. But if there is anything wrong with the mainspring the works will not go. Just so it is with the heart in religion. It is the mainspring of life to the soul.

What is the furnace to the steam engine?

> It is the cause of all its motion and power. The machinery may be properly made. Every screw, and valve, and joint, and crank, and rod may be in its right place. But if the furnace is cold and the water is not turned into steam, the engine will do nothing. Just so is it with the heart in religion. Unless the heart is lighted with fire from on high, the soul will not move.

> Would you know the reason why such multitudes around you take no interest in true religion? They have no real concern about God, or Christ, or the Bible, or heaven, or hell, or judgment, or eternity. They care for nothing but what they shall eat, or what they shall drink, or what they shall put on, or what money they can get, or what pleasure they can have. It is their heart which is in fault! They have not the least appetite for the things of God.

> They are destitute of any taste or inclination for spiritual things. They need a new mainspring. They need a new heart. "Therefore is there a price in the hand of a fool to get wisdom, seeing he has no heart unto it" (Proverbs 17:16).

> Would you know the reason why so many hear the Gospel year after year, and yet remain unmoved by it? Their minds seem like Bunyan's "slough of despond." Cartloads of good instruction are poured into them without producing any good effect. Their reason is convinced. Their head assents to the truth. Their conscience is sometimes pricked. Their feelings are sometimes roused.

Why then do they stick fast? Why do they tarry? It is their hearts which are in fault! Some secret idol chains them down to the earth, and keeps them tied hand and foot, so that they cannot move. They need a new heart. Their picture is drawn faithfully by Ezekiel, "They sit before you as my people, and they hear your words - but they will not do them - for with their mouth they show much love - but their heart goes after their covetousness" (Ezekiel 33:31).

II. I will now show you, in the second place, the heart that is WRONG in the sight of God. There are only two sorts of hearts, a right one and a wrong one. What is a wrong heart like?

What does the Scripture say about the natural heart?

It says many things which are deeply solemn, and painfully true. It says that "the heart is deceitful above all things, and desperately wicked" (Jeremiah 17:9). It says that "every imagination of the thoughts of the heart is only evil continually" (Genesis 6:5). It says that "the heart of the sons of men is full of evil" (Ecclesiastes 9:3).

It says that "From within, out of the heart of man," as out of a fountain, "proceed evil thoughts, adulteries, fornications, murders, thefts, covetousness, wickedness, deceit, lasciviousness, an evil eye, blasphemy, pride, foolishness. All these evil things come from within" (Mark 7:21). Truly this is a humbling picture! The seeds of these things are in the heart of everyone born into the world. Surely I may well tell you that the natural heart is wrong.

But is there no one common mark of the wrong heart, which is to be seen in all whom God has not changed? Yes! there is; and to that common mark of the wrong heart I now request your attention. There is a most striking and instructive figure of speech, which the Holy Spirit has thought fit to use, in describing the natural heart. He calls it a "stony heart" (Ezekiel 11:19).

I know no emblem in the Bible so full of instruction, and so apt and fitting as this one. A truer word was never written than that which calls the natural heart a heart of stone. Mark well what I am going to say; and may the Lord give you understanding!

(a) A stone is HARD. All people know that. It is unyielding, unbending, unimpressible. It may be broken - but it will never bend. The proverb is world-wide, "as hard as a stone." Look at the granite rocks which line the coast of Cornwall. For four thousand years the waves of the Atlantic Ocean have dashed against them in vain. There they stand in their old hardness, unbroken and unmoved. It is just the same with the natural heart. Afflictions, mercies, losses, crosses, sermons, counsels, books, tracts, speaking, writing - all, all are unable to soften it.

Until the day that God comes down to change it, it remains unmoved. Well may the natural heart be called a heart of stone!

(b) A stone is COLD. There is a chilly, icy feeling about it, which you know the moment you touch it. It is utterly unlike the feeling of flesh, or wood, or even earth. The proverb is in everyone's mouth, "As cold as a stone." The old marble statues in many a cathedral church have heard the substance of thousands of sermons. Yet they never show any feeling. Not a muscle of their marble faces ever shrinks or moves. It is just the same with the natural heart.

It is utterly destitute of spiritual feeling. It cares less for the story of Christ's death on the cross, than it does for the last new novel, or the last debate in Parliament, or the account of a railway accident, or a shipwreck, or an execution. Until God sends fire from heaven to warm it, the natural heart of man has no feeling about religion. Well may it be called a heart of stone!

(c) A stone is BARREN. You will reap no harvest off rocks of any description. You will never fill your barns with grain from the top of Snowdon or Ben Nevis. You will never reap wheat on granite, or slate, or on flint. You may get good crops on Norfolk sands, or Cambridgeshire fens, or Suffolk clay, by patience, labor, money, and good farming. But you will never get a crop worth a farthing off a stone. It is just the same with the natural heart. It is utterly barren of penitence, or faith, or love, or fear, or holiness, or humility.

Until God breaks it up, and puts a new principle in it, it bears no fruit to God's praise. Well may the natural heart be called a heart of stone!

(d) A stone is DEAD. It neither sees, nor hears, nor moves, nor grows. Show it the glories of heaven, and it would not be pleased. Tell it of the fires of hell, and it would not be alarmed. Bid it flee from a roaring lion, or an earthquake, and it would not stir. The Bass Rock and Mount Blanc are just what they were 4000 years ago. They have seen kingdoms rise and fall, and they remain utterly unchanged. They are neither higher, nor broader, nor larger than they were when Noah left the ark. It is just the same with the natural heart. It has not a spark of spiritual life about it. Until God plants the Holy Spirit in it, it is dead and motionless about real religion.

Would you know the reason why it is so difficult to do good in the world? Would you know why so few believe the Gospel, and live like true Christians? The reason is, the hardness of man's natural heart. He neither sees nor knows what is for his good. The wonder, to my mind, is not so much that few are converted, as the miraculous fact that any are converted at all.

I am not greatly surprised when I see or hear of unbelief. I remember the natural heart is wrong.

Would you know the reason why the state of people is so desperately helpless, if they die in their sins? Would you know why ministers feel so fearful about everyone who is cut off unprepared to meet God? The reason is, the hardness of man's natural heart. What would a man do in heaven, if he got there, with his heart unchanged? By which of the saints would he sit down?

What pleasure could he take in God's presence and company? Oh no! it is vain to conceal it. There can be no real hope about a man's condition, if he dies with his heart wrong. I leave this point here. Once more I press the whole subject of my paper upon your conscience. Surely you must allow it is a very serious one. Is your heart right? Is it right in the sight of God?

III. I will now show you, in the last place, the right heart. It is a heart of which the Bible contains many pictures. I am going to try to place some of those pictures before you. On a question like this, I want you to observe what God says, rather than what is said by man. Come, now, and see the marks and signs of a right heart.

(a) The right heart is a "NEW heart" (Ezekiel 36:26). It is not the heart with which a man is born- but another heart put in him by the Holy Spirit.

It is a heart which has new tastes, new joys, new sorrows, new desires, new hopes, new fears, new likes, new dislikes. It has new views about the soul, and sin, and God, and Christ, and salvation, and the Bible, and prayer, and heaven, and hell, and the world, and holiness.

It is like a farm with a new and good tenant. "Old things are passed away. Behold all things are become new" (2 Corinthians 5:17).

(b) The right heart is a "BROKEN and CONTRITE heart" (Psalm 51:17). It is broken off from pride, self-conceit, and self-righteousness. Its former high thoughts of self are cracked, shattered, and shivered to atoms. It thinks itself guilty, unworthy, and corrupt. Its former stubbornness, heaviness, and insensibility have thawed, disappeared, and passed away. It no longer thinks lightly of offending God. It is tender, sensitive, and jealously fearful of running into sin (2 Kings 22:19). It is humble, lowly, and self-abased, and sees in itself no good thing.

(c) A right heart is a heart which BELIEVES on Christ alone for salvation, and in which Christ dwells by faith (Romans 10:10; Ephesians 3:17). It rests all its hopes of pardon and eternal life on Christ's atonement, Christ's mediation, and Christ's intercession. It is sprinkled in Christ's blood from an evil conscience (Hebrews 10:22). It turns to Christ as the compass-needle turns to the north. It looks to Christ for daily peace, mercy, and grace - as the sun-flower looks to the sun. It feeds on Christ for its daily sustenance, as Israel fed on the manna in the wilderness.

It sees in Christ a special fitness to supply all its needs and requirements. It leans on Him, hangs on Him, builds on Him, cleaves to Him, as its physician, guardian, husband, and friend.

(d) A right heart is a PURIFIED heart (Acts 15:9; Matthew 5:8). It loves holiness, and hates sin. It strives daily to cleanse itself from all filthiness of flesh and spirit (2 Corinthians 7:1). It abhors that which is evil, and cleaves to that which is good. It delights in the law of God, and has that law engraved on it, that it may not forget it (Psalm 119:11).

It longs to keep the law more perfectly, and takes pleasure in those who love the law. It loves God and man. Its affections are set on things above. It never feels so light and happy as when it is most holy; and it looks forward to heaven with joy, as the place where perfect holiness will at length be attained.

(e) A right heart is a PRAYING heart. It has within it "*the Spirit of adoption whereby we cry, Abba Father*" (Romans 8:15). Its daily feeling is, "*Your face, Lord, will I seek*" (Psalm 27:8). It is drawn by a habitual inclination to speak to God about spiritual things - weakly, feebly, and imperfectly perhaps - but speak it must.

It finds it necessary to pour out itself before God, as before a friend, and to spread before Him all its needs and desires. It tells Him all its secrets. It keeps back nothing from Him. You might as well try to persuade a man to live without breathing, as to persuade the possessor of a right heart to live without praying.

(f) A right heart is a heart that feels within a CONFLICT (Galatians 5:17). It finds within itself two opposing principles contending for the mastery - the flesh lusting against the spirit, and the spirit against the flesh. It knows by experience what Paul means when he says, *"I see a law in my members warring against the law of my mind"* (Romans 7:23). The wrong heart knows nothing of this strife. The strong man armed keeps the wrong heart as his palace, and his goods are at peace (Luke 11:21).

(g) Last - but not least, the right heart is HONEST, and SINGLE, and TRUE (Luke 8:15;1 Chronicles 12:33; Hebrews 10:22). There is nothing about it of falsehood, hypocrisy, or image-acting. It is not double or divided. It really is what it professes to be, feels what it professes to feel, and believes what it professes to believe. Its faith may be feeble. Its obedience may be very imperfect. But one thing will always distinguish the right heart. Its religion will be real, genuine, thorough, and sincere.

A heart such as that which I have now described, has always been the possession of all true Christians of every name, and nation, and people and tongue. They have differed from one another on many subjects - but they have all been of a "right heart."

They have some of them fallen, for a season, like David and Peter - but their hearts have never entirely departed from the Lord. They have often proved themselves to be men and women laden with infirmities - but their hearts have been right in the sight of God. They have understood one another on earth. They have found that their experience was everywhere one and the same. They will understand each other even better in the world to come. All that have had "right hearts" upon earth, will find that they have one heart when they enter heaven.

CONCLUSION

(1) I wish now in conclusion to offer to every reader of this paper, a QUESTION to promote self-inquiry. I ask you plainly this day, "What is your heart? Is your heart right or wrong?"

I know not who you are into whose hands this paper has fallen. But I do know that self-examination cannot do you any harm. If your heart is right, it will be a comfort to know it. *"If our heart condemns us not, then have we confidence towards God"* (1 John 3:21). But if your heart is wrong, it is high time to find it out, and seek a change. The time is short.

The night comes when no man can work. Say to yourself this very day, "Is my heart right or wrong?" Think not to say within yourself, "There is no need for such questions as these. There is no need to make such ado about the heart. I go to church or chapel regularly. I live a respectable life. I hope I shall prove right at last."

Beware of such thoughts, I beseech you - beware of them if you would ever be saved. You may go to the best church on earth, and hear the best of preachers. You may be the best of churchmen, or the soundest member of a chapel. But all this time, if your heart is not right in the sight of God, you are on the high road to destruction. Settle down to quiet consideration of the question before you. Look it manfully in the face, and do not turn aside. Is your heart right or wrong?

Think not to say within yourself, "No one can know what his heart is. We must hope the best. No one can find out with any certainty the state of his own soul." Beware, I say again - beware of such thoughts. The thing can be known. The thing can be found out.

Deal honestly and fairly with yourself. Set up a 'trial' on the state of your inward man. Summon a jury.

Let the Bible preside as judge. Bring up the witnesses. Inquire what your tastes are - where your affections are placed - where your treasure is - what you hate most - what you love most - what pleases you most - what grieves you most. Inquire into all those points impartially, and mark what the answers are. *"Where your treasure is there will your heart be also"* (Matthew 6:21).

A tree may always be known by its fruit, and a true Christian may always be discovered by his habits, tastes, and affections. Yes! you may soon find out what your heart is, if you are honest, sincere, and impartial. Is it right or wrong?

Think not to say within yourself, "I quite approve of all you say, and hope to examine the state of my heart someday. But I have no time just at present. I cannot find leisure.

(2) I wish, in the next place, to offer a SOLEMN WARNING to all who know their hearts are wrong - but have no desire to change. I do it with every feeling of kindness and affection. I have no wish to excite needless fears.

"Without holiness no man shall see the Lord" (John 3:3; Matthew 18:3; Hebrews 12:14). It is not enough to have our sins pardoned, as many seem to suppose. There is another thing needed as well as a pardon, and that thing is a new heart. We must have the Holy Spirit to renew us, as well as Christ's blood to wash us. Both renewing and washing are needful before anyone can be saved. Can you suppose for a moment, that you would be happy in heaven, if you entered heaven without a right heart?

A sheep is not happy when it is thrown into the water. A fish is not happy when it is cast on dry land. And men and women would not be happy in heaven, if they entered heaven without right hearts. My warning is before you. Harden not your heart against it. Believe it. Act upon it. Turn it to account. Awake and arise to newness of life without delay. One thing is very certain. Whether you hear the warning or not, God will not go back from what He has said. "If we believe not, He abides faithful - He cannot deny Himself" (2 Timothy 2:13).

(3) I wish, thirdly, to offer COUNSEL to all who know their hearts are wrong - but desire to have them made right. That counsel is short and simple. I advise you to apply at once to the Lord Jesus Christ, and ask for the gift of the Holy Spirit. Entreat Him, as a lost and ruined sinner, to receive you, and supply the needs of your soul. I know well that you cannot make your own heart right. But I know that the Lord Jesus Christ can. And to the Lord Jesus Christ I entreat you to apply without delay.

If any reader of this paper really wants a right heart, I thank God that I can give him good encouragement. I thank God that I can lift up Christ before you, and say boldly, Look at Christ - Seek Christ - Go to Christ. For what did that blessed Lord Jesus come into the world?

For what did He give His precious body to be crucified?
For what did He die and rise again?
For what did He ascend up into heaven, and sit down at the right hand of God?
For what did Christ do all this - but to provide complete salvation for poor sinners like you and me - salvation from the guilt of sin, and salvation from the power of sin, for all who believe!

Oh, yes! Christ is no half Savior. He has *"received gifts for men, even for the rebellious"* (Psalm 68:18). He waits to pour out the Spirit on all who will come to Him. Mercy and grace - pardon and a new heart, all this Jesus is ready to apply to you by His Spirit, if you will only come to Him. Then come - come without delay to Christ. What is there that Christ cannot do? He can create. By Him were all things made at the beginning. He called the whole world into being by His command. He can quicken.

He raised the dead when He was on earth, and gave back life by a word. He can change. He has turned sickness into health, and weakness into strength - famine into plenty, storm into calm, and sorrow into joy. He has wrought thousands of miracles on hearts already. He turned Peter the unlearned fisherman into Peter the Apostle. He turned Matthew the covetous publican into Matthew the Gospel writer.

He turned Saul the self-righteous Pharisee into Paul the Evangelist of the world. What Christ has done once, Christ can do again. Christ and the Holy Spirit are always the same. There is nothing in your heart that the Lord Jesus cannot make right. Only come to Christ.

If you had lived in Palestine, in the days when Jesus was upon earth, you would have sought Christ's help if you had been sick. If you had been crushed down by heart-disease in some back lane of Capernaum, or in some cottage by the blue waters of the sea of Galilee, you would surely have gone to Jesus for a cure. You would have sat by the way-side day after day, waiting for His appearing. You would have sought Him, if He did not happen to come near your dwelling - and never rested until you found Him.

Oh, why not do the same this very day for the sickness of your soul?

Why not apply at once to the Great Physician in heaven, and ask Him to *"take away the stony heart and give you a heart of flesh?"* (Ezekiel 11:19). Once more I invite you. If you want a "right heart," do not waste time in trying to make it right by your own strength. It is far beyond your power to do it. Come to the great Physician of souls. Come at once to Jesus Christ.

(4) I wish, lastly, to offer an EXHORTATION to all whose hearts have been made right in the sight of God. I offer it as a word in season to all true Christians. Hear me, I say to every believing brother or sister. I speak especially to you. Is your heart right? Then be thankful. Praise the Lord for His distinguishing mercy, in *"calling you out of darkness into His marvelous light"* (1 Peter 2:9). Think what you were by nature.

Think what has been done for you by free undeserved grace. Your heart may not be all that it ought to be, nor yet all that you hope it will be. But at any rate your heart is not the old hard heart with which you were born. Surely the man whose heart is changed ought to be full of praise. Is your heart right? Then be humble and watchful.

Oh, keep your heart with all diligence! Watch and pray lest you fall into temptation. Ask Christ Himself to keep your heart for you. Ask Him to dwell in it, and reign in it, and garrison it, and to put down every enemy under His feet. Give the keys of the citadel into the King's own hands, and leave them there. It is a weighty saying of Solomon, *"He who trusts in his own heart is a fool"* (Proverbs 28:26).

Is your heart right? Then be hopeful about the hearts of other people. Who has made you to differ? Why should not anyone in the world be changed, when such a one as you has been made a new creature? Work on. Pray on. Speak on. Write on. Labor to do all the good you can to souls. Never despair of anyone being saved so long as he is alive.

Surely the man who has been changed by grace ought to feel that there are no desperate cases. There are no hearts which it is impossible for Christ to cure.

Finally, let me entreat all right-hearted readers to look onward and forward to the day of Christ's second coming. A time draws near when Satan shall be bound, and Christ's saints shall be changed - when sin shall no more vex us, and the sight of sinners shall no more sadden our minds - when believers shall at length attend on God without distraction, and love Him with a perfect heart. For that day let us wait, and watch, and pray. It cannot be very far off. The night is far spent. The day is at hand. Surely if our hearts are right, we ought often to cry, "Come quickly - come Lord Jesus!

Measuring The Christ Quotient (CQ)

♛ C+Morality
"Queen Esther"

> *"When Esther's words were reported to Mordecai, he sent back this answer: "Do not think that because you are in the king's house you alone of all the Jews will escape. For if you remain silent at this time, relief and deliverance for the Jews will arise from another place, but you and your father's family will perish. And who knows but that you have come to your royal position for such a time as this?" Then Esther sent this reply to Mordecai: "Go, gather together all the Jews who are in Susa, and fast for me. Do not eat or drink for three days, night or day. I and my attendants will fast as you do. When this is done, I will go to the king, even though it is against the law. And if I perish, I perish." So Mordecai went away and carried out all of Esther's instructions."*

> *Esther 4:14-17 (NIV)*

We save the best measure for last. The moral to our overall leadership story. What do you do, when answering God's call to your moment of truth becomes a matter of life and death, potentially costing yours? What do you say, when your silence and holding of your peace comes with a heavy price that your own people have to pay? What move do you make, when your position of privilege in the palace no longer shields you from being above the law? Where do you go when your background check comes to the forefront?

The call of God brings us to a "such as this" moment of truth for Esther. Esther is the Jewish maiden who became queen of Persia and rescued her people from a murderous plot to annihilate them. The story of Esther begins with a king's banquet. King Ahasuerus (also called Xerxes) was the son of the famed Persian king Darius

I, who is mentioned in Ezra 4:24; 5:5-7; 6:1-15; Daniel 6:1, 25; Haggai 1:15; and 2:10.

The empire of King Ahasuerus was enormous; in fact, it was the largest the world had ever seen. Persia covered the area now known as Turkey, as well as Iraq, Iran, Pakistan, Jordan, Lebanon, and Israel; it also encompassed sections of modern-day Egypt, Sudan, Libya, and Saudi Arabia. As with most of the pagan Gentile kings of that day, King Xerxes enjoyed putting on public displays of his wealth and power, which included feasts sometimes lasting as long as 180 days.

Evidently, during the feast that is mentioned in Esther 1:10-11, the king requested that his wife, Queen Vashti, come before the entire gathering of officials to show them her great beauty wearing her crown. The speculation is that King Xerxes wanted Vashti to appear wearing *only* the crown. Queen Vashti refused the king's request, and he became enraged.

King Xerxes consulted his advisers in the law who declared that Vashti had wronged all the people of the land. They feared that the women of Persia would hear of Vashti's refusal to obey her husband and begin to despise their own husbands. They suggested the king issue a decree throughout the land that Vashti could never again enter his presence. The king did so, proclaiming the edict in all the provincial languages.

With Vashti vanquished, the king was without a queen. Xerxes' attendants suggested he make a search for beautiful virgins throughout the land to find a new queen. Josephus, the Jewish historian, records that King Ahasuerus chose a total of 400 women to fill the harem and act as candidates for the new queen (Esther 2:1–4). The women were to undergo a year's worth of beauty treatments before meeting the king (verse 12). Esther, a Jewess whose Hebrew name was Hadassah, was chosen as one of the virgins (verse 8).

Until the time that the virgins were brought to the king, they were kept in the harem under the care of Hegai (Esther 2:8); after their meeting, because they were no longer virgins, they were moved to the area set aside to house the concubines—or mistresses—where they were put under the watchful eye of another eunuch, named Shaashgaz (verse 14).

Esther had been living in the citadel of Susa, where the king also lived. She was the cousin of a Benjamite named Mordecai, who was also her guardian, having adopted her as his own daughter when her parents died. Mordecai held some type of official position within the Persian government (Esther 2:19). When Esther was chosen as a candidate for queen, Mordecai instructed her not to reveal her Jewish background (verse 10). He also visited the king's harem daily to see how Esther was doing (verse 11).

When Esther's turn to be with the king came, "she asked for nothing except what Hegai the king's eunuch, who had charge of the women, advised. Now Esther was winning favor in the eyes of all who saw her" (Esther 2:15). She also won the king's favor: he "loved Esther more than all the women," and he made her queen (Esther 2:17). It seems that Esther, in addition to having "a lovely figure and [being] beautiful" (verse 7), was submissive in following the advice of wise counselors and quite winsome in every way.

As the story progresses, it also becomes evident that God was at work through the whole process. Sometime later, Mordecai was sitting at the king's gate and overheard an assassination plot against Xerxes. He reported it to Queen Esther, who reported it to the king and gave Mordecai the credit. The plot was foiled, but the event was largely forgotten (Esther 2:21–23). We see in this event Esther's continued connection to Mordecai as well as her integrity. Both Mordecai and Esther honored the king and wanted to protect him from his enemies.

After this, the king appointed an evil man over his affairs. His name was Haman, and he despised the Israelite people. Haman was a descendant of Agag, king of the Amalekites, a people who were Israel's sworn enemy for generations (Exodus 17:14-16), and bigotry and prejudice against Israel were deeply rooted within Haman's darkened heart. In his hubris, Haman commanded the royal officials at the king's gate to kneel down and honor him, but Mordecai refused. The royal officials spoke to Haman about this, being sure to tell Haman that Mordecai was a Jew.

Haman wanted not only to punish Mordecai but "sought to destroy all the Jews, the people of Mordecai, throughout the whole kingdom of Ahasuerus" (Esther 3:6). King Xerxes allowed Haman to do as he pleased in the matter, and a decree went out to all the provinces that on a certain day, which had been chosen by lot (or *purim*), the people were "to destroy, to kill, and to annihilate all Jews, young and old, women and children, in one day" (Esther 3:13). The people were bewildered, and there was great mourning among the Jews (Esther 3:15; 4:3).

Queen Esther was unaware of the plot against the Jews, but she found out when her maids and eunuchs told her that Mordecai was in distress. Esther sent a messenger to Mordecai to find out what was wrong. Mordecai sent his cousin a copy of the edict and asked her "to go into the king's presence to beg for mercy and plead with him for her people" (Esther 4:8). Now, there was a law against entering the king's presence uninvited, and Esther had not been invited by the king for the past thirty days.

Through her intermediary, Esther reported to Mordecai her seeming inability to help. He responded, "Do not think to yourself that in the king's palace you will escape any more than all the other Jews. For if you keep silent at this time, relief and deliverance will rise for the Jews from another place, but you and your father's house will perish. And who knows whether you have not come to the kingdom for such a time as this?" (Esther 4:13–14). In a great display of faith, Esther agreed. She asked the Jews to fast for her for three days while she and her maids also fasted. "Then I will go to the king, though it is against the law," she said, "and if I perish, I perish" (Esther 4:16).

When Esther approached the king, she was literally risking her life. But Xerxes "was pleased with her and held out to her the gold scepter that was in his hand," a sign that he accepted her presence (Esther 5:2). She invited Xerxes and Haman to a banquet that day. The king called for Haman and came to the meal where he asked what she would like, "even up to half the kingdom" (verse 6). Esther invited the two men to attend another banquet the following day where she would present her request (verse 8). The men agreed.

Xerxes had difficulty sleeping that night and ordered the record of his reign to be read to him. Amazingly, the account he heard was that of Mordecai uncovering the assassination plot and saving the king's life. Meanwhile, Haman went home, gathered his friends and wife, and told them how honored he had been. But he had seen Mordecai on the way home, which had dampened his spirits. His wife and friends suggested Haman build a gallows on which to hang Mordecai (Esther 5:9–14). Haman followed their advice and built the gallows.

Just as King Xerxes was mulling over the fact that he had not honored Mordecai for his life-saving act, Haman came in to talk to the king about hanging Mordecai. The king asked for Haman's opinion about how to honor a man whom "the king delights to honor" (Esther 6:6). Haman, thinking Xerxes was referring to him, suggested parading the man through town wearing a royal robe and riding on a horse the king had ridden while proclaiming, "Thus shall it be done to the man whom the king delights to honor!" (Esther 6:9). Xerxes ordered Haman to do this immediately for Mordecai.

Haman obeyed the king and honored the man he hated the most. He then told the events to his wife and friends. With more foresight than they probably realized, "his wise men and his wife Zeresh said to him, 'If Mordecai, before whom you have begun to fall, is of the Jewish people, you will not overcome him but will surely fall before him'" (Esther 6:13).

The king's eunuchs arrived and took Haman to Esther's banquet (verse 14). There, Esther told the king that her people had been sold to be annihilated. Showing great respect and humility, Esther said that had they only been sold into slavery, she would have held her peace, "because no such distress would justify disturbing the king" (Esther 7:4). The king was aghast that someone would dare to do such a thing to his queen's people (verse 5). Esther revealed the man behind the plot to "this vile Haman" (verse 7).

Xerxes exited the banquet enraged. Haman stayed behind to plead with Esther for his life. When the king reentered the room and saw this, he thought Haman was molesting Esther and ordered Haman to be killed on the very gallows he had built for Mordecai (verses 8–10).

After Haman was dead, Xerxes gave Esther all of Haman's estate and gave Mordecai his signet ring, essentially giving Mordecai the same authority in the kingdom Haman previously had. The decree that had gone out from Haman, however, was irrevocable. Esther again pleaded with the king to intervene. Xerxes ordered another decree to be written to counter the first: this one gave the Jews the right to defend themselves against any who would attack them. Now there was joy throughout the provinces. Many even became Jews out of fear. Some enemies did attack on the previously appointed day, but the Jews were victorious over them (Esther 8).

Esther's bravery and faith in God are a testament to the trust this young woman had in the living God. Her life is a lesson in God's sovereignty over His creation. God maneuvers every aspect of life to position people, governments, and situations for His plan and purpose. We may not know what God is doing at a particular moment, but a time might come when we realize why we have gone through certain experiences or met certain people or lived in certain areas or shopped in certain stores or taken certain trips.

The time may come when everything comes together, and we look back and see that we, too, were in the right place at the right time, just as Esther was. She was in the harem "for such a time as this."

She was made queen "for such a time as this." She was strengthened and prepared to intercede for her people "for such a time as this" (Esther 4:14). And she was faithful to obey. Esther trusted in God and humbly served, no matter what it might cost. Esther is truly a reminder of God's promise, as written in Romans 8:28: "And we know that God causes all things to work together for good to those who love God, to those who are called according to His purpose."

Esther's faithful actions of morality, integrity and courage under fire provides us with the blessed assurance and encouragement that responding to God's call is a matter of eternal life after death. It reminds us that doing or saying the right thing, at the right time is not always popular. Speaking truth to power may have life or death consequences, but ultimately bears Kingdom implications and Heavenly rewards.

Christ ↑ Type

Samson

> *"The angel of the LORD appeared to her and said, "You are barren and childless, but you are going to become pregnant and give birth to a son."*

Judges 13:3 (NIV)

Like Christ, Samson is one of the few in Scripture whose birth was divinely preannounced to his parents, sharing this quartet of an honor with Isaac and John the Baptist. Samson was born a Nazirite, meaning he was "separated" or "set aside" for God. Like Christ, this is no mere distinction.

Though we draw the line between them there.

As a matter of conduct and discipline, the similarities between these two leaders ends where the other begins. Discipline is the test and obedience the measure of our love for the Father. Where Christ consistently passed with flying colors on both accounts, Samson failed time and time again.

As leaders, we must determine to lead our own lives well, following a moral compass and code of conduct, before expecting anyone else to follow us continually. Leaders go through ups and downs, but at some point what goes up has to stop coming down.

Samson began his leadership journey as a very disciplined man. He was able to delay his own, immediate gratification with the exception of his weakness for women. As he moved further along his leadership continuum, Samson violates his Nazarite code of conduct. Nazarites were strictly forbidden to consume wine and partake in sexual immorality. Samson delighted, and over-indulged in both.

> *"The fuller the cup the more easily is it to spill the contents. The higher the spiritual privilege the more need for lowliness of walk before God. The stronger we are the greater the temptation to trust in our strength. The more frequently the Spirit of God moves us, the more powerfully will the world and flesh oppose us. The life of Samson alternates with light and shade. A Nazarite who seemed to be partially unconscious of the sacredness of his life, a fatal flaw in his character as a servant in the work of God."*

> *- James Smith*
> *(Samson's Life & Death)*

In the end, it was his weakness for the Philistine women that did him in. His passion for women and obsession over Delilah superseded God's expressed will. This is a clear violation of the G-code. Let Samson and his sordid relationship with Delilah be a warning that goes beyond the theatrical for men in positions of leadership.

Despite his birth being preannounced by an Angel of the Lord and in spite of having the Spirit of the Lord upon him, Samson's sexual yearnings of the flesh controlled his life (1 John 2:16). He was a brave heart in battle but weak in the knees when it came to women (Proverbs 5:3; 6:32; Matthew 5:28).

There are many valuable lessons to glean from Samson. Though born with unlimited potential, Samson limited his opportunities because of sin. As leaders, the deeper we allow ourselves to be seduced by the glamour and allurement of sin, the more blind we become. Samson was spiritually blind, long before his eyes were gouged out

(Judges 16:21). Sin binds us, then blinds us beyond the point of no return.

By all accounts, Samson could have been one of Israel's greatest leaders, yet turned out to be one of the worst. He learned the hard way that trust is the very foundation of genuine leadership. As we can all attest, people are willing to forgive the occasional mistake or see past shortcomings based on ability. However, they won't stick around for long, and trust someone who routinely falls short on character.

"Signs of Leaders in Trouble"

Source: Maxwell Leadership Bible

Leaders who find themselves on shaky ground usually exhibit one or more of the following signs which point to an erosion of trust:

1. *Failing to address glaring weaknesses.*

   Samson struggled with sexual impurity. He asked for a pagan wife, slept with prostitutes, and ultimately Delilah destroyed him. Any time a leader neglects to repair his character flaws, they become more flagrant.

2. *Counting on deception to safeguard themselves.*
   People who flirt with disobedience often deceive others to protect themselves. Samson liked using riddles to outwit

others. He didn't tell the whole truth, which would eventually lead to distrust and betrayal.

3. *Acting impulsively.*
   Time after time, Samson displayed his impetuosity. He chose his wife rashly. He made wagers without thinking. And more than once his impulsive spirit led him into a bloody battle. A leader who cannot control his temper endangers both himself and others.

4. *Are overcome by an area of weakness.*
   Sin eventually consumes anyone who gives it free rein. Samson met his match in Delilah. The deceiver was deceived; the seducer, seduced. He lost a dangerous game and it cost him everything.

5. *Misuse their God-given gifts.*
   Samson possessed immense strength and godly anointing, but he took both for granted. Many times, Samson exploited his God-given gift, intended for the deliverance of his people, for personal revenge. When a leader misuses God's gifts, serious consequences follow.

"When Leaders Lose Their Teachability"

Samson's self-centered, undisciplined and arrogant nature made him unteachable. What happens when leaders lose their teachability?

1. *They lean on their own strength and understanding.*

   Unteachable leaders lose touch with God and His people. They lean on their own strength and do not seek guidance from God or others.

   Samson repeatedly used brute force and violence to cope with difficulties.

Worse still, Samson never acknowledged God as the source of his strength. He went from a man of anointing to a man of arrogance.

2. *They fail to learn from their mistakes.*
A person's life runs uphill or downhill, depending on whether he falls forward or backward. It's only a mistake if you fail to learn from it. Samson's life reveals no record of improvement, only downward spiral. For leaders to learn from their mistakes they must be...

• Big enough to admit mistakes. Samson blamed everyone else for his problems. He never once admitted his sin or humbled himself before God.

• Smart enough to profit from them. It's one thing to know you're wrong; it's another to figure out *why* you erred.

• Strong enough to correct them. If you can't implement necessary changes, you can't improve yourself or your situation.

3. *They react rather than lead.*
While good leaders are proactive, unteachable people almost exclusively react. When Samson saw the daughter of Timnah, he immediately asked for her in marriage. When his wife married his best man, he burned down the Philistine's fields. Samson over-reacted, over and over again, right up to his death.

4. *They are easily defeated.*
Unteachable people always lose. Even great talent (like Samson's) can only take a person so far. Samson's character flaw, left unrepaired because of an unteachable spirit, led to moral erosion and unchecked sin – which led to his eventual destruction.

Discipline alone does not qualify an individual for leadership, he or she should not expect to remain in the position very long without it. More government leaders have fallen from poor discipline than poor policies. More business owners have squandered their careers from the lack of discipline and negative lifestyle behaviors, than the lack of positive cash flow. More prominent figures have lost their fortunes playing with harlots, than playing the stock market.

More men of the cloth have stain glassed their ministries and innocent lives of others in a moment of instant gratification, than they have actually saved in their congregations. Like Christ, Samson performed amazing exploits. *"He rent a young lion like a kid"* (Judges 14:6). *"With the jawbone of a donkey he slew a thousand men"* (Judges 15:15). *"He carried away the gates of the city of Gaza"* (Judges 16:3).

Like Christ, Samson came to fulfill God's promise: *"One man of you shall chase a thousand"* (Joshua 23:10) - both proving it is as easy for God to work with one man as with three hundred (Judges 7:7). Samson, though, had no followers. He asked for none.

Like Christ, Samson knew his key to victory came from the secret place of strength in the Lord. However, only One of them carried his strength to overcome His enemies. The other divulged the trade secrets to his, while pillow talking and sleeping with the enemy. Samson not only cut his hair but apparently bumped his head and forgot *who* his source of strength was altogether.

Like Christ, Samson's story is one of devotion to the Father. However, only One of them would maintain his vow of godly devotion. The other abandoning his in devotion to other gods. One leading to an expected end. The other leading to a tragic one.

Samson's life begs the introspective question, "how much do we really love God?"

In our heart of hearts, is He really the Lord operating over our lives, or is she running it? Does He sit on the throne of our hearts, or does Delilah occupy it? Do we thirst for Him, or lust for her? Do we honor God every day, or just on Sunday? If He is our Lord, why do we struggle so hard to obey His commands but acquiesce so easily to everyone else's demands?

Not to mention, there are plenty of basic instructions in the Word of God we routinely disregard. For example, take our earlier admonition to pursue peace with all people. How's that working out for you, today?

We live in the age of grace. But, God's grace should not be viewed as a personal line of credit, and we're always teetering at the limit of our available balance. Grace is the vehicle that obedience licenses us to drive in. Let us serve God honorably, acceptably with reverence and godly fear.

> *"What shall we say [to all this]? Should we continue in sin and practice sin as a habit so that [God's gift of] grace may increase and overflow?*
>
> *Romans 6:1 (AMP)*

Too often we only want the Santa Claus part of God that serves us best. For goodness sake. We wish for His love, grace and mercy to fall on us and His justice and wrath to be poured out upon those we disagree with. But God is all, or nothing at all. We would be wise to remember that He is not a cheap idol of a pagan god to be tempted and trifled with. He is Almighty God. All souls belong to Him.

In the end, His consuming fire will burn the dross, and sinful places of our lives, so that we come out as pure gold (Luke 3:16-17). We would be wise to take heed so His will can be done in our lives. We better recognize so His purpose will prevail and we may serve Him better. If only Samson's superhuman strength had supernaturally served him better. Instead, the lustful desires of the flesh would be his kryptonite.

If only Samson had properly managed the affairs of his heart.

"Then she said to him, "How can you say, 'I love you, 'when your heart is not with me? You have mocked me these three times and have not told me where your great strength lies." When she pressured him day after day with her words and pleaded with him, he was annoyed to death. Then [finally] he told her everything that was in his heart and said to her, "A razor has never been used on my head, for I have been a Nazirite to God from my mother's womb. If I am shaved, then my strength will leave me, and I will become weak and be like any [other] man."

Judges 16:15-17 (AMP)

Samson was not a giant; his great strength did not, therefore, lie in an arm of flesh. No human muscle can be developed into spiritual power. The secret of his great strength lay in the presence of the Almighty Spirit of God within him, as one consecrated to the will of God. "You shall receive the power of the Holy Spirit coming upon you, and you shall be witnesses unto Me" (Acts 1:8). This is still the secret of the great strength of any servant of Jesus Christ, and it may be yours. This great strength cannot be purchased by intellectual wisdom or social position. It is the gift of God (Acts 8:18-20), and should be to our souls what our physical strength is to our bodies, only in a superhuman degree, the mighty power of God.

Code of Conduct

Leadership Summary

• **If we want our organizations, cultures, teams and ministries to thrive, we must bring these words to life within the context of the code by which we conduct ourselves**. We must fundamentally honor our agreements, respect our associations, value our people and keep our word as if God is signing off on every move. If God is our silent partner and seed investor, we must bring Him into the valuation equation. We must give rise to a new definition of what it is to go by the book. We must encode the basics of faith back into our operational DNA.

• **The G-code is identifying the presence of God within the structural composite of our marketplace activity and enterprise solutions**. This is not at all scientific, but certainly microscopic. We must view our businesses through the lens of our being living, breathing organisms with the ability to mutate God's Kingdom principles in the form of our daily operations. In other words, I do the right thing, and the next right thing that follows, not only to please my manager but to be pleasing to God. I do right by my staff because I want to be right with God. Because I'm a believer, I truly believe that He sees all.

• **Psychologist Jesse Bering schools a group of unsuspecting, early childhood learners in New Zealand on the cognitive science of religion and innate nature of the G-code through an experiment called "the empty chair effect."** The hypothesis simple, yet profound. Bering and his PhD students Jared Piazza and Gordon sought to validate their sound premise: When no other actual person is around, and we're tempted to do something we know that we shouldn't, the illusion of a supernatural watcher should meaningfully influence our behavioral decision making.

• We **must understand honor means everything to our Father**. We must be willing to place God's office atop our building directory. If God truly is our silent partner and seed investor, we must factor Him, our faith, our character and our integrity into the valuation equation. Seriously. We must no longer view our faith in God as somehow being separate from, offensive and a threat *to* the workplace. We must begin to have the courage to abandon the lewd desire to always have "the best of both worlds," while leaving God's Kingdom out of it.

• **It is in the maturing of our discipline, and putting away of the childish things we do in the flesh, that makes us fit for reasonable service in partnership with the Holy Spirit**. This is not a natural phenomenon but the byproduct of supernatural discipline.

When the fighter is ready, the trainer appears. Ready or not, we've all experienced the rod of correction and discipline of our Heavenly Father. Perhaps, in rebellion though, we stopped short of the realization that it was His chasing and chastening that followed. Not the other way around. One makes us run *from* Him. The other makes us run *to* Him.

• **Because our ways are not the Father's, we naturally consider discipline as the correction of a wrong**. Paul urges the church of Corinth to walk their faith life out "with the same discipline of an athlete." Not constantly beating yourself up. Edifying yourself, your church or your organization requires a different kind of discipline. One beats you down, the other builds you up.

• **Before muscles can build memory, they must first remember what it feels like to be torn**. Matters of discipline produce hardship and require the full training commitment of obedience and perseverance. Like a sparring prize fighter, obedience calls for us to focus on our techniques and see past the pain in the process to the victorious outcome. Jesus is our undisputed example.

• **Christ fought the good fight to the finish on the cross**. He received His rank, earned His title and took His rightful place at the right hand of God the Father. We, too, must endure the battles, tests and bouts with temptations in this life by looking to our heavenly reward and taking up our rightful position as more than conquerors. Like Christ, we hold the belt of truth up high and do so by (voluntarily) surrendering our fight with the flesh.

• **The discipline we walk with today will yield** *"the peaceable fruit of righteousness to those who have been trained by it"* **tomorrow**. This, regardless of what we are currently going through on the job, or being out of a job. Whether our leadership and character is undergoing fiery trial, or under pressure, we look to our head trainer who put our fight plan together in the first place. Like a good boxer, we trust our cornerstone as He instructs through the later rounds.

• **Like a good trainer, God recognizes our weaknesses and our fight or flight tendencies.** Ultimately, it is by our faith and trust in Him, not by our good works alone, that we are declared victorious. When in doubt, we remember those nervous moments when we were on the ropes, dancing around the ring of doubt and fear. Falling victim to our bad habits. It was His voice that urged us to get back to fighting squarely in the middle of the ring. It is then we recollect to our senses that our success and body of work is not solely based on our own skills and abilities.

• **Obedience is what God is looking for the most from His prize fighters**. He is responsible for the tale of the tape. Our job is to stay obedient to it. In the middle of the fight, there are times His instructions may look like anything BUT a winning strategy. But, His ways are not our ways. His reach is far higher and much longer than ours. We throw a lot of punches but he lands more. We take comfort in the fact that it is in obedience to the bruising of our reproof and the taking of cuts from our correction that we are commended, and made fit for the fight.

• **Inevitably, there are times we must submit ourselves in obedience to correction**. No matter what level of the game we're on, we are subject to a higher authority. By submitting ourselves to God's correction and subjecting our leadership to Him as a matter of conduct we, in turn, level the playing field by subjecting ourselves to those we are leading. The active component in the definition of submission is in the *"sub"* portion. It is performed in the act of *"coming under"* someone else's mission. His or hers. Them or theirs. Anyone else but ours.

• **Correction is intended to earnestly advise, not ridicule**. The intent is to course correct toward faithful action. This is what makes great coaches and allows supervisors to supernaturally transform themselves. If we take time to think on the transformative impact made on us by these individuals, and rod of correction they applied to motivate us, very often their words of rebuke actually stirred up conviction in us, bringing us through our false pride to true repentance.

• **To repent, is to change course - not to feel sorry, or ashamed, or embarrassed but to be convicted about going in the right direction when all signs are pointing opposite**. If we never get to the place of repentance and remain defensive beyond the point of no return, our conduct never changes and we miss the opportunity to grow further in the Spirit. Pursuing peace with those we work or partner with means training ourselves in the forgiveness of others and asking others to forgive us. Otherwise, bitterness, resentments and the lack of forgiveness in our work environments runs wide and deep like the roots of the mulberry tree.

• **It's the little things that add up to a culture of feedback and thriving team dynamic**. It's the minor adjustments to our attitude, hearts and minds that make us better co-workers, better managers, better partners, better collaborators. It's the major corrections we make to the activity errors in our personal life that do the work of transforming us more and more into the professional image of Christ.

• **We are genetically predisposed to many things**. A predisposition doesn't always cause a trait to develop, but instead tends to *contribute* to its development. There are many contributing factors, not the least of which is our environment. Therefore, we may be predisposed to something that never actually develops. Like good, and evil. Faith is an innate, learned behavior.

• **The "*self*," is a collection of living cells**. We could very well be called the "*cellf*." Every cell has a job and a function. They move, think, see, laugh and talk. When they come together, they make us. When you think you're hungry, it's your cells that are growling. When you wake up with the urge for a Morning Joe or tobacco, it's your cells making a fixed decision *for* you. Same goes for all of our addictions, afflictions, temptations, triggers and so on. This is what it means to be a slave (*in*slaved), or prisoner to sin. To master one's *self*, is to master "our*cellves*."

• **The Bible teaches us that the heart is the part of us at which God especially looks**. "Man looks at the outward appearance - but the Lord looks on the heart." Man is naturally content with the outward part of religion, with outward morality, outward correctness, outward regular attendance on means of grace. But the eyes of the Lord look much further. He regards our motives. He "weighs the spirits." (Proverbs 16:2.) He says Himself, "I the Lord am the searcher of the heart, the tester of the thoughts" (Jeremiah 17:10).

• **More encouraging empathy trends and new theories have emerged across the leadership landscape.** One such noteworthy theory indicates *"need-based leadership"* is the shift we need. As Dr. Greg Sumpter highlighted for *SmartBrief*, "need-based leadership can be simply defined as a relationship whereby the leader's responsibility is to meet the needs of those in their care."

• **Queen Esther's faithful actions of integrity and courage under fire provide us with the blessed assurance and encouragement that responding to God's call is actually a matter of eternal life after death**. It reminds us that doing or saying the right thing at the right time is not always popular. Speaking truth to power may have life or death consequences. Both, ultimately bearing Kingdom implications and accruing heavenly rewards.

• **Like Christ, Samson is one of the few in Scripture whose birth was divinely preannounced, sharing this quartet of an honor with Isaac and John the Baptist**. Samson was born a Nazirite, meaning he was "separated" or "set aside" for God. Like Christ, this is no mere distinction. Though we draw the line between them there.

• **There are many valuable lessons to glean from Samson**. Though born with unlimited potential, Samson limited his opportunities because of sin. As leaders, the more we allow ourselves to be seduced by the glamour and allurement of sin, the more blind we become. Samson was spiritually blind, long before his eyes were gouged out (Judges 16:21). Sin binds us, then blinds us beyond the point of no return.

• **We live in the age of grace**. God's grace should not be viewed as a personal line of credit, teetering on the edge of the available balance. Grace is the vehicle that obedience licenses us to drive in. Here, we referenced Romans 6: *"What shall we say then? Shall we continue in sin that grace may abound? God forbid! How shall we who died to sin live any longer in it?"* Let us serve God honorably, acceptably with reverence and godly fear.

APPENDIX

Being a leader takes courage, discipline, and determination. While a great leader can bring great success, it also comes at the cost of being judged and overwhelmed. The Bible speaks of so many wonderful leaders and how God blessed them for their work. We have captured just a few.

There are many verses and Scriptures that God spoke to encourage men and women who choose to step up and lead. If you are striving to be a leader or if you are looking for inspiration along the way, these Bible verses about leadership should help!

Galatians 6:9

9 Let us not become weary in doing good, for at the proper time we will reap a harvest if we do not give up.

Hebrews 13:7

7 Remember your leaders, who spoke the word of God to you. Consider the outcome of their way of life and imitate their faith.

Isaiah 41:10

10 So do not fear, for I am with you; do not be dismayed, for I am your God. I will strengthen you and help you; I will uphold you with my righteous right hand.

James 1:12

12 Blessed is the one who perseveres under trial because, having stood the test, that person will receive the crown of life that the Lord has promised to those who love him.

James 3:1

1 Not many of you should become teachers, my fellow believers, because you know that we who teach will be judged more strictly.

James 4:10

10 Humble yourselves before the Lord, and he will lift you up.

Jeremiah 1:5

5 "Before I formed you in the womb I knew you, before you were born I set you apart; I appointed you as a prophet to the nations."

John 3:30

30 He must become greater; I must become less."

Matthew 7:12

12 So in everything, do to others what you would have them do to you, for this sums up the Law and the Prophets.

Matthew 20:26

26 Not so with you. Instead, whoever wants to become great among you must be your servant,

Philippians 2:3

3 Do nothing out of selfish ambition or vain conceit. Rather, in humility value others above yourselves,

Philippians 2:4

4 not looking to your own interests but each of you to the interests of the others.

Philippians 4:13

13 I can do all this through him who gives me strength.

Proverbs 4:23

23 Above all else, guard your heart, for everything you do flows from it.

Proverbs 22:29

29 Do you see someone skilled in their work? They will serve before kings; they will not serve before officials of low rank.

1 Timothy 3:2

2 Now the overseer is to be above reproach, faithful to his wife, temperate, self-controlled, respectable, hospitable, able to teach,

1 Timothy 4:8

8 For physical training is of some value, but godliness has value for all things, holding promise for both the present life and the life to come.

1 Timothy 4:12

12 Don't let anyone look down on you because you are young, but set an example for the believers in speech, in conduct, in love, in faith and in purity.

2 Timothy 2:15

15 Do your best to present yourself to God as one approved, a worker who does not need to be ashamed and who correctly handles the word of truth.

Psalm 37:5

5 Commit your way to the LORD; trust in him and he will do this:

Romans 8:28

28 And we know that in all things God works for the good of those who love him, who have been called according to his purpose.

Proverbs 27:23-24

23 Be sure you know the condition of your flocks, give careful attention to your herds; **24** for riches do not endure forever, and a crown is not secure for all generations.

Mark 10:42-45

42 Jesus called them together and said, "You know that those who are regarded as rulers of the Gentiles lord it over them, and their high officials exercise authority over them. **43** Not so with you. Instead, whoever wants to become great among you must be your servant, **44** and whoever wants to be first must be slave of all. **45** For even the Son of Man did not come to be served, but to serve, and to give his life as a ransom for many."

John 13:13-17

13 "You call me 'Teacher' and 'Lord,' and rightly so, for that is what I am. **14** Now that I, your Lord and Teacher, have washed your feet, you also should wash one another's feet.**15** I have set you an example that you should do as I have done for you. **16** Very truly I tell you, no servant is greater than his master, nor is a messenger greater than the one who sent him. **17** Now that you know these things, you will be blessed if you do them.

Ephesians 4:11-16

11 So Christ himself gave the apostles, the prophets, the evangelists, the pastors and teachers, **12** to equip his people for works of service, so that the body of Christ may be built up **13** until we all reach unity in the faith and in the knowledge of the Son of God and become mature, attaining to the whole measure of the fullness of Christ. **14** Then we will no longer be infants, tossed back and forth by the waves, and blown here and there by every wind of teaching and by the cunning and craftiness of people in their deceitful scheming. **15** Instead, speaking the truth in love, we will grow to become in every respect the mature body of him who is the head, that is, Christ. **16** From him the whole body, joined and held together by

every supporting ligament, grows and builds itself up in love, as
each part does its work.

Titus 1:7-14

7 Since an overseer manages God's household, he must be
blameless—not overbearing, not quick-tempered, not given to
drunkenness, not violent, not pursuing dishonest gain. **8** Rather,
he must be hospitable, one who loves what is good, who is self-
controlled, upright, holy and disciplined.9 He must hold firmly
to the trustworthy message as it has been taught, so that he can
encourage others by sound doctrine and refute those who oppose
it. **10** For there are many rebellious people, full of meaningless talk
and deception, especially those of the circumcision group. **11** They
must be silenced, because they are disrupting whole households by
teaching things they ought not to teach—and that for the sake of
dishonest gain. **12** One of Crete's own prophets has said it: "Cretans
are always liars, evil brutes, lazy gluttons." **13** This saying is true.
Therefore, rebuke them sharply, so that they will be sound in the
faith **14** and will pay no attention to Jewish myths or to the merely
human commands of those who reject the truth.

ABOUT THE AUTHOR

Erin O. Patton is the Founder of New Birth Institute. As an author, teacher and counselor, he is passionate, divinely purposed and driven toward maximizing God-given human potential. His work fosters thriving cultures within communities, organizations and family structures with an emphasis on Leadership development.

After forging a success path as a C-Suite executive for global corporations including Nike, Inc. and launching a series of start-up businesses driving social impact, he answered the call to Ministry. Erin graduated from Northwestern University's Medill School of Journalism and received his MBA from the Cox School of Business at Southern Methodist University before pursuing his Master of Divinity (MDiv) with a concentration in Leadership from the Fuller Theological Seminary.

CPSIA information can be obtained
at www.ICGtesting.com
Printed in the USA
LVHW050200220322
714005LV00005B/130

9 781662 844218